MEANINGS
OF MOBILITY

MEANINGS OF MOBILITY

Family, Education,
and Immigration in the
Lives of Latino Youth

Leah Schmalzbauer

Russell Sage Foundation
New York

The Russell Sage Foundation

The Russell Sage Foundation, one of the oldest of America's general purpose foundations, was established in 1907 by Mrs. Margaret Olivia Sage for "the improvement of social and living conditions in the United States." The foundation seeks to fulfill this mandate by fostering the development and dissemination of knowledge about the country's political, social, and economic problems. While the foundation endeavors to assure the accuracy and objectivity of each book it publishes, the conclusions and interpretations in Russell Sage Foundation publications are those of the authors and not of the foundation, its trustees, or its staff. Publication by Russell Sage, therefore, does not imply foundation endorsement.

Library of Congress Cataloging-in-Publication Data

Names: Schmalzbauer, Leah, author.
Title: Meanings of mobility : family, education, and immigration in the lives of Latino youth / Leah Schmalzbauer.
Description: New York : Russell Sage Foundation, [2023] | Includes bibliographical references and index. | Summary: "How do low-income Latino youth experience educational mobility? How do they understand it in relation to social mobility more generally? And what does their educational mobility mean in the context of their socially marginalized families and communities? *Meanings of Mobility* explores these questions. It centers on the life histories of sixty low-income Latino youth, most of whom are the first in their immigrant families to go to college in the United States, and all of whom have now graduated or are set to graduate from Amherst College, one of the most selective private colleges in the United States. Over the past twenty years, shifts in the admissions policies of highly selective schools like Amherst, in partnership with privately funded recruitment initiatives, have reshaped the race and class composition of the U.S. educational elite. Although Latinos continue to be underrepresented in elite colleges and universities, their numbers are robust compared to years past. Yet, we know little about this new Latino demographic. Shifting away from a deficit-based focus on those Latino youth who do not make it to or through college, Schmalzbauer focuses instead on those who have made it, with the dual goal of bringing attention to and complicating the understanding of their educational success. The author seeks to better comprehend what factors have helped them succeed and what further supports they need"—Provided by publisher.
Identifiers: LCCN 2023002174 (print) | LCCN 2023002175 (ebook) | ISBN 9780871548009 (paperback) | ISBN 9781610449212 (ebook)
Subjects: LCSH: Social mobility—United States. | Hispanic American youth.
Classification: LCC HN59.3 .S38 2023 (print) | LCC HN59.3 (ebook) | DDC 305.23089/68073—dc23/eng/20230414
LC record available at https://lccn.loc.gov/2023002174
LC ebook record available at https://lccn.loc.gov/2023002175

The paper used in this publication meets the minimum requirements of American National Standard for Information Sciences—Permanence of Paper for Printed Library Materials. ANSI Z39.48-1992.

Text design by Suzanne Nichols.

RUSSELL SAGE FOUNDATION
112 East 64th Street, New York, New York 10065

To Steve, Micah, and Zola
I love you

And to my students,
who inspired and guided this project
from beginning to end

Contents

About the Author

LEAH SCHMALZBAUER is Karen and Brian Conway '80, P'18 Presidential Teaching Professor of American Studies and Sociology at Amherst College.

Acknowledgments

MANY, MANY PEOPLE contributed to this project. My intent is to acknowledge every one of them here, but no doubt I will overlook someone. My apologies in advance if that happens.

I want to first and foremost thank the youth who participated in this study and their families who welcomed me into their homes and shared their stories with me. Getting to know my participants through our interviews and time together has indelibly marked me as a sociologist, writer, teacher, and mother.

I am also grateful to the many students who worked with me on this project through the Amherst College Greg Call Internship Program and whose intellectual labor, insight, and creativity fueled the research and inspired my writing: Alelí Andrés, Eve De Muheto, Tacia Diaz, Nate Edisis, Jeanyna Garcia, Sofia Guerra, Elliott Hadwin, Kat Mendoza, Lea Morín, Jonatan Ortega, Leslikarina Patino, Jeremy Paula, Manuel Rodriguez, Alyssa Snyder, Ana Vieytez, Elaine Vilorio, and Erika Zambrano. My thanks go out as well to the students who contributed to this research through their participation in my Mellon-funded seminar, "The Meanings of Mobility": Alelí Andrés, Tacia Diaz, Paola Garcia-Prieto, Jeremy Margolis, Julia Prestfelder, Emily Ratte, Silvana Romero, and Alyssa Snyder.

Alelí Andrés and Manuel Rodriguez coauthored stand-alone journal articles with me from this research. I could not be prouder that they are both now pursuing doctorates in sociology. Our discipline is lucky to have them! Parts of the article I wrote with Manuel, "Pathways to Mobility: Family and Education in the Lives of Latinx Youth," are included in the book's introduction and first chapter.

Thanks to Traeci Stevens, who did the majority of the transcription work for this project. I will forever be in awe of her speed and accuracy.

Amherst College generously supported the research and writing of this book. In addition to paying my student research assistants, the Faculty

Research Award Program funded my first years of interviews, travel, and fieldwork. I also benefited from the William R. Kenan Professorship and the Karen and Brian Conway '80, P'18 Presidential Teaching Professorship, as well as from a year of paid research leave during which I drafted the manuscript.

The dean and provost of Amherst College, Catherine Epstein, encouraged this project from its inception. I am grateful for her leadership and vision and for the time she took to read some of my writing, give feedback, and guide me toward historical information about the college. Matthew McGann, Amherst's dean of admissions, was also a tremendous support. He too read parts of my manuscript and made sure I had access to the college's latest admissions data and policy decisions. Mike Kelly, the head of the Archives and Special Collections, helped me locate materials to historically contextualize this study. Hanna Bliss, the director of immigration services at Amherst, helped me understand the college's immigration policies. Jesse Barba, the director of institutional research, shared data with me on Latino student enrollment and graduation rates. And Dawn Cadogan, the sociology librarian during the bulk of my work on this project, helped me find real-time data on COVID and its impacts on Latino communities. Karen Graves gracefully and efficiently facilitated the accounting end of my research. I am also forever grateful for my generous, smart, and engaged colleagues in American Studies, Anthropology and Sociology, and Latinx and Latin American Studies. Special thanks to Karen Sanchez-Eppler and Pawan Dhingra for reading and providing feedback on my earliest writing from this project, and to Pawan for helping me think through critical decisions at various points during the research and writing.

When I was hired at Amherst, I did not truly understand what it meant to be working at a "research college." I now do. In addition to the generous financial and collegial support the college has given me for my work, I have benefited from fantastic grant-writing and management support. I credit Mary Strunk and Lisa Stoffer, who were in the Department of Sponsored Research and Grants at the time, and who helped me secure my first major external grant, a Presidential Authority Grant from the Russell Sage Foundation. They helped me hone my research idea, smooth my writing, clarify my research design, and ultimately submit a proposal that was viable and exciting. Darlene Sliwa helped me create the budget for my grant, and then Darlene and Michael Stein magically made the management of my grant easy and stress-free.

I will forever appreciate the Russell Sage Foundation for awarding me a Presidential Authority Grant, which allowed me to bring a COVID angle into my research. RSF's director of publications, Suzanne Nichols, offered project-changing advice by urging me to incorporate my COVID research into the manuscript I already had planned, instead of writing a second stand-alone book. I am certain this insight made for a better and more impactful final product. Thank you also to Suzanne for making the publication process seamless, efficient, and clear.

When I received my RSF grant, I invited Alyssa Snyder and Elaine Vilorio, both of whom had worked with me as undergraduates, to be my post-bac research assistants. I am indebted to them for saying yes! I could not have completed the COVID portion of this research without them. They assisted me with interviews, helped me code and analyze interview transcripts, and walked me through the technical challenges of doing research over Zoom. Though they were both once my students, I now consider them peers and trusted friends.

After I completed a draft of my manuscript, I asked Elaine and another former student, Jeremy Margolis, if they would read it and provide comments. They enthusiastically agreed. The feedback they provided was invaluable.

Years ago I read the book *Divided by Borders* by Joanna Dreby and was awed by the depth of the research and the humanity of the writing. I am grateful that Joanna has since become a dear friend and close collaborator. Our regular writing and research meetings nurtured my confidence as I moved through the writing of this book. Joanna read the first draft and provided generous and detailed feedback that helped clarify my arguments and gave me the encouragement I needed to stay true to my writing style.

Family and kin have been essential sources of love, encouragement, and insight over the course of this project. My "posse"—Sheila Jaswal, Solsiree del Moral, and Josef Trapani—kept me energized and smiling, especially during those times when I was feeling especially anxious and unsure. My in-laws, Phil and Ellie Bruner, Ben and Carolyn Opps, Rick Bruner and Jim Sparks, and my nieces and nephews, Maizy and Miller Opps and Victor and Olympia Schmalzbauer Sparks, and my stepdad, Vincent Graziano, were consistent sources of encouragement, perspective, and fun. My sister, Anna Schmalzbauer, provided love, good judgment, and wisdom that guided and grounded me, especially during the most isolating times of the COVID pandemic. There are no words to capture the gratitude I have for my parents, Gary Schmalzbauer and Leone Medin. This is a book about family and educational mobility, and their experiences as working-class, first-generation college students who were motivated to ensure their own children's mobility inspires everything that I do. My mom also regularly serves as one of my most trusted readers and editors.

Thanks to my Australian Shepherd, Rocky, who kept me company on the many runs and hikes during which I sorted through my ideas for this book, and who slept at my feet during most of my writing.

Finally, my deepest gratitude goes to my husband, Steve Bruner, and my children, Micah and Zola Schmalzbauer Bruner. To them I say, thank you for putting up with my quirks and "sociology alerts," for grounding me, for encouraging me to take risks, for modeling discipline and resilience, and for patiently listening to my ideas and Steve for reading drafts of my work. Thank you for bringing an abundance of joy, insight, and meaning to my life. I love you!

Introduction

GABY LOOKED OVER her shoulder as she patiently waited for the remaining students to filter out of the classroom. After the last student had left, she slowly pulled a chair away from the heavy oak seminar table and sat down next to me. Though smiling, her face suggested unease. "I'm struggling," she said, tears enveloping her striking brown eyes. "You know, getting here was always the dream, and I've made it. But . . ." She paused. "Everything is still so hard."

We had just finished reading Pierrette Hondagneu-Sotelo's seminal work, *Doméstica*, a rich sociological portrayal of the lives of Latina immigrant domestic workers in California. Gaby had connected to the book in a deeply personal way.[1] Her mom was a domestic worker, also in California. *Doméstica* validated the anger that Gaby felt when she thought about the disrespectful ways in which some of her mom's employers had treated her, as well as her resentment toward the wealthy children her mom had taken care of, children who had gotten more of her mom's time and attention than she had. Ironically, she now found herself at a school in which many of her classmates could have been those wealthy children. "I felt really seen when I read this book," Gaby explained, "but it also reminded me what a different world I'm living in now. It's hard to make sense of it all."

There was more. Gaby was struggling to balance her evolving passions and interests with the responsibility she felt to her family. Her parents' migration from Nicaragua to the United States in the 1980s and her mom's grueling work cleaning houses and caring for other people's children were sacrifices that had paved the way for her educational success. Now Gaby was pondering what it meant to make the most of her opportunities—to make good on her parents' sacrifices. Specifically, she was contemplating dropping her premed major to nurture her own passions, which she had discovered to lie in the humanities. Yet she feared that doing so would let her parents down.

While Gaby was growing up in the early 2000s, her parents had presented her with limited examples of professional success. She should be a doctor or a lawyer, they told her, the only high-status careers they knew about, as they had not gone to college. Unfortunately, Gaby did not want to be either. Thus her angst. "I don't want to be a doctor," she sighed, "but I owe them. This isn't just about me." After pausing to take a deep breath and collect her thoughts, Gaby continued, sharing with me the narrative that she had heard regularly throughout her childhood. "Education is the pathway to success. This is why we came here. Your job is to make the most of it." As we talked that cold spring morning, the weight of this narrative felt especially heavy. Gaby sensed a growing divide between her parents' belief in education as the key to success and her own day-to-day experiences navigating an elite educational space that often felt oppressive. While she worried about her family's economic survival, she had classmates who were heading off to spring break on the family jet. Could education be an equalizer when their starting points were so different? She was beginning to have second thoughts.

There were also new, more complicated feelings swirling around in Gaby's head and heart. It wasn't just the responsibility she felt to her family or the inequalities she was observing that were causing her stress. It was also "this place" and the way she felt it had changed her. She explained that when she first arrived at Amherst College in 2014, she felt "poor," "dumb," and "beaten up." As such, she kept the transfer tabs for University of Southern California and University of California, Los Angeles, open on her computer and counted down the days until she could go home to her family. But then, when she did go home, she was caught off guard. Everything felt different. It didn't take long for her to realize that it was not home or her family that had changed—she had changed. Tears welled up again as she explained, "Home almost doesn't feel like home anymore."

Gaby, a student in my "Latino Immigration" seminar, had a background similar to those of the youth whose stories structure this book. Gaby's father immigrated to the United States without documentation and with few resources, but with big dreams of providing a better future for his family. Gaby was raised in a low-income, predominantly Latino community. She had two siblings: an older brother who was born and raised in California, and a half-sister who stayed in Nicaragua after her mom migrated to the United States. Gaby was the first in her family to go to college. Indeed, her parents did not finish high school. Neither did her brother. Getting into a good college had long been Gaby's dream, as well as her parents' dream. They all believed that college was the pathway to a better life. By this measuring stick, she had made it. And yet, "the dream," as she noted when we first started talking, had gotten more complicated as she neared the top of the educational mobility ladder and transitioned into a place that was thousands of miles and many social worlds away from her family and community. It was Gaby and the many other Latino students I met during my first years teaching at Amherst College who inspired me to write this book, exploring their pathways to and experiences of educational mobility.

I moved to Amherst College in 2014 from Montana State University, where I taught for ten years. While in Montana, I was part of a university-community collaboration focused on mentoring Latino youth. Through that project I got to know several high-performing young Latinos with college aspirations. When it came time for them to apply for college, they never looked further than Montana's state colleges and universities, intuiting that high tuition costs prohibited any other options. I supported their strategy. It had not occurred to me then that a fully funded, private elite education was a possibility for low-income—and in some cases undocumented—Latino youth. If I, a professor, did not know about these opportunities, how were first-generation college students to know? Yet, when I got to Amherst, my immigration classes were full of students who were in many ways like my Montana mentees. They were low-income, Latino, first-generation college students, and some were undocumented or had the temporary protected status for undocumented youth of Deferred Action for Childhood Arrivals (DACA). I wanted to know: How did they get here? What pathways led them far from home to an elite liberal arts college in western Massachusetts?

There were other questions occupying my thoughts during my first years on campus. Amherst had done what few other schools in the country had to increase educational access for high-achieving, low-income youth, including those who were undocumented. There was so much to celebrate about this accomplishment. Yet it took only a few conversations with students like Gaby to realize how much I, and many of those with whom I worked, had underestimated the challenges that still faced students after they made it to the top of the educational ladder. In many ways, my Latino students were thriving. Most were getting good grades, forging new friend-ships, raising their voices in activism, and taking advantage of every opportunity presented to them. And yet, as Gaby admitted, "this is really hard." I wanted to know more. How were low-income Latino youth expe-riencing educational mobility? How did they understand it in relation to social mobility more generally? And what did their educational mobility mean in the context of their socially marginalized families and commu-nities? This book explores these questions.

I centered my study on the life histories of sixty low-income Latino youth, the vast majority of whom were the first in their immigrant families to go to college in the United States. All of them have now graduated or are set to graduate from Amherst College, one of the most selective private colleges in the United States. I conceptualize their educational mobility trajectories as exceptional. Consider the overall mobility picture for low-income youth. According to the sociologist Sara Goldrick-Rab, 74 percent of low-income ninth-graders of all racial and ethnic backgrounds aspire to and expect to attend college, yet only 51 percent of children from low-income families ever make it to any sort of higher education institution, including community college.[2] More sobering still, only two in five children from low-income families receive a degree of any sort within six years, including associate degrees and certificates. Latinos' college attendance has notably increased over the past decade, but they still have the lowest college completion rates of all racial-ethnic groups.[3] Undocumented Latino youth face even more formidable barriers to college completion.[4]

Yet, while collective Latino mobility stagnates, over the past twenty years shifts in the admissions policies of highly selective schools like Amherst, in partnership with privately funded recruitment initiatives, have reshaped the race and class composition of the U.S. educational elite.[5] Latinos continue to be underrepresented in elite colleges and universities.[6] Nevertheless, their numbers are robust compared to years past.[7] Yet we know little about this new Latino demographic. This book helps fill this conspicuous gap. Shifting away from a deficit-based focus on those Latino youth who do not make it to or through college, I focus instead on those who have made it, with the dual goal of bringing attention to, and complicating the understanding of, their educational success. I seek to better comprehend the factors that have concretely supported their success, as well as the additional supports they need. Scholars, policymakers, and leaders within higher education have much to learn from those who have shared their stories with me.

The life histories I collected inspire three related arguments. The first is that the positive relationship between education and social mobility is at least partly an ideological construct. The participants in this study initially bought into this belief system, but as they moved along their educational pathways to and through Amherst, their experiences generated a more critical understanding of mobility. As such, while my findings suggest that educational mobility was indeed likely to lead to social mobility for most of the participants, this relationship is not nearly as direct or smooth as they were socialized to believe. Second, while mobility discourses tend to center individual meritocratic ideals, youth's pathways to and experiences of mobility were supported by and encased in family and community. In other words, for them, educational mobility was a relational process. In some ways it was collaborative and empowering, and in other ways it was complicated and imbalanced. But no matter its expression, family and kin networks were central to how youth understood and experienced their education, as well as how they thought about their future. And third, place—specifically, the geographic locality in which my participants came of age—shaped their educational pathways and experiences of educational mobility in important ways. Place also influenced how they navigated their relationships with family from afar and how they thought about their future.

The chapters that follow offer insights into how to support aspiring youth in ways that are attuned to the complexities of inequality and the centrality of family in their lives. They also shed light on where institutions of higher education and broader social policies are falling short in supporting aspiring youth as they move through their college years, making plans and setting goals for the future. Although the qualitative data in this book are confined to low-income Latino youth, the findings offer a window into the experiences of all low-income youth, especially those from immigrant families who are navigating the complexities of educational mobility. Indeed, an understanding of the pathways to exceptional educational mobility and the impact of this mobility on individual and family well-being is critical for informing policies that will increase equity and inclusion.

FAMILY AND THE EDUCATIONAL MOBILITY OF THE LATINO SECOND GENERATION

As was true for Gaby and her family, the youth and parents I interviewed for this book expressed a strong belief in education as the key to social mobility. The youth shared that they had been motivated since a young age by the ideology that education is the key to pulling themselves up by their bootstraps. They are not alone. Research has found this belief to be hegemonic among immigrants.[8] The conflation of education and social mobility is reasonable. Statistics show quite clearly that those with a college degree generally do better financially than those without it, and that those with a degree from an elite institution do even better still.[9] It thus makes sense that educational attainment is commonly used as a predictor of the social mobility of second-generation immigrants.[10]

Yet this conflation is also problematic. While I do not intend to refute the value of a college education in terms of the mobility prospects it offers to aspiring Latino youth, the relationship between education and social mobility is much more complicated and less secure than popular discourse and statistics alone suggest. Indeed, the relationship was simultaneously inspiring and promising as well as extremely challenging and uncertain for the youth and families discussed in this book. Although the vast majority of participants found that their position at Amherst had given them more opportunities than they ever would have imagined, most also came to recognize that their educational status was still not enough to override all aspects of their subordination, at least not in the short term. When I interviewed them, they were set to graduate from one of the top schools in the country, but they were still poor. They still confronted racism. And those who were undocumented or who had undocumented family members still feared deportation. And so, despite the persistence of societal messages touting their imminent entry into the upper class and the enduring faith of their parents, teachers, and mentors in the correlation between education and social mobility, over time most youth had learned not to assume that their educational mobility would automatically translate into wealth and well-being.

Recent research lends credence to such misgivings. Elizabeth Armstrong and Laura Hamilton, in their ethnography of female students' social pathways through a large American university, find that the most promising path for future social mobility is through the "party pathway" of sorority membership and participation in university-sanctioned social traditions.[11] This pathway tends to benefit the most class-privileged students while further marginalizing those from the working class, who feel disconnected from this form of social life. Armstrong and Hamilton conclude that instead of disrupting social hierarchies, university life in many ways magnifies them.

Relatedly, María Rendón, in her research with young, inner-city, second-generation Mexican men, finds that no matter what their educational trajectory has been, most ultimately converge in the working class.[12] Some of her participants attended college and passed their classes, but failed to connect with institutional actors who could help them transfer their college attendance into future mobility. Without these relationships, they were unable to make the leap from educational mobility to social mobility. Hard work and good grades, while laudatory and meaningful in their lives, were not enough to launch them into the middle class.

Recent research by Raj Chetty and colleagues, published in an Opportunity Insights report, lends further credence to the conclusions reached by Armstrong and Hamilton and by Rendón.[13] Chetty and his colleagues find that who one's friends are matters most for low-income youths' shot at upward economic mobility. Those who make cross-class friendships—specifically, low-income youth who have middle- and upper-class friends—have a much clearer path to upward mobility than those whose friendship networks are segregated by social class.

Indeed, relationships matter. Yet mobility discourses tend to center individualism. The well-trodden discourse of the American Dream is a good example. The Dream discourse assumes that individuals are autonomous, and that all those who work hard have the ability to "pull themselves up by their bootstraps" on their own. In contrast, the educational mobility of the Latino youth I interviewed was enabled through a deeply relational and collaborative process. Their pathways to Amherst were paved with overlapping support networks rooted in family and community, and family and community continued to be central to how they experienced and understood their educational mobility after arriving at Amherst.

As such, it is not surprising that the vast majority of the youth I interviewed gave generous credit for their academic success to family sacrifice.[14] The psychologists Susan Sy and Jessica Romero have termed this "familismo," which they conceptualize as a cultural trait unique to Latino families.[15] Many of the participants in this study, both youth and their parents, similarly touted Latinos' unique cultural commitment to family. Yet in this book I operate from the premise that instead of being an essentialist cultural trait unique to Latinos, strong family ties are a product of immigration, which causes families to serve as a critical site of survival and mobility.[16] Immigration both generates and depends on strong family ties, which are, in turn, an important part of the educational mobility story of the second generation. This is not a uniquely Latino phenomenon.

Nazli Kibria, in her influential book *Family Tightrope*, for example, writes of the sacrifices and loyalties within Vietnamese immigrant families. She finds that even though Vietnamese women have more individual opportunity in the United States than in Vietnam, they maintain a loyalty to patriarchal family norms as a way to push back against the broader forms of immigrant marginalization their families are facing. Kibria aptly concludes that instead of drawing on culture to explain these strong ties, "immigrant families must be analyzed in relation to the external structural conditions encountered by immigrants in the host society."[17] Family and kin relationships become central to survival in the context of hostile contexts of immigrant reception.

Similarly, Cati Coe, writing about Ghanaian immigrant families, argues that when families lack necessary social supports and are thus left on their own "to figure it out," they "respond by adapting their existing beliefs, practices, and resources of family life . . . to their migration experience."[18] In other words, families develop different cultural frameworks and practices—what Coe calls "repertoires"—in order to respond to and survive in the face of structural challenges connected to their immigrant realities.

Immigrants from Latin America have also developed cultures of loyalty, collectivity, and knowledge sharing in order to survive in a society that has too often been hostile to their presence. As an example, immigrant family members, parents in particular, have developed the tradition of passing down to their children wisdom that they gained through their own migration and that helps youth survive and thrive. Norma Marrun finds that Latino students gain resilience, inspiration, and life-guiding information from their immigrant parents who use storytelling and *consejos* (advice infused with cultural values) to set high educational expectations and offer robust support for their children.[19] Many of these stories and *consejos* were inspired by the challenges and sacrifices that characterized their own migration to the United States.

Robert Smith similarly has argued that the second generation is motivated by an "immigrant bargain," in which immigrant parents expect their children to pay them back for the sacrifices implicit in immigration by achieving educational success.[20] And indeed, the participants in this study, like immigrant youth from other backgrounds, talked about this "bargain" as a driving motivation for their educational success.[21] The narrative of the immigrant bargain suggests that parents do everything in their power to foster success—including, for some, allowing their children to move away to pursue educational opportunities.[22] Children, for their part, strive to repay their parents for their sacrifice by achieving educational success. Just like Gaby, participants spoke of this bargain as central to their educational pathway and to how they thought about their responsibility to family. Yet, importantly, research suggests that the immigrant bargain bears fruit only when coupled with strong social supports.[23] Indeed, family, while critically important, is not enough. Among the youth in my sample, strong family networks overlapped with community and school-based networks to support their educational mobility.

While family is certainly central in the lives of immigrant youth, I do not intend to paint an overly romantic image of immigrant families. Family relationships, like all relationships, are imbued with power and differential interests and can get messy. In other words, immigrant family networks are not inherently supportive. They can also act as forms of social control, especially in families with high expectations of reciprocity.[24] These expectations of, and commitments to, reciprocity, which were common among study participants, came with a cost. Gaby, for example, felt a lot of stress because of the obligation she felt to her family.[25] Heightening her stress was her feeling that few of her peers and professors understood why she was so loyal.

Adding further stress, as Gaby and the other students in this study moved up the educational mobility ladder, they developed a more sophisticated understanding of the inequalities in opportunities and security that structured their relationships with family and kin. This understanding was similar to what Leisy Abrego terms the "relational legal consciousness" developed by U.S. citizen children with undocumented family members.[26] Abrego reports that her research participants, though formally privileged as citizens, often cited guilt, responsibility, and fear as emotions connected to their citizenship. These feelings arose because close family ties led them to internalize their family members' vulnerability and other experiences of being undocumented. Similarly, though participants in my study ultimately moved away from home to attend a college rooted in wealth and prestige, they continued to absorb the struggles and marginalization of the family members they left behind. They never lost sight of their families' struggles because they internalized those struggles as their own.

Not only did youth in my study internalize the social positions and struggles of their family members, but most of them also came to critically understand the social inequalities at the root of them. In the study conducted by Joanna Dreby and her colleagues, youth with U.S. citizenship who moved to Mexico with their deported parents came to understand the implications of inequalities in citizenship status through their migratory experiences.[27] Specifically, through their migration, they came to recognize that they had protections that their parents lacked. They also learned that the protections they enjoyed in the United States were not necessarily available to them in Mexico. Correspondingly, as youth in my study moved away from home and into an elite educational environment, they developed a more critical understanding of their educational privileges in relation to their family members' marginalization. They also came to see their own relative disadvantage in comparison to their wealthy, non-Latino White peers.

I argue that youth's critical understandings of inequality become more finely tuned as they are further immersed in contexts of wealth and Whiteness, where their abstract knowledge of inequality becomes an intimate part of their experience. Academic exposure to theories of inequality and marginalization further heightens their consciousness. Many thus come to comprehend the roots of the social inequalities that shape their families' struggles and opportunities, a realization that is both empowering and discouraging.

While the youth in this study became more cognizant of the structural aspects of their families' marginalization, they continued to reap inspiration from their families' sacrifices and struggles. They remained committed to their education because it was still the only avenue they saw in which they had a chance of uplifting their families. They also continued to pursue their education because it was meaningful in their lives, although it did require that they learn how to navigate the gaps between their individual interests and desires and the needs and expectations of their families. This was a lot to juggle. Remember that Gaby was ambivalent about turning away from her premed major to pursue her newly discovered passion for the humanities in large part because she knew she was the only one in her family with a shot at a financially lucrative career. As she said, "This isn't just about me." Gaby felt that she owed her family, especially her parents. She also came to understand that paying them back would be more difficult than her parents assumed.

A heavy sense of responsibility, mixed with an emotional stew of guilt, inspiration, hope, and fear, often accompanies this deepening consciousness. Thus, while the stories in this book celebrate the rich opportunities that educational mobility has created in the lives of low-income Latinos and the critical safety nets it has helped to weave, they also reveal that educational mobility can heighten inequalities and shift relationship dynamics within immigrant families and communities. Nevertheless, the individuals and families whose stories I share persisted and resisted, rewriting discourses of mobility and success in the process.

The stories in this book also suggest that geographic locale, or "place," influences the direction of educational mobility pathways as well as how youth experience these pathways. This is to say, where one is born matters, where one grows up matters, and where one's parents migrated from matters.[28] Place shapes the security, opportunities, networks, and information to which one has access, as well as the ways in which one experiences the transition away from home and into and through college and beyond.[29] Place also impacts the ways in which upwardly mobile youth think about family and home as they travel on their educational journeys and construct their plans and aspirations.

Smith's subtle insight that parents of aspiring children let them move away from home to attend college signals the importance of place in terms of educational mobility.[30] According to Krista Mattern and Jeff Wyatt, only 14 percent of American youth travel more than five hundred miles to attend college, and only 4 percent travel more than one thousand miles.[31] In comparison, Latino youth travel an average of only thirty-nine miles. For the vast majority in this study, moving far away from home to attend Amherst came with its own challenges connected to youth's responsibilities within their families.[32] Moving away also introduces another layer of relationality, namely, that which exists between places. Leaving home for school often means moving into a new climate, topography, demographic context, and built environment as well as confronting new cultural and sensual experiences. This is to say, the distance between home and school is not only geographic but also social.[33]

LATINO YOUTH IN ELITE SPACES

Although the youth in this book successfully accessed elite higher education, new barriers presented themselves as they moved through college—yet another way in which educational mobility proved to be more complicated than they had originally assumed. As Anthony Abraham Jack pertinently asserts, "Access alone is not enough for fostering inclusion and generating mobility."[34] A growing body of research suggests that adapting to an elite educational environment can be difficult, especially for students from working-class backgrounds.[35] And to be sure, the life histories I collected show that achieving educational mobility does not preclude the emotional challenges of moving between what can be radically different contexts of home and school, nor does it mitigate students' accompanying need to develop strategies to navigate the new and sometimes hostile social terrain of elite higher education.

As an example, the low-income students interviewed by Elizabeth Aries a couple of decades ago—also at Amherst College—reported that they did not recognize themselves or their backgrounds in the college's values and traditions, which were centered on the upper class.[36] Students told her that they found the environment to be unfamiliar and unsettling. Although they sensed the social inequality that structured the campus, their feelings of alienation were intensified by not having the space or the language to talk about it.

Making the situation even more challenging, Aries learned, was that students' identification with "home" changed while they were in college.[37] Here again, place matters: these students experienced their lives as split between two different social and material worlds. Although most worked hard to maintain strong family and kin relationships across what they recognized to be growing intrafamily and community inequalities, those who did still felt a sense of loss. Remember Gaby's words: "Home almost doesn't feel like home anymore." Like Gaby, other youth in this study struggled emotionally when those very family members who had been key to their survival and mobility could not understand what their lives were like in their new social and material world. Educational mobility, it seems, can come with a familial price.

This price is incurred as students come to see and understand their working-class families through a different lens. Allison Hurst, in her study of first-generation college students, blames colleges and universities for the way they relate to working-class students.[38] By suggesting that membership in the middle and upper classes should be aspiring students' end goal, Hurst argues, college messaging inadvertently puts down working-class cultures and jobs, alienating students who come from those backgrounds. Low-income students ultimately find themselves in a "class limbo." While striving to move up, they may feel they have betrayed their working-class families and communities.

Jack's research with low-income students at an Ivy League university identifies additional cultural and structural challenges facing low-income students.[39] He finds that entry into the elite educational sphere can be socially jarring, as there is an assumption of high levels of cultural capital and familiarity with academic practices like attending office hours, applying for summer internships, and negotiating with professors; these practices, however, are unfamiliar to many low-income individuals. Moreover, Jack finds that low-income students, despite living on elite campuses, may continue to struggle with structural violence connected to poverty, such as bouts of hunger or homelessness. Structural violence becomes apparent when newly diversified schools blindly assume a baseline of privilege in their student bodies, like not having to stay in the dormitory or use the dining hall during school vacations. Despite the diversification of elite higher education, I would suggest, some policies are still rooted in the assumption that students are middle- or upper-class.

Importantly, Jack argues, low-income students' experiences are differentiated by their precollege educational paths. He terms the students who attend preparatory programs that habituate them to an elite environment the "privileged poor." He finds that these students are incorporated into an elite environment more easily than the "doubly disadvantaged," who come from underfunded public high schools. In related work, Jack and Zennon Black find that while the privileged poor experienced attendance at an elite college as the organic next step on their mobility pathways and felt at ease and motivated to engage in the diverse community, the doubly disadvantaged tended to feel alienated.[40] They responded by drawing moral boundaries between themselves and more privileged students, withdrawing from campus life in the process. In this book, I pay close attention to the differential experiences of youth who are part of the privileged poor and those who are doubly disadvantaged. My findings are in line with Jack and Black's, in that those who came to Amherst from preparatory schools seem to have had an easier time and been more engaged in campus life than those who did not. That said, having an easier time did not erase their families' struggles or the responsibility they felt to ease them.

In my research, I learned that race matters too for youth's incorporation experiences. Terah Venzant Chambers and her colleagues suggest that "racial opportunity costs" be considered a means of understanding the trade-offs implicit in the high academic success of students of color.[41] They conclude that the "price" of success often includes intense psychological and social unease, specifically the stress of feeling isolated and misunderstood. To be sure, elite schools, notwithstanding their increasing focus on diversity, are not immune to racism.[42] Yung-Yi Diana Pan and Daisy Verduzco Reyes, for example, find that elite institutions, despite their efforts to bolster supports for students of color, inadvertently "ascribe" non-White students as "other."[43] The Latino students they interviewed experienced this ascription as alienation and exclusion. My participants had similar experiences.

This is all to suggest that diversity narratives and policies, however well intentioned, may actually mask inequalities and hinder belonging for the most marginalized.[44] Natasha Warikoo, in her study of diversity initiatives at Harvard and Brown, similarly finds that while an appreciation of diversity is increasingly central to an elite identity, and while the students she interviewed celebrated being part of a diverse campus, they expressed ambivalent support for redistributive policies and demonstrated little understanding of the structural inequalities framing their lives.[45]

Despite the many challenges faced by low-income students in the context of elite higher education, they find ways to survive and thrive, often by forming affinity groups.[46] And indeed, the youth in this study resisted marginalization by finding community with other Latino students, working-class students, and students of color. Having moved away from their families and communities, they created new kin networks that were key to their social survival and well-being.

Through it all, relationships matter. A lot. My participants experienced the elite environment of Amherst College through a relational lens. They did not leave home, family, or community behind when they arrived on campus. Instead, their familial and kin relationships, as well as the sounds, smells, and tastes of home, contextualized how they responded to their new educational home, and how they envisioned and strategized their postcollege futures.

THE STUDY

In centering the lives of Latino youth, my intent was to let their stories, experiences, and insights guide my writing and ultimately, in turn, to guide readers. I quote extensively from life history interviews, focus groups, and ethnographic family case studies that I conducted between 2016 and 2021. I edited the excerpts for length and, when necessary, for readability.

The core interview sample comprises sixty youth who occupied intersecting social positions. They all identified as low-income and, as such, were eligible for federal Pell grants or full financial assistance from Amherst

College. They were also the first in their families who were on course to graduate from college in the United States. They represented a mix of immigration statuses (U.S. citizen, permanent resident, undocumented, and DACA), they were members of mixed-status and U.S. citizen families, and they were part of families whose members had changed statuses over time. Throughout the book I pay close attention to how legal status shapes mobility pathways, experiences, and general family well-being. Participants identified as women, men, and nonbinary, and they represented a range of Latino backgrounds from diverse U.S. geographic locations (see appendix A).

All of the students I interviewed for this book were on track to graduate from college. At Amherst, this did not make them exceptional. Amherst's general graduation rate within six years is in the ninetieth percentile. For 2016, the most recent year for which there are data, 92 percent of Amherst students had graduated within six years. For this same year, the graduation rate for Latino students was 96 percent. Yet if we focus on the four-year graduation rate—that is, on those who graduated without taking a leave of absence—the numbers are lower: 85 percent for all students and 81 percent for Latino students. In other words, although this book focuses on Latino students who had "made it," this category encompasses the vast majority of entering students at Amherst. As I hope this book will make clear, however, "making it" was no easy feat for study participants. From what I have learned in this study, I imagine that those who did leave Amherst, whether to transfer elsewhere or to stop their studies altogether, did not do so flippantly. Indeed, a few of the youth you will get to know in this book took multiple leaves en route to graduation, and there were times when they did not know how they were going to get through.

Throughout the book, I analyze students' experiences and achievements in relation to those of their families. Similarly, Cynthia Feliciano argues that to truly measure the educational mobility of second-generation immigrant youth, we should analyze their success in comparison to their parents' educational attainment in the home country.[47] According to Feliciano, almost all immigrants to the United States are positively selected for immigration—that is, they have more education than the average citizen in their home country. But levels of selectivity differ quite a bit between immigrant groups. The children of immigrants who have high selectivity, tend to have greater educational advantage in the United States than do those with low selectivity. To ground this, Asian immigrants tend to have high selectivity, while Latin American immigrants tend to have low selectivity. The vast majority of the parents of youth in this study attained only a high school degree or lower in their home country (see appendix A). This is to say, they had education levels below or right around the averages of their home countries. Thus, even when analyzed in a transnational context, the youth in this study did not grow up with relative educational or class advantage.

Although I sought out students who identified as low-income, Latino, and first-generation college students, I left other parameters of the sample open in order to explore additional factors that might prove to be important. For example, upon noticing that place was emerging across the interviews as an influence on participants' educational pathways, I conducted two focus groups. The five members of the first group were students who grew up in global cities with robust immigrant communities—New York, Houston, Los Angeles, and Boston. The second included five students who grew up in smaller cities, towns, or rural areas—Oklahoma City, southern New Jersey, rural North Carolina, Wyoming, and West Texas. Chapter 1 delves into the impact of place on youth's pathways to Amherst.

With ten participants, I also completed "family constellation interviews" that included at least one parent and a sibling.[48] I selected these families for geographic diversity and for siblings who were on varied educational trajectories. Eight families lived in or adjacent to major cities or immigration hubs, and two of the families were located in remote areas. Seven of the families included siblings who were on similar educational trajectories, while three of the families included siblings who were on diverging tracks in which one sibling was not expected to graduate from a four-year college.

In addition to interviewing family members, I undertook "domestic ethnography," spending a day with nine of the families in their homes and exploring their communities with them as my guide.[49] The time I spent with students and their families in their communities was invaluable, as it allowed me to see students "at home" and thus to better understand their experiences of moving between the worlds of home and school. The tenth constellation interview took place during the COVID-19 pandemic and thus over Zoom.

When COVID-19 struck the United States in the spring of 2020, the world was turned upside down for the participants in this study, as was true for many people. The geographic distance that I typically found to be common between upwardly mobile students and their families evaporated when Amherst closed and students went home. The informal ethnographic observation I was able to do while teaching remotely was informative. Peering through a Zoom lens into the lives of my Latino students, I was able to see the chaos and heightened insecurity that COVID had sparked. Many had returned to crowded homes with little private space for study or class participation, and they faced increased financial and domestic responsibilities. These students told me that they felt the worlds of home and school colliding even more than normal as they tried to center their academic work in a context in which it felt wholly disconnected and pragmatically unimportant.

Soon after the start of the pandemic, Latino students who lived in COVID hotspots like New York, Los Angeles, and Houston started to report sick family members, revealing yet another way in which place mattered in their lives. Many had family members who were essential workers, and I witnessed how quickly COVID could spread through multi-generational immigrant households. Additionally, emails I received from students who had recently graduated and were immersed in graduate school or professional lives revealed that the stakes of their success seemed higher than ever. Their commitment to family continued to serve as a source of both motivation and stress.

My observations and conversations during the early weeks and months of the COVID pandemic confirmed that this study needed to include youth's experiences dealing with the public health and economic crisis spawned by the virus. Did their educational mobility protect them in the context of the pandemic? What impact did the pandemic have on their role within their family? Was it affecting their aspirations and future plans? From December 2020 to December 2021, I did two additional rounds of in-depth interviews with forty of my original sample of sixty partici-pants. I had conducted all of the original sixty interviews in person, but I did these follow-up interviews over Zoom. I have attempted to incor-porate the COVID crisis organically into this book. It enters for the first time, as a shock of sorts, in chapter 5, and then weaves its way through the final three chapters. This progression mirrors the way it appeared in and then occupied the lives of my participants.

Throughout this research, I prioritized learning about the meaning that educational mobility has had in the lives of my participants and their families. Life history interviews allowed me to guide them through their childhood and adolescence by prompting them to tell me stories about the relationships, experiences, and places that mattered most to them. Most of the formal interviews I completed, including the COVID interviews, lasted between two and four hours, while some lasted between five and six hours. I had multiple interactions with most participants. A life history approach also allowed me to analyze mobility from the perspective of my participants and to gain an understanding of how they defined and understood their success—or in the case of family members, their chil-dren's or sibling's success. It also enabled me to put the key relationships, institutions, places, and experiences that shaped their mobility trajectories into a larger social-historical context.

The bulk of this study was based at Amherst College, where I am a faculty member. When I first started talking to colleagues about my research, they commonly asked: Are you going to identify Amherst? Why not use a pseudonym as most authors do? I thought seriously about these important questions and sought counsel from trusted mentors and authors. Ultimately, I decided I needed to name Amherst. Indeed, it is the intimate relationship I have with Amherst, as well as the trust I have built with Latino students on campus, that made this research possible. Just as the substantive argument in this book is centered on relationships, so too are the methodology and project construction. These are relationships I was able to build only because of my insider position at the college. Amherst's institutional review board, along with the students and parents I interviewed, approved this approach.

My position as an Amherst College faculty member also gave me unique ethnographic insights that helped contextualize the interviews. For example, my position allowed me to spend countless hours listening to Latino students talk informally about the complex combinations of opportunities and challenges implicit in their educational experiences. Although I do not draw from these informal conversations directly in this book—except for the couple of situations in which the student later joined the project as a participant (as Gaby did)—these conversations provided invaluable context and validation to the data I collected in the formal interviews.

I considered sampling outside of Amherst but decided, after analyzing preliminary interviews, that Amherst, and specifically its social structures and policies, had shaped participants' experiences in particular ways that I wanted to hold constant. Containing the research to Amherst allowed me to track the impact of Amherst's policies on the mobility pathways of students and the well-being of their families. And yet, importantly, because Amherst is part of a growing network of colleges and universities that have prioritized need-blind admissions and implemented equity and inclusion policies, the insights the research yields and the policy implications I discuss in the conclusion extend far beyond the confines of Amherst College.

Finally, my faculty position at Amherst enabled me to collaborate with student research assistants who were invested in this topic. From the project's inception, I worked with a small rotating team of students, the vast majority of whom were low-income children of immigrants and the first in their family to go to college. My student collaborators worked with me to develop the literature review, hone thematic developments, code and analyze blinded interview data, and do some of the interviewing and focus groups. A few research assistants also participated in the life history interviews. Most of them were social science and humanities students who had some training in research methods. Still, I did qualitative methods and ethics training with all of them. For five years, our research team met weekly to discuss our work and share insights. These meetings and the relationships I built with research assistants were among the most rewarding aspects of this project. Their contributions to this project were invaluable (see appendix B for more detail).

Of course, situating this research in my job site also presented risks and complications. I have been critically aware since this project's beginning that my position as a faculty member doing research with students, if not regulated, could put unintended pressure on them. As such, I put protections in place. For example, my research assistants recruited all interview participants. Also, while several participants had taken a class with me, I never conducted interviews with a student who was currently enrolled in a class with me or intended to take a class with me in the future (though in the latter case there was one exception). Because the majority of participants were third- or fourth-year students when the interviews took place, by the time their interviews were transcribed and analyzed they had already graduated. All of the names I use in this book are pseudonyms, and I have changed or generalized other identifying information when asked to do so by participants.

I also tried to be reflexive about my positionality, both in my conversations with students and in the analysis of the data. I am White, non-Latino, from a middle-class background, and with no recent immigrant family history. And yet I shared with my students the experience of being new to Amherst College and feeling like an imposter in that elite space. Coming to Amherst from Montana State and having attended a public undergraduate university, I too was unprepared for the social distance I had to overcome to feel at home at Amherst. Yet, while I may have shared the imposter syndrome with most of my participants, I was privileged in many ways that they were not. In addition to my race and class privilege, I had family who lived with me, and I was tenured, a status that brought me the security of knowing I had many years, if it were to take that long, to find my social place in the Amherst community. The student participants, in contrast, were transitory and away from their family support networks.

As I approached and moved through this project, I drew on the only antidote to my privilege I know: a mix of reflexivity and intentional humility. I entered this research with a commitment to contributing to scholarly and policy discussions that would increase access to and better the experience of educational mobility for the Latino second generation. Throughout I have worked hard to listen and learn, never losing sight of the unique privileges that paved my way into the lives and worlds of the participants in this study.

As a final note, readers have by now noted that I have chosen to use "Latino" instead of "Latinx" or "Latine" in my writing. I truly struggled with this decision, and I am still not sure I got it right. Mostly, I was influenced by the family members I interviewed, the vast majority of whom (meaning all but siblings who also attended highly selective schools) did not use "Latinx" or "Latine" and instead used "Hispanic" or "Latino" when they spoke with me. I am aware that the use of "Latinx" or "Latine" can signify "elite." While this characterization fits the educational status of the majority of my study participants, it does not for most other people in their lives. Ultimately, I have chosen not to use "Latinx" or "Latine" because of the class exclusivity of the term at the time I did this study, as revealed across my interviews.

A NOTE ABOUT AMHERST COLLEGE

Amherst College is consistently ranked at or near the top of all liberal arts colleges in the United States. In 2022 it had an admission rate of only 7 percent. In this respect, it is exclusive. Amherst is also one of the most diverse of the highly selective colleges in the United States. In the 2021–2022 academic year, 49 percent of the student body identified as U.S. students of color, 15 percent were first-generation college students, and 21 percent were Pell grant–eligible, an indication that they came from the lowest economic strata in the country. During this same academic year, Amherst became one of the first private colleges in the country to end legacy admissions, a long-standing policy that gave an admission boost to the children of alumni. In this way, Amherst has established itself as an institution that seeks not only to attract the "best and the brightest" but also to make an Amherst education accessible independent of background or ability to pay its steep bill, which was approximately $80,000 in the 2021–2022 academic year.

Yet Amherst has not always been diverse or progressive. Founded in 1821 to serve "indigent young men of piety and talents" seeking positions in the Christian ministry, Amherst supported cohorts of men of modest means, mostly White, for the first fifty years. This student population changed, as it did with many colleges, in the late 1800s, when college became not only about intellectual endeavors but about social networking and fun.[50] For the next century and a half, Amherst students were predominantly White men who came from families with high financial or cultural status. It was not until the 1970s that Amherst enrolled its first small cohort of Latino students, and the overtly hostile reception they were met with persisted into the 1990s.[51] Women were not accepted into the college until 1975. Amherst became the progressive institution it is today through the combined hard work and bold leadership of several of the college's deans and presidents and, most importantly, the activism and leadership of marginalized students.[52]

Currently, Amherst College is one of only six U.S. institutions of higher education that are need-blind in their admission process and that meet the full financial need for all students, regardless of citizenship status. The other five schools are Harvard, the Massachusetts Institute of Technology, Dartmouth, Yale, and Princeton. The generous financial aid that Amherst provides makes it likely that low-income students will graduate debt-free, barring any personal loans they elect to take on. As at other highly selective schools, Amherst recruitment initiatives target students who might not otherwise know that, if admitted, Amherst will meet their full need with financial aid. The college committed to further enhancing financial aid when it ended legacy admissions in 2021. Specifically, as the policy now stands, 80 percent of U.S. households would be eligible to send a student to Amherst who, once admitted and enrolled, would receive a scholarship that covers full tuition. Furthermore, students from families earning less than the median U.S. household income—that is, between $67,500 and $141,000—typically receive a scholarship that covers not only full tuition but also housing and meals. Amherst's recruitment efforts include outreach to high schools and community colleges throughout the United States as well as partnerships with privately funded "pipeline programs," typically located in global U.S. cities, that support high-achieving youth's access to elite schools. Where and how recruitment happens is important, as most U.S. high school students who would qualify for full tuition grants from elite colleges do not even apply.[53]

Elite schools like Amherst are unique in the ways they bring individuals from different race, class, gender, and immigration backgrounds into the same residential community. But intentional diversity does not dismantle deep-rooted inequalities that frame institutional life and individual experiences.[54] Although Amherst is celebrated as one of the most diverse and policy-progressive institutions in the country—as indicated by its receipt of the prestigious 2016 Cooke Prize for Equity in Educational Excellence—inequality continues to frame students' lived campus experiences.[55]

For example, while over half of Amherst's students receive financial aid and over 20 percent are Pell grant–eligible, around 20 percent of students come from the top 1 percent of the income hierarchy.[56] Of course, these data, published in 2017, were calculated before several of the key changes noted earlier were taking effect, and so we can imagine that the disparity curve has flattened a bit. Still, it holds that while Amherst is need-blind for all students, low-income Latinos, especially the undocumented, represent only a small slice of the general student population. And despite Amherst's progressive policies, deep structural divides persist amid its great diversity of students.

In November 2015, a small group of Black women students organized a protest in Amherst's Frost Library in solidarity with those who had been impacted by racist incidents on campuses around the country, most notably at the University of Missouri. What was initially planned as an hourlong event turned into a multiday sit-in after students of color spontaneously started sharing testimonies of their experiences of racism at Amherst. The college would never be the same again. What soon came to be known as "The Uprising" forced Amherst to publicly confront its racist roots. The process that followed and continues to this day has been tense and painful at times, yet also healing and generative. Many of the programs that the college now has in place to support students who come from marginalized backgrounds came out of The Uprising. To be sure, there is still much work to be done to make Amherst a truly inclusive community.[57] It is my hope that this book will contribute to the important work that is underway at Amherst and other institutions committed to bolstering diversity and equity and fostering inclusion.

AN OUTLINE OF THE BOOK

The chapters that follow draw from life history interviews and focus groups to pave a chronological road through the educational lives of low-income Latino youth at Amherst College, highlighting their evolving experiences of educational mobility and its relationship to their prospects for and perspectives on social mobility.

Chapter 1 describes the various pathways to educational mobility that led my participants from their home communities to Amherst. This chapter reveals the ways in which youth participants and the key actors in their lives—parents, teachers, mentors—bought into a belief system that equates education with social mobility. The chapter reveals that the prescriptive formula at the heart of this ideology—that a combination of hard work, good grades, and individual sacrifice leads to mobility—is incomplete. Instead, the overlapping social networks of family and kin, local schools and communities, and elite recruitment organizations are key to students' ability to achieve exceptional educational mobility. This chapter also focuses on the critical impact of place on both network access and youth's experience of their educational pathways.

Chapter 2 takes the reader into the experiences of these Latino youth as they left home and transitioned into and through their new world of Amherst College. It documents and explores the challenges that students faced as they confronted wealth and Whiteness, often for the first time. It is about the initial disappointment they felt when they got to campus and their belief in meritocracy was challenged, and their critical understanding of social inequality honed. The chapter also shows the strategies that students used to survive, thrive, and resist in a context that often felt alienating and exclusive.

In chapter 3, I bring family back to the fore as I look at the impact of youth's transition into elite higher education on their closest relationships. Here students realized the high, though unforeseen, familial price of educational mobility. Specifically, this chapter delves into how youth's relationship with "home" evolved, and sometimes fractured, as they developed new perspectives on their social world and advanced their critical understanding of their place in the world and their family's place.

Chapter 4 explores the impact of educational mobility on sibling relationships. Here I show how youth struggled to inspire their siblings with the message that education is "the way out," while simultaneously feeling disconnected from family and ambivalent about the mobility formula they preached. I structure this chapter around three sibling pairs. Two of these pairs included siblings who were on diverging educational pathways. That is, while one sibling was set to graduate from Amherst College, the other was unlikely to ever graduate from college or even to achieve any educational credentials beyond high school. The third pair included siblings who were on similar pathways, both having made it to and through elite colleges. My goal with this chapter is to provide an intimate look into the different ways in which educational mobility can impact intragenerational family relationships and shape the consciousnesses of family members.

Chapter 5 discusses how COVID impacted educational mobility pathways and experiences. It reveals the important ways in which place shaped the initial impacts of the virus on participants, while also exploring the economic and mental health impacts on youth over the first year and a half of the pandemic. This chapter also looks at the new family responsibilities that emerged in the lives of participants and the ways in which their educational mobility helped them fulfill them. It brings in the perspectives of youth who were students at Amherst when the pandemic began as well as the views of those who had recently graduated.

Chapter 6, the last empirical chapter, looks at the ways in which educational mobility shaped and shifted the hopes and aspirations of these Latino youth. It shows that, at the end of the day, they held on to the belief that education leads to social mobility, though they had gained a critical consciousness of inequality through the process. Their goals reflected this duality. This chapter pays special attention to how illegality and COVID framed their aspirational lives and how they responded.

The book concludes with a summary of the key themes that emerged in my data and a discussion of their policy implications for higher education. Throughout this book I aim to show my readers how larger social, economic, and legal forces shape the daily lives of aspiring youth and their families.

Chapter 1 | Pathways to Amherst

NOEL WAS BORN in 1999 on the outskirts of Denver, Colorado, which at the time was a new destination for Mexican immigrants. Most of them were drawn to the area by its abundant and relatively high-paying construction work. Noel had fond memories of Colorado, where he lived in a tight-knit trailer park that was home to many of his family and kin. As he remembered it, his early childhood was structured by school, family, and play, all of which brought him great joy. When Noel was ten, he was invited to join a program at the local Boys & Girls Club whose mission was to encourage gifted low-income youth to start thinking about college. One of Noel's fondest childhood memories was the trip he took with this group to the University of Colorado. "That's when I decided I was going to college," he told me.

Life was more difficult for Noel's mom, Suzy. A single mom during much of Noel's early childhood, she worked long hours and struggled to make ends meet. When I interviewed her in 2019, she told me, "When I was pregnant, I remember thinking, 'How am I going to support a child?' There was no option. I had to figure it out. But it was really difficult." Yet, despite her struggles, she always found the time and energy to encourage Noel toward educational success. If he misbehaved, for example, she punished him by making him work on his multiplication tables or his cursive writing. She laughed as she admitted that the strategy had failed miserably. As she had quickly learned, schoolwork was not an appropriate punishment for Noel—he loved it too much.

Suzy was born in rural Kansas, where her parents were migrant agricultural workers. She lived there until she was ten, at which time she returned "home" with her mother to a small town in Durango, Mexico. As a child and teenager, Suzy was a strong student, with dreams of college and a career as a teacher. Her life, however, took a different path. When she was eighteen, her dad told her to pack a small bag for a trip to Colorado, where they had extended family. Suzy assumed that they were just going for a visit. When they arrived, her father shocked her with the news that she would have to stay, live with her uncle, and get a job so she could send money home to her mom and younger siblings. Suzy's smile disappeared and tears emerged as she relayed the painful memory. After a moment of pensive silence, she wiped her eyes. She then explained that it was because she had to sacrifice her own dreams for her family's well-being that she was so committed to giving her children more opportunity. Noel was born three years after Suzy moved to Colorado.

When Noel was five years old, Suzy repartnered, had another child, then repartnered again. While still only in elementary school, Noel began taking on child-care responsibilities at home. Then, when Noel was in middle school, the Great Recession hit. Noel's stepdad, Tomás, also a migrant from Mexico, lost his job and decided to move the family to West Texas, where he and Suzy both had family and the economy promised more opportunity. Noel was sad to leave Colorado, he told me, but understood that the move was necessary for the family's financial well-being. In Texas they settled in a predominantly working-class Latino community at least three and a half hours from any major city. This place that would be Noel's home until he left for college shaped his educational pathway in important and distinct ways.

I visited Noel and Suzy at their home in December 2019. Getting there was no easy feat. To travel at a reasonable price, I flew into Austin, rented a car, and then drove three and a half hours through the plains of Texas to their small brick house. The region where they settled is flat and expansive. Sparsely populated towns fit seamlessly with the desert plants and trees that dot the dry, rugged landscape. Their community is surrounded by ranchland and a growing number of oil fields. Railroad tracks divide it, marking the boundaries of its two high schools. Noel attended the smaller, poorer high school, where the majority of his classmates were Latino, mirroring the demographics of the area, though he also had non-Latino White and Black peers. Noel described his high school community as tight, because "we were united by social class. We were all poor." Across town, wealthier families who were mostly connected to the oil industry and ranching attended the much larger and better-resourced high school.

When Noel and his family first arrived in West Texas, many Latinos in the area worked in the meatpacking industry. Although the region's transition to an oil economy soon thereafter opened up new job opportunities, none offered a secure living wage. Noel's stepdad worked in meatpacking and then became a truck driver, a typical job progression for Latinos in the area. Suzy, who by that time had two more young children, tended to things at home. Money was tight. Noel remembered worrying a lot about his family's finances and wondering if or how he would ever be able to afford college.

Throughout it all, school was Noel's haven. From his first year in Texas, his grades put him at the top of his class, and his teachers noticed. He was recruited for the math team as an eighth-grader. As a freshman, he joined the marching band and formed close bonds with classmates during their 6:00 AM practices and raucous performances at the notorious Friday night football games. When he was a sophomore, Noel stepped onto his school's limited Advanced Placement track. When he aced AP Calculus the next year, his math teacher sat him down and explained that while there were no more math opportunities at his high school, she thought he had the smarts and maturity to complete advanced calculus on his own. So he did. When he couldn't pay the bill for his AP texts and tests, it was paid by an anonymous donor, who Noel thought might have been his eleventh-grade physics teacher, one of his many supporters.

Throughout high school, Noel had a number of committed mentors cheering him on toward college, pointing him mostly toward local and regional state schools; a few encouraged him, however, to broaden his horizons and consider Texas A&M or the University of Texas, both of which were a few hours away. None mentioned the possibility of leaving Texas or attending a private school. Noel thought that they didn't know it was an option. Through it all, Suzy and Tomás, while supportive of Noel's college aspirations, were not directly engaged in his education. They were operating in survival mode at the time, and there was no easy way for them to connect with the school community. Also, they didn't speak English, and only a few of Noel's teachers spoke Spanish.

Noel remembered that when the time came to take the PSAT in his junior year, his first formal step toward college, he paused when he got to a question on the registration page about whether he wanted his scores shared with colleges and universities around the country. He decided to check the box. After Noel placed in the ninety-ninth percentile on the test, which included a perfect performance in math, he got a letter from Amherst College inviting him to apply and offering him a paid trip to visit campus. Similar letters came in shortly thereafter from Washington University, Williams College, and others. Noel was floored. Never having heard of any of these schools, he did not know what to make of the offers. For the first time he realized that there might be college opportunities beyond West Texas that he and his teachers had not considered even possible.

Noel remembered this time in his life with crystal clarity. He recalled the vice principal's exuberant response when he shared his college invitations with her. In all her years of teaching, she had never had a student receive this kind of attention from private schools. He remembered her advice: "Noel, you need to think big. You need to take advantage of all of these opportunities. Don't let anyone limit your dreams." Noel took her words to heart. After that conversation, he clearly recalled, he looked around his high school lobby at the military recruiting tables and college flags from regional Texas colleges and thought, *Wow, I can't believe this is happening. I might have a ticket that could take me beyond West Texas*. Noel's love of his small town and loyalty to Texas were unwavering. Nonetheless, he longed to explore new places and opportunities. He still wondered what would have happened if he had not checked that box.

Noel's pathway to Amherst was similar in important ways to the pathways of most of the research participants in this book. His family and kin formed the base of his educational trajectory. Starting when he was a young boy, they provided security and support, taught him resilience, and instilled high educational expectations. But the support of family was not enough. Noel was also immersed in robust local school and community networks, first in Colorado and then in Texas, in which cross-class actors—community leaders, teachers, and school staff—identified his talents and gave him individually focused encouragement and mentorship that guided him toward college. But even this support and guidance were not enough. Noel then needed to simultaneously leverage the support and expectations of both his immigrant family and his mentors in order to access and then navigate elite college recruitment networks. For Noel, accessing and then navigating these networks was tricky, and the stakes of each decision he made were high.

It is here, in his access to and navigation of elite networks, that Noel's story diverges from the experience of most of the other youth I interviewed. Whereas most had access to teachers, advisers, or mentors who were able to connect them with elite educational opportunities, Noel tapped into the elite college recruitment network only after checking the right box on the PSAT registration form. Their very different experiences in accessing recruitment networks shows that where one grows up matters.

Indeed, the life histories I collected reveal that place is a critical factor shaping youth's ability to leverage their family and institutional networks to tap into elite recruitment networks. Specifically, youth who grew up in global cities (New York, Boston, Los Angeles, Chicago, Miami, Houston) that are hubs for financial and educational capital as well as for immigration tended to have readier access to cross-class actors who could connect them with elite recruitment networks than did those who grew up in secondary cities, suburbs, or remote areas.[1] This accords with Caroline Hoxby and Christopher Avery's finding that while most U.S. high school students who would qualify for full tuition grants from highly selective schools do not apply, those who do tend to be from major urban areas.[2] Meanwhile, rural youth tend to apply to local state schools.

In the pages that follow, I explore the roles of family, community, and elite networks in youth's pathways to exceptional educational mobility, paying special attention to variations by place. All three networks proved necessary to secure a pathway to Amherst.

FAMILY SUPPORT AND THE IMMIGRANT BARGAIN

Family support was critical to the success and well-being of all my participants. Whether they were from cities, suburbs, or small towns, most grew up in areas they described as poor or working-class, with weak social infrastructures. In these challenging social contexts, family networks provided basic security. Families who were able to provide this security had access to housing and food, basic protections that cannot be assumed to be present for all immigrant families. Additionally, for all but a couple of my participants, parents served as important sources of motivation and resilience. Some version of the immigrant bargain had been struck in the majority of their narratives. Youth spoke about being inspired, and at times burdened, by their parents' great sacrifices and high expectations. Their parents strongly believed that their child's elite education would lead to social mobility for the whole family, and the youth felt the pressure to make this come true.

Antonio was only four years old when he left rural Oaxaca with his young mother and uncle. Their destination was a small Mexican enclave in southern New Jersey where his grandparents had settled a few years earlier. Antonio's memories of his early childhood were transnationally scattered. He remembered the dusty roads in his southern Mexican village and the warm feeling of being surrounded by family. His memories of leaving his village, however, were vague, as were his memories of their border crossing and initial settlement in the United States. He told me that the only clear recollection he had from that time was his unwavering faith in his mom; he knew that as long as they were together, he would be okay.

In the United States, Antonio's mom was "always, always, always working." He paid close attention to her work ethic and determination, and as he grew older he began to be inspired by her *consejos*. "To be successful," she would tell him, he would "have to work harder than everyone else" and "be better than exceptional." He would have "to be perfect." She also told Antonio that education was the only ticket she could offer him out of a life of financial insecurity. "We didn't have that much money, but when it came to education my mom . . . held nothing back. She was, like, if I have to work these hours for you to be able to do the projects that you need to do, I'll give it to you. . . . I didn't have that many clothes or toys . . . but when it came to education . . . she was open to whatever I needed."

When Antonio learned that he was undocumented, he finally understood why his mom's tone was always serious when she delivered her advice, and why she had set the bar so high. Coming from an undocumented, working-class family shaped Antonio's goals and ideas of success. He was still quite young when he set the goal of repaying them by doing well in everything. The immigrant bargain became the elixir for his dreams and the emotional fuel driving him to pursue an elite education.

Alberto was born in Guatemala. Like Antonio, he came to the United States, undocumented, with his mother when he was only a toddler. They settled in Houston, where they had family and there was a large Guatemalan community. Alberto spoke emotionally about the risks that his mother took and the suffering she endured leaving Guatemala and coming to the United States in order to secure a better life for him. A junior when I first interviewed him, he credited his mom for his educational drive and opportunities. "I think it [her immigration story] really pushed me to try to do my best . . . to please her because I knew how much she had sacrificed. . . . My mom tried to get me into really good schools so I could have a good education." Indeed, they were both committed to the idea that Alberto's educational success was the only way they could achieve a better life.

Parents coupled their belief in education as the key to mobility with rules to ensure that their children stayed serious and focused. Iván's story serves as an example. He grew up in the Bronx. His mom was Honduran and his dad Puerto Rican. He wanted to spend his afternoons playing sports with his friends, but his mother did not allow it until he could assure her that his homework was done, and done well. "She'd always ask me . . . 'Did you finish your homework? . . . You can't go outside until you finish your homework.' . . . She was always lurking there. If I got anything below a ninety she'd be disappointed." Miguel shared a similar story. He grew up in a multigenerational Dominican household in New York City. "My mom was really . . . strict about certain things, so that helped me to focus a lot on school. I loved video games . . . but my mom prohibited me from playing video games during the weekdays. I couldn't touch them. . . . I had to study."

A central part of parents' commitment to and sacrifice for their children's education was making sure that their children did not have to work outside the home. Only seven of the sixty youth I interviewed had a job during high school. Several told me that they wanted to work but their parents would not allow it, and the few who did work told me that they had to talk their parents into allowing it. Parents wanted their children's priority to be school. Most of the families could have used the extra income, but not letting their children work was part of parents' sacrifice.

Paola's parents, both Mexican, worked extra shifts so that she could focus solely on school. According to Paola, "School was always the most important. My mom used to say . . . 'The only thing you have to do is school. We're working our asses off so that you can go to school.'" Beatriz heard a similar narrative. She migrated from Brazil with her parents and brother when she was in elementary school. After overstaying their tourist visa, they became undocumented and life was a constant struggle. Beatriz wanted to work in order to ease her family's financial stress, but her parents would not allow it.

> My mom would always say . . . "I don't want you to work, I just want you to study. I don't want you cleaning houses like we're cleaning houses. I want something better for you. I want you to excel in school." . . . And I always wanted to prove to my parents that . . . cleaning houses and doing all these humiliating jobs was going to be worth it. . . . I was going to make them proud.

Parents validated their children's interpretation of their messaging. In my conversations with them, they talked about their own need to work when they were children. Indeed, most said that they could not remember a time in their childhood when they weren't engaged in work, such as caring for children, vending goods on the streets, or working in the fields. College had not been an option for these parents. They wanted a different path for their children.

Remember that Noel's mother Suzy had wanted to study beyond high school, but she never had the opportunity. Instead, her parents made her work to help support her younger siblings. After settling in Colorado, she vowed that she would never let work get in the way of her children's education.

> My childhood was really difficult. . . . I wanted to continue studying. I wanted to be a teacher. But there was never an option because I had to work and help with everything at home. (crying) . . . I always tell Noel that my sacrifice is not for me, it's for him. The only thing I want is for my children to have more opportunity. I never pressure Noel, but I tell him that his responsibility is school. Mine is the house. . . . The only thing he has to do is focus on his education.

Noel told me that he never let himself lose sight of how much his mom had to give up so that he could have the opportunities she missed.

Miguel's mom, Elaine, went to high school in the United States after migrating from the Dominican Republic as a teen. She wanted to go to college, but her formal education came to a halt after high school graduation. Like Suzy, she had no option but to get a full-time job. She had no safety net, and her family was counting on her to pitch in financially. She found work as a waitress at an Ivy League club in New York City, a job she has now held for over twenty years. It was there, waiting on wealthy, high-status alums of prestigious universities, that she committed herself to laying a path for her children to achieve the same status. Elaine made sure that they attended the best public schools available, and she kept an eye out for scholarship opportunities for private programs. At home, she set strict rules so that school always came first. "I am very strict. [I told my kids,] 'You don't have to help me out with the house. . . . I want you to do . . . your homework. Your [job is to be] a good student, and I take care of everything else. I don't care if I have no sleep. . . . But you have to do well in school.'" Elaine found a lot of pleasure in now being able to share with the customers she served that her son graduated from Amherst and her daughter from Brown.

Pablo and Aurelia both migrated from Guanajuato, Mexico, to California. Pablo came first, enduring a brutal border crossing, followed by sleeping in his car for three months while he worked in the fields of southern California. Both Pablo and Aurelia regret that they never had the opportunity to study beyond primary school. They vowed to do whatever they could so that their son Omar—a participant in this study—and their other children would not have the same limitations. In their minds, that meant making sure school was always their top priority. When I interviewed them in the summer of 2018, Aurelia told me:

> We always told our kids that education was the most important thing. We never let them work. We worked so they could focus on school. Well, sometimes they would work a bit with my husband during vacations, but never during school. They always wanted to work, to help. But we only let them do a little bit . . . enough so they know how hard it is and how little it is paid. This helps them understand what opportunities they have.

Pablo and Aurelia parented strategically, allowing their children to work only once in a while in order to teach them about the difficult reality of hard physical labor and to nurture their belief that an education was the way to a better future.

While themes of family sacrifice and support are threaded throughout the life histories I collected, I also encountered some resentment and frustration on the part of youth. Indeed, sacrifice and high expectations can exert pressure. Yet even those youth experiencing resentment remained committed to the immigrant bargain. Ben, for example, came to the United States with his mom on a tourist visa during the Colombian civil war. Although he understood and appreciated his mom's desire to provide him with security and opportunity, he begrudged her decision to migrate without documentation. Still, he wanted to honor her sacrifice.

> I've really resented my mom for putting us in this situation. . . . I love my mom and the sacrifices she made, but I don't trust her judgment. . . . Like around DACA. . . . That's when . . . my resentment was really building. . . . Still . . . I want to come out of this [college] with a financially stable position where I can support my mom and insulate her from any other troubles . . . because of the . . . sacrifices she's made to help me get here.

Youth mentioned other resentments, most having to do with their parents' inability to help them with schoolwork or navigating the education system. This resentment was most noticeable among those who lived in remote areas that were ill equipped to support immigrant youth and help them flourish in school. Brenda, for example, grew up in the rural Mountain West. Hers was one of the few immigrant families in the area. With no teachers or staff at her school who spoke Spanish, it was difficult for her parents to engage with her education. "I kind of had resentment towards my parents for not being involved in school, and helping me when I needed it. I remember having a lot of friends saying, 'Oh, I had my mom look over my essay and she helped me write it up.' And I'd be like, 'She did what?' It was just hard for them [her parents] to be involved."

The same was true for Noel and Kevin, who similarly remembered being frustrated that their parents could not support them, even though they understood why. As noted at the start of this chapter, Noel grew up in new immigrant destinations in Colorado and Texas. Kevin, born in Mexico, spent most of his childhood in Oklahoma. Their parents, while supporting their drive to be top students, were otherwise disengaged from their education, partly owing to communication and cultural barriers, but also because of their unrelenting work schedules and low educational levels. Noel "loved" school, he said, "but they were just never able to help me. . . . I asked for first-grade math help, and they couldn't help me because their education is very minimal. . . . So it's that resentment . . . for not being able to . . . support me and not being involved." Similarly, when Kevin won a school spelling bee, he recalled, "I actually started crying, because I realized my parents weren't in the audience, and I was mad. . . . But they had to work. They had kids to take care of and they had responsibilities. . . .

And it's this sense of remorse, or just being mad, but also understanding it's not their fault." Noel and Kevin both understood why their parents could not be involved in their schoolwork and activities, but that didn't alleviate their frustration and sadness.

Even more common than feelings of resentment toward their parents were the tensions that arose, youth noted, over their leaving home to attend college. The parents I interviewed told me that letting their children leave was one of the most difficult sacrifices they had to make. Youth, in turn, talked about the emotional repercussions of their decision. Layla grew up with a single mom in New York City. Her story mirrors what I heard in many interviews. When Layla was applying to colleges outside of New York, her mom would say, "Oh my God, that's so far away." She would then pause, and say, "But if that's what you want to do, then you can do it."

Geographic distance meant different things depending on a family's ability to traverse it. Of the parents I interviewed, seven visited Amherst, but only one visited during the heart of their child's four years there. The rest went only for graduation. Letting their children move far away to attend Amherst was especially hard for undocumented parents, who could not travel by plane for fear of deportation. When Isabela, for example, was invited to visit Amherst from Orange County, California, her mom, Victoria, though supportive of the trip, was anxious. Victoria remembered the experience vividly: "It was difficult when she left the first time to visit the school. . . . My soul wanted to go with her. . . . But what if . . . the moment I get on the plane I get deported? . . . Thanks to God she called me and said, 'Mom, I am here at the school.' I was able to breathe."

Not only is travel dangerous for the undocumented, but it is prohibitively expensive for those who live on limited incomes and do not have flexible work schedules. Lisa's mom, Leona, for example, was undocumented and worked in a job that gave her no time off. When Lisa was accepted into Amherst, Leona, who lived on the outskirts of Washington, D.C., described the moment as "very sad, very depressing." But she also understood that the move was necessary for Lisa's success. "I was not going to oppose that. 'As long as it is for your own good, go on ahead. Do it,' I tell her. 'Absorb everything that you can.'" Leona never visited Amherst.

Making the decision to move far from home to attend school was also uniquely difficult for students and parents who had never known anyone else who had done so. Lucy, for example, grew up in the rural South. She was raised by her mother and grandmother, both of whom were born in the United States. Her dad was deported to El Salvador when she was quite young. The oldest child in a multigenerational household, Lucy bore a lot of family responsibility and had strong emotional bonds with her mother and grandmother. When she was applying to colleges, her mom told her to aim high. When Lucy was accepted into Amherst, her mom was overcome with conflicting emotions:

> When I told her . . . she went into the bedroom and closed her door, and she didn't talk to me for the rest of the night. I thought she was mad at me. She came out the next morning and . . . said, "I'm so proud of you, but this is so hard for me. You are my whole world. . . . I don't know what I'm going to do without you here, but I would never do anything to try and keep you here."

No one in Lucy's family had ever known someone who voluntarily moved away from home. "This is not what people in our family do. This is not what people from our community do. It's a lot of sadness. . . . There's this big fear that now that I'm gone, I won't ever want to come back." Lucy's community was small, rural, and populated mostly with families who had been there for generations. Leaving felt like breaking a deeply engrained social norm, like a betrayal of sorts.

Lucy's experience resonated with Noel, who explained that "leaving Texas for college is not something people in my community do. . . . To make this big migration to Amherst puts a lot of pressure on those of us from rural communities. To experience social mobility, you have to be prepared to leave your roots behind." Noel had thought a lot about what it would take to move up the class ladder, and he had recognized that if he stayed in West Texas, his opportunities would be limited. As such, he was ambivalent about his loyalty to his community. Texas was home, and he loved it, but he also yearned for more than his town could offer him.

Suzy, Noel's mom, was also ambivalent:

> When he decided to apply to go to school in Massachusetts, I couldn't understand. "Why don't you stay close to home?" I asked. I didn't understand why he would want to go to the other side of the world. . . . He explained that Amherst was a school with a lot of prestige, and it was really expensive, but if he got in he was promised a scholarship. I told him that if he got in, "*Adelante* [Go ahead]." And when he got the letter of acceptance, I cried, because it's so far away. (*cries*) But I supported him. For me it was very difficult. But I told him, "If you want to go, you must go. . . . It's your future."

All of the parents in this sample had left family behind themselves to come to the United States, and so they understood how hard the separation would be. Most, like Suzy, came to recognize that the opportunity formula had not changed from when they themselves embarked on their immigrant journey: social mobility required geographic mobility.

There were other youth, like Noel, who talked about the conflicting feelings of "wanting out" of the remote area where they lived, wanting to chase their dreams, and yet feeling the emotional weight of their parents' sadness mixed with their own love for and commitment to home. Brenda, for example, had known for a long time that she would have to leave her small town to have a better life. She described the emotional labor of explaining to her parents why leaving was the best decision:

> Once I realized I could leave, I wanted to leave. . . . And I told them . . . "I'm going to start the college application process, and I want you to know that the colleges I'm applying to are far away." . . . My dad was really quiet, and he was like, "Why do you want to go so far away?" And I was like, "Because that's where the opportunities are. . . ." After [I] explain[ed] my reasoning, they . . . recognized . . . they came to a whole new country and left their family members. Now . . . I have to make my own sacrifices to help them.

No matter how difficult it was for students to leave home, ultimately what made the decision manageable was their commitment to family betterment. Everyone, even those with complicated family relationships, talked about educational mobility as a family pursuit, and one that they believed would lead to social mobility for the whole family. As Brenda succinctly put it, "I have watched my dad work himself to death. . . . That's my drive. . . . I know education is our way out."

SCHOOL AND COMMUNITY NETWORKS

Although family provided youth with critical support and motivation, family alone was not enough to enable their educational mobility. A pathway to an elite education required strong social supports that enabled youth to develop their educational capacities and to be recognized as high-performing by cross-class institutional actors who were willing and able to guide them toward college.

Rendón differentiates between the family networks that ensure social reproduction by fulfilling basic human needs from the leveraging networks typically found on a local institutional level that enable social mobility.[3] In particular, she argues that cross-class ties that connect high-achieving marginalized youth with educational information and opportunities are essential.[4] Similarly, Vivian Louie, in her study of second-generation, college-attending Dominicans and Colombians, found that while youth were motivated by the narrative of the immigrant bargain, their educational success was the product of "constellations of support" that extended well beyond family and kin to include institutional and community actors.[5]

For the youth I talked to, committed mentors were typically at the center of their extrafamilial constellations of support.[6] Lacking deep stores of social capital in the context of their immigrant families, youth received help from mentors who served as cross-class actors. Teachers, counselors, and community members identified potential in these youths and then went above and beyond to help them develop and achieve their educational goals. In many interviews, students referred to their mentors as "life changing," or as being "the reason I am here today."

Participants almost universally credited one or more teachers for giving them the confidence to aim for a highly selective school. Just having good relationships with teachers, however, was not enough. Most described special, persistent, individualized attention and guidance from their teachers. A couple of participants either did not feel supported by teachers or had negative experiences with school leaders, but these youth had other cross-class institutional or community actors in their lives who provided special backing and guidance.

Fiona grew up in the Bronx. When her grandmother had a stroke, her family returned to Mexico for about a year. Fiona's transition back to the United States after that time was difficult. Although she was a U.S. citizen, her parents were undocumented, and the family was separated during their travels: Fiona and her brother traveled with an aunt back to New York, while her parents had to make a dangerous desert crossing and were detained. Fiona told me that she was traumatized by the separation as well as by abuse by an uncle while she was in Mexico, abuse that she was told not to talk about. Her first months back in the United States, she said, were "awful." Only a second-grader, she was bullied by other students because of her dark skin and struggles with English. Still, she was a good student. Ultimately, it was a supportive teacher who turned school into a safe place for Fiona, and education into a family pursuit.

> Then I went to third grade, and I had a really good teacher. He was Mexican. And he was really nice to me. . . . He was like, "You've got to go to the library, you've got to be really proactive." . . . So my mom would take us to the library, like all of the time. We literally knew the librarian. She [the librarian] would say, "Let's read this book," . . . and she'd give us tickets to the museum, or she'd give us tickets to, like, see a play, or stuff like that.

With the encouragement of Fiona's third-grade teacher and the community librarian, she and her brother pursued middle school with an enthusiasm and seriousness that they maintained throughout high school. Although neither applied to selective New York City high schools, they both did well academically and ended up college-bound, Fiona to Amherst via QuestBridge and her brother to the City University of New York.

For the vast majority of participants, family support was strong and steady, but a couple had parents who were less than enthusiastic about their child's educational pursuits. In these rare cases, teachers and mentors played an even more important role, especially in high school. Angelica's story serves as an example. She grew up in Santa Ana, California, in what she described as a "very traditional" and patriarchal Guatemalan and Mexican family. Although she was a top student, her parents, both of whom had only a primary school education, did not have high expectations for her because she was a girl. They agreed that she should go to college, but they did not want her to leave home. She was expected to help with the cooking, cleaning, and caring for her younger siblings. A teacher inspired Angelica to pursue a highly selective college in spite of her parents' reservations.

> He said, "What are your goals?" . . . No one had ever asked that. . . . I didn't have an answer for him. . . . He had . . . my transcript in front of him, and he's like, "Why aren't you dreaming big? Why aren't you thinking about college?" . . . I was like, ". . . I'm going to get my diploma and I'm going to get a job." He's like, "No, you are capable of more than that. You are a star. You need to dream bigger." He gave me hope. . . . He stuck with me.

With the support of this teacher, Angelica eventually persuaded her parents to allow her to leave home for school. Her case shows that some people can make it without enthusiastic parental support if their basic needs are met and their constellation of extrafamilial support is strong.

Teachers not only inspired confidence in these students but also provided them with hands-on support, such as giving them extra attention and spending individualized time with them to develop their academic skills and shape them intellectually by exposing them to new ideas and ways of thinking. Iván credited his favorite high school teacher for nurturing his scholarly aptitude. While growing up in the Bronx, Iván attended an elite preparatory school in Manhattan on a scholarship. It was a tough transition, and it took him a while to feel like he belonged at the school and to gain the confidence to aim for a highly selective college. He was among many of the participants in this study who reflected on how important it was that being from a background similar to his own made this teacher relatable, a role model, and capable of fostering what Smith terms an "in-group identity."[7] Teachers with backgrounds similar to their students' could nurture the belief that educational mobility was key to social mobility by sharing their own story of success:

> I remember, every day before track practice, I would go to his office. . . . He was the first administrator in the school that knew what it was like to be growing up in the Bronx. . . . So I felt very comfortable with him. . . . I saw him as a role model. . . . He had Mexican parents and a working-class background. Him growing up in the Bronx and then going to Cornell and then doing these amazing things . . . that's the trajectory that I wanted.

Nora similarly spoke about the importance of having teachers in her school who looked like her, understood her life and background, and were living proof that upward mobility was possible through education.

> I feel like a lot of kids come into college [and] go through this Black 101 process, or Latino 101. . . . There are self-esteem issues, because you never saw yourself represented. . . . And I didn't have that. The cool kids looked like me. . . . The smart kids looked like me. And I had teachers of color that went to really good schools, Columbia and University of Chicago and Colgate. So we knew about these schools, because we had teachers who had gone to these schools and they were invested in us.

These teachers also helped prepare students by letting them know that the transition into an elite White space would be difficult. They assured their students that they would get through it and that they would be more resilient because of it. Nora and Iván both drew on this inspiration and wisdom as they made their way to and through Amherst.

Although supportive teachers and mentors were essential to educational success, the extent of that support varied depending on where youth grew up and what kind of high school they attended.[8] Students who attained scholarships to preparatory schools or who attended specialty public high schools with high college placement rates enjoyed the most support on their way to Amherst. Students who lived in remote areas and students in large urban schools whose academic potential was initially overlooked had to be uniquely creative and resilient to secure their pathways. Indeed, most students who grew up in a global city were able to put themselves on the path to educational mobility by following a pretty straightforward formula of parental support plus an invested teacher or two. Those living in more remote or marginalized contexts had a much more difficult time.

For example, as I noted in the introduction, after Noel completed the last of the AP math classes that were available in his remote Texas high school, his teacher, though encouraging, told him that if he wanted to continue, he would have to do so by himself. "She told me what chapters to study. And I just had to learn things like Taylor polynomials and . . . polar coordinates . . . on my own." He aced the advanced calculus course that he took elsewhere.

There were also outliers who faced an overtly hostile climate at school. Importantly for each of these students, an invested adult from the community was there to buffer the hostility and offer support. Kevin, for example, faced discrimination by administrators in his Oklahoma high school. "For my high school it was just me against the administration. . . . They would take the opportunity to tokenize me . . . but when I asked them to advocate for me . . . I remember the principal looking me dead in the eye and was like, . . . 'You can advocate for yourself.'" Ultimately Kevin found a supportive network and mentorship through his school dance troupe, which he credited for his academic success.

Antonio also faced hostility in his southern New Jersey high school. "Even though it was overwhelmingly a minority school, their White students were the ones who they championed. . . . I mean, I was there too, but I was an afterthought." So Antonio sought mentorship elsewhere. A distant cousin who lived in the apartment above him had graduated from the same high school years before and was the first from the community to attend an Ivy League school. He advised Antonio about what classes to take and was the first to explain that there were private colleges that offered full funding for undocumented students. His guidance, combined with unwavering support from his mom and grandparents, helped Antonio survive and thrive in school despite a lack of encouragement from teachers and school leaders.

Youth's life histories confirm that while their families provided the base for their educational mobility, additional support was necessary and came generally from teachers, community members, or in rare cases extended family or others outside the direct community. Most notably, educational mobility was supported by cross-class actors who consistently gave aspiring youth individualized attention, provided guidance, and instilled the skills and confidence necessary for them to access higher education networks. But as I mentioned earlier, even this additional support was not enough to secure a pathway to an elite school.

PLUGGING INTO THE ELITE COLLEGE NETWORK

All the participants in this study excelled in high school, by which time most of them had their sights set on college. Yet most did not know the differences between types of colleges, nor did they understand the ins and outs of financial aid. They had heard that Ivy League schools were the best, and that private schools were prohibitively expensive. Unsurprisingly, then, most would have applied only to local public colleges without the intervention of mentors or programs committed to assisting first-generation college students in navigating college admissions. None would have employed a nuanced application strategy.

This pattern maps onto Hoxby and Avery's finding that most high-performing students who would qualify for full tuition grants from highly selective schools do not apply because they do not know that this support exists. Instead, they apply to nearby public schools, and most go into debt to attend them.[9] What differentiates the majority of my participants from their high-performing peers is that, beyond having both family support and teachers and mentors whose backing they could leverage to create a college pathway, they participated in programs connecting them with elite college networks and alerting them to schools with need-blind admissions. The rare ones who lacked this support learned about highly selective schools via mailings after being identified as high achievers by their standardized test scores. The fact that the students with the most tenuous paths to Amherst were all from remote areas further suggests the key role of place in connecting youth to elite college networks.

Those with the clearest and most direct road to Amherst participated in private pipeline programs. One of the best-known pipeline programs is Prep for Prep in New York City. Miguel was selected for Prep for Prep while he was still in middle school, following a rigorous testing process. Once accepted, he participated in extracurricular tutoring and mentoring, including a rigorous academic summer program in middle school. The program culminated in a full-tuition grant to an elite preparatory high school. Not only did Prep for Prep put Miguel on a path to excelling academically, but it gave him the cultural capital and confidence to navigate the process by connecting him with multiple mentors and cross-class guides committed to his educational success.

Most participants, however, did not enter a pipeline program in middle school, nor did they receive a scholarship to attend an elite preparatory school. Instead, they connected with organizations in high school that helped them better understand and navigate the higher education landscape. Omar moved to Evanston, Illinois, from the Central Valley of California with his Mexican parents, Pablo and Aurelia, and two siblings when he was a teenager. Evanston is a first-ring suburb of Chicago, home to Northwestern University, and the base for Evanston Scholars, a program that matches highly educated professionals in the community with high-performing, low-income students. Omar credited Evanston Scholars with his admission to Amherst.

My sophomore year I had no idea what was happening. Other people were starting to talk about college. . . . My parents had told me to study and work hard and get an education. Yeah, I'll go to college, but like, where am I going to go? . . . How do I apply? When do I apply? . . . That was all just a blur. . . . I applied [for Evanston Scholars] my sophomore year. . . . This program assigns you a mentor. . . . I described to him what kind of school I wanted. . . . And he was like, okay, this one, this one, this one. . . . He helped me throughout the entire process. . . . I don't think I would be here if I hadn't gotten a chance to be in that program.

Although Pablo and Aurelia had minimal formal education, Pablo was a self-taught math whiz who had worked with Omar on his math tables starting when he was very young. His father's organic smarts, good teaching, and incredible work ethic prepared and inspired Omar to do well in school. Pablo and Aurelia always told Omar he had to go to college. Aurelia, who worked as a custodian at a prestigious school in Chicago, could picture her children in a similar environment, and so she pushed them to do well and aim high. Omar responded, staying up late into the night so he could have the kitchen to himself to study. But ultimately it was his teachers and the mentors he met through Evanston Scholars who steered his ambition, work ethic, and extraordinary academic performance onto a path to an elite school.

Sandra also got help from a pipeline program. She grew up in Newark, New Jersey, and was raised by a single mom from Colombia. Sandra's mom did everything she could to nurture Sandra's educational opportunity: for instance, she took a cleaning job in the local Catholic church when Sandra was young so that Sandra could go to the parish's elementary school for free. When the free parochial education ended in middle school, however, Sandra had no option but to attend her local, underresourced high school. Soon thereafter, Sandra was identified as a promising student by one of her teachers and invited to join a program called LEEP—Law and Education Empowerment Project. LEEP helped Sandra improve her academic skills and navigate the college admissions landscape. It also introduced her to professional mentors, all of whom were successful attorneys.

LEEP was a college-bound program that I started my eighth-grade summer. . . . I really don't think I would have been here at Amherst without them. . . . They told me about Amherst, told me about schools like Amherst. . . . They explained things a lot more than I would have gotten in my high school because there were so many kids. I would go after school two times a week, and . . . we'd do debate and then Saturday was writing class.

Sandra had long been supported by strong family and community networks, but LEEP enabled her to see the world of elite education for the first time and to realize that it was within her reach. The exposure inspired her, for sure, but more importantly, LEEP provided her with the pragmatic guidance to translate her family and community support into a concrete pathway to Amherst.

Ultimately, as these examples illustrate, students must have simultaneous support from multiple networks to achieve exceptional educational mobility. Cross-class actors helped participants leverage their academic success and family and community support to access the recruitment networks of elite colleges. I saw this leveraging at play in the experiences of those who learned about pipeline programs from teachers. For example, it was a teacher's suggestion that Alberto apply for a summer enrichment program at Rice that initially plugged him into the elite college network. "The first year ends and I have all As . . . and I don't have anything planned for the summer. . . . One of my teachers is like, 'There's this program at Rice that I think you would be interested in, it's a weeklong thing.' And I was like, 'Yeah, I have nothing else to do.' And my mom was thrilled. 'Oh, you're going to be at Rice University!'"

Once the program at Rice ended, Alberto was invited to join Emerge, a pipeline program that exposed him to highly selective schools and assisted him throughout the application process. "Emerge . . . took us on a tour after sophomore year to visit schools. . . . So I visited Harvard, Brown, Brandeis, Tufts . . . these elite schools. And you know we're talking to college counselors and college students." Emerge also informed Alberto, who has DACA status, about which schools provided need-blind aid independent of legal status. This knowledge, combined with his mom's enthusiastic support, paved his pathway to Amherst.

Ricardo was also connected to a pipeline program by one of his teachers. Although Ricardo did well in school and his parents stressed the importance of education, he was unsure of how school would fit into his life. He grew up in an industrial hub outside of Chicago. His parents, both immigrants from Mexico, worked in low-wage jobs, and money was always tight. The youngest of four, Ricardo watched his siblings struggle in school. He also witnessed his sister get pulled into a street gang. Because he knew he was needed at home, he thought that if he did go to college, he would stay close. So when a Chicago-based pipeline program hosted a recruitment event at his high school, Ricardo did not attend. The next day, upon hearing that Ricardo missed the event, one of his teachers dragged him into the high school college counselor's office to get information about the program. Ricardo described his teacher's persistence:

My teacher introduces herself to the college counselor, and tells her I need an application. She [the counselor] was like, "Oh, did he go to the Family Reunion Night last night? That's the requirement, that's where you get the application." This is when my teacher started lying for me (*laughs*). She was like, "Ricardo needs an application. He couldn't go last night because his parents were both working a second shift. He needs an application right now or else this is going be the biggest mistake that you've ever made."

The counselor gave Ricardo an application, which he successfully completed with his teacher's support. Ricardo was accepted into the program and then connected with a mentor who taught him about highly selective, need-blind schools and helped him through the application process. Ricardo credits both the program and his persistent teacher with changing his life.

The most common pipeline program that came up in my study was QuestBridge, an extraordinarily competitive program that helps match high-achieving students from low-income backgrounds with the nation's top schools, which commit to offering them scholarships. Angelica first learned about QuestBridge from a classmate who had been accepted into the program the previous year. Angelica applied to QuestBridge's College Prep Program, which took her to Stanford the summer after her junior year. She told me that visiting Stanford opened her eyes to a new world. "That was the first time I was on a college campus. We got lost. . . . It was huge. It was beautiful." The next year Angelica applied to QuestBridge's College Program and was matched with Amherst.

Tito also was accepted to Amherst via QuestBridge. Born in Peru, Tito was undocumented for most of his childhood, and he had never known anyone who went to college. But both of his parents were determined that he get an education. The small town in central Florida where he lived was worlds away from Miami and the extracurricular support programs for high-achieving youth that could be accessed there. So even though his parents were enthusiastic about him going to college, he did not know how to get there. Still, he was an excellent student and had dreams of attending medical school. After a stressful process that resulted in the approval of his U.S. residency while in high school, Tito felt a world of possibility open up to him. But he did not know how to take advantage of it. He figured that he would apply to a state university. Just when he was about to embark on this plan, a guidance counselor who had just learned about QuestBridge, and who saw potential in Tito, invited him to a meeting to talk about his college plans. That meeting changed everything.

She called me into her office . . . and she was like, "Well, Tito . . . you had really good grades. I just wanted to check up on you and see where you're thinking of going to college." And I said . . . I was going to apply to UF [University of Florida]. And she's like, "Well, have you ever thought about going out of state?" . . . And then . . . she was like, "Have you heard about QuestBridge?" . . . So I looked it up . . . and . . . I decided to apply.

Tito did not have to persuade his parents about leaving home to go to school. They supported him doing whatever he needed to do to get ahead.

Several students, though they had teachers or mentors who encouraged them toward college, had no one in their network with specific knowledge of pipeline programs or highly selective schools and need-blind admissions. These students, all of whom lived in a remote area, were like Noel in that they learned about highly selective schools only because they performed well on a college preparatory exam.

For example, Ben, a DACA student, had his sights set on attending college but knew little about the options available. Like Tito, he lived in a small Southern town and figured he would apply to a state university, hoping he would find a way to pay for it. He assumed that his DACA status would prohibit him from attending an expensive school because he would have no access to financial aid. He had never heard about need-blind admissions. But then, after doing really well on the ACT, Ben started getting mailings from top-ranked schools, inviting him to apply. Ben explained that "Amherst reached out to me with the diversity open house. So I applied. I just got mailings . . . based on AP scores and ACT scores. And then QuestBridge sent me a mailing . . . [and] told me to apply."

> Those mailings were really important . . . as a source of information. . . . I especially started getting them after I took my ACT. . . . I was getting, like, random schools. . . . I really only read the ones of . . . the prestigious schools that I had heard about abstractly. . . . [My] teachers didn't have much of an idea, counselors, not much of an idea. . . . Getting that high score on the ACT kind of made me realize that there might be more open doors.

Despite family support, good grades, and enthusiastic teachers, Ben was cut off from cross-class actors who could connect him with an elite recruitment network. And no one in his family or community networks knew about need-blind admissions. His test scores were the only mechanism available as a point of access. He told me how grateful he was that he paid attention to what had seemed at first to be random college mailings that, in a harried moment, he just might have thrown away.

Indeed, place shaped elite network access in critical ways. Those who grew up in a global city were the most likely to have teachers and mentors who were aware of elite college pipelines and recruitment networks.

Some of those teachers and mentors had accessed the same pipelines or networks themselves. It also seems that, just by living in a densely populated area that was a hub for capital, universities, and progressive educational policies, those who grew up in a global city were more likely to encounter information about elite educational opportunities, even if not directly from teachers or mentors. Angelica, for example, had a high school classmate who told her about QuestBridge and encouraged her to apply.

Those who lived in a global city or another place where cross-class actors understood the complex landscape of higher education were the most likely to participate in pipeline programs that helped them navigate the college application process. One of the most important pieces of information communicated by these programs was the availability of full tuition grants for high-performing, low-income students. For study participants, this information changed everything and opened up a world of new opportunity and possibility. Students who grew up in a remote area were the least likely to get such guidance and thus had the most precarious journeys through the college selection and application process. Indeed, some were able to access an elite recruitment network only because of a singular decision they had made, like checking the right box on a college admissions test form or not throwing away a mailing. But even in these lucky cases, family and local community support systems were there to push them along.

WHEN NETWORKS CONVERGE IN PLACE

The youth in this study all thrived academically in high school and had family support, and most of them had the social capital to alert them to highly selective schools with need-blind policies. Only when family networks, local school networks, and elite recruitment networks converged, however, was their entry into a highly selective college possible. The ways in which this convergence occurred—that is, how youth experienced their pathways to Amherst—varied in large part because of where they grew up and what networks they could access.

Family served as the critical base on which their academic success was built. The vast majority of parents prioritized their children's education and were committed to the immigrant bargain.[10] They enacted the bargain in particular ways: enforcing homework and, in most cases, prohibiting their children from working during high school, even if the family needed the money. Instead, they carried the family's heavy financial burden by working longer hours or cutting back on expenses. Through their actions, parents inspired their children and passed along expectations and wisdom.

Family support was essential to the educational pathways of the vast majority of my participants, but not enough by itself. Youth also needed to be recognized by teachers or school leaders as exceptional students in order to continue their educational ascent. With generous, individualized attention, teachers motivated youth, validating the messaging they received from their parents that education was the key to mobility. Teachers also provided logistical and strategic guidance, sharing knowledge about college options and helping students navigate the path to get there. Many teachers also informed students about pipeline programs. Youth who lacked teacher or local school supports spoke about other individuals in their community networks who made up for the deficit, confirming the importance of cross-class actors on their pathways.

Participants who were privileged with access to pipeline programs described them as life-changing. For some youth, a pipeline program provided the opportunity to attend a private preparatory high school where they attained the academic and social capital that helped them access Amherst. More often, such programs connected working-class students with professional mentors who had attended highly selective schools themselves. Latino youth talked about these mentors as providing inspiration and practical support. At the very least, access to pipeline programs gave students basic information about schools with need-blind admissions policies. Those with pipeline program support were the best prepared for the college admissions process.

Place mattered a lot in students' ability to leverage their family and community networks to access elite recruitment networks. Place also influenced how youth experienced their mobility pathways. It is not surprising to me that the vast majority of students who apply to highly selective schools have grown up in a major metropolitan area.[11] The capital concentrated in major cities attracts skilled professionals, many of whom are graduates of highly selective schools.[12] These professionals are the kinds of mentors who guided many of the youth I met in this project. Similarly, many of the most supportive teachers of global city–based participants were graduates of highly selective schools. Those teachers who were Latino or from a similar background inspired confidence in youth by fostering an in-group identity. Students from a geographically remote area were much less likely to have access to pipeline support or teachers and counselors who knew about elite schools and need-blind admissions. For most of them, test scores were what initially connected them to elite recruitment networks, suggesting that non-urban youth may be at a disadvantage compared to youth in large urban areas.

Finally, I found that youth who grew up in a global city were much more likely to have been exposed to others from a background similar to their own who had left home to attend a highly selective school than were those who grew up in a secondary city or a more remote area. This exposure broadened their perspective and ultimately made it easier for them to leave home, and easier for their parents to let them leave. This is not to suggest that global cities are a bastion of opportunity for all. There are many in these places who fall through the cracks. Yet, in my sample at least, global cities were shown to provide many more opportunities than did other places.

As the next chapter reveals, getting accepted to Amherst and then leaving home were just the first legs of a long and rewarding but arduous educational journey. The challenges of transitioning into the new world of elite education caught many youth off guard, revealing to them—often for the first time—the complex and not always certain relationship between educational and social mobility.

Chapter 2 | A New World

GLORIA GREW UP on the South Side of Chicago in a small, modest house framed by a steep stoop and a tidy yard. Its fading yellow paint suggested the persistence of hope and optimism in a context of hardship. Gloria's immediate neighborhood didn't bustle or buzz. It had few businesses and no parks or public gathering spots. Gloria recalled that when she was a child, gangs occupied the streets. It was much quieter now, those neighborhood gang members having aged out of street life and into factory and service work. A few blocks away was the neighborhood known as Mexican Village. There the streets seldom slept. Gloria spent many of her childhood weekends in "the Village" with her grandparents, aunts, uncles, and cousins, enjoying the strong bond of her extended immigrant family as she took in the scents and sounds of Mexican Chicago. For Gloria, this was home, and it was difficult to leave. Her belief in the promise of social mobility via a college education eased the pain of leaving a bit. Still, nothing was simple about the radical transition that Gloria had to make away from the working-class immigrant world she had always known and into a new world of elite opportunity and expectations.

> I decided I just had to jump in and not think. . . . I didn't allow myself to think about the fact that I was going to be alone, that I didn't have anybody. I just thought about the fact that it was going to be full tuition and I knew that it was a good opportunity and that it was a good school. And then, as I did more research, I was like, "Holy shit, it's a really good school!" So I knew that I was going into something good, but I didn't want to think about leaving. . . . I started crying on the plane because I was like, "What did I get myself into? I don't know anybody." I actually got to Amherst the day before everyone else because the plane ticket was weird. I remember getting here and feeling really alone. I met one new friend that day who is Puerto Rican. She was there with her dad, and they were really nice. . . . She became one of my best friends. Then, the next day, I saw everyone's parents come

drop them off, including my roommate's. And I remember thinking, "Why couldn't my family come? Why am I setting up my room by myself and everyone else is getting taken out to dinner?" That was something that really hurt. It was a huge thing. It's still something that I remember. And even now, when Parents' Weekend comes around, and things like that, I still wish that they could come. Or thinking about graduation, I wonder, "Are they going to be able to come then? Will they meet this place?" It's literally two different worlds that I go across.

Gloria's pathway to Amherst had not been easy, but her transition into Amherst, and her journey there, were in some ways even more difficult and complicated. Poised at the top of the educational mobility ladder, Gloria realized that she was entering a radically different social world, one characterized by wealth, Whiteness, assumptions of citizenship, and an abundance of resources and support such as she had never known before. Gloria's parents had worked their entire adult lives—her mom in restaurant kitchens and her dad in factories—to give their children the opportunity to go to college, and for as long as Gloria could remember she had been relentlessly striving to be a college-worthy student. With that challenge behind her, Gloria was now enthused and ready to take this next big step. Yet her entry into the world of elite education did not make her able or even willing to leave her old world behind. She had to learn how to live in both worlds, and how to navigate the expectations of a space structured by inequality.

Gloria's story of educational mobility is nuanced and complex. Like all the individual life stories I collected for this book, it is not generalizable. Yet it encapsulates important themes woven throughout all of those stories. For the vast majority of youth in this study, educational mobility forced them to juggle the divergent realities, norms, and expectations of home and school. Indeed, for most of them—especially the "doubly disadvantaged"—incorporating themselves into Amherst required, for the first time, that they confront privilege and inequality, directly and intimately, in their academic and residential lives.[1]

In the process, youth developed what Mary Romero conceptualizes as a "double consciousness": the critical perspective that youth embody when their lives straddle contexts of privilege and subordination.[2] For my participants, surviving and thriving at Amherst required learning the ins and outs of an elite education. While doing so, however, they continued to embody the lessons and experiences they had gleaned from growing up in working-class immigrant families and communities. As they began to understand the depth and complexity of American inequality in the course of navigating both realities, they also began to realize how much they would have to overcome to reach the social and material status of their more privileged peers.

CONFRONTING WEALTH AND WHITENESS

The majority of participants in this study grew up in areas that were pre-dominantly Latino and working-class. With the exception of those who attended a preparatory or specialty high school, most did not know any non-Latino Whites, aside from teachers and school administrators, before going to college. Fewer still had anyone in their inner circle who was wealthy. Their segregated lives map onto the demographic reality of the United States. Despite civil rights legislation and social justice–based move-ments and advocacy, the United States remains a highly segregated country. In addition to growing up in race- and class-segregated spaces, many par-ticipants were among the five to six million youth in the United States from a mixed-status family, or they grew up in a community where an undocu-mented legal status was common.[3] Thus, when they arrived at Amherst, they were confronted with the intersecting privileges of wealth, Whiteness, and assumptions of U.S. citizenship for the first time.

Elite institutions of higher education are unique in their relatively recent commitment to bringing together diverse student bodies in residential environments.[4] Until 1975, all of the students at Amherst College were men, and until efforts were undertaken, beginning in the 1990s, to diversify the student body, most students were White and wealthy. So much has changed. In 2021, Amherst College boasted a student body in which 62 percent were receiving grant-based aid and 15 percent were first-generation college students. What is more, Amherst is on the tipping point of becoming a majority-minority campus in terms of race. And yet, as I detail in the intro-duction, this diverse demographic landscape remains rooted in a structure of inequality that privileges the norms of Whiteness. This is to say, while Whiteness might not be visible in the college's demographic statistics, it has deep cultural roots. It reveals itself in who claims which spaces and how comfortably they do so; in the informal codes that prescribe how students should speak, dress, and present themselves in classrooms and other college spaces; and in how they should interact with faculty and staff.

There are also vast class divides on campus. As noted in the introduc-tion, whereas during the time of my research 20 to 30 percent of Amherst students came from the lowest income strata in the United States, 20 percent came from the top 1 percent—a vast divergence in terms of social class.[5] Such polarization within a small residential community has experiential implications. As Cesar, one of my participants, explained it to me, "I think a lot of people can't fathom how rich some people are. And there are also people who can't fathom how poor other people are . . . and that creates this weird divide."

For most of the youth who participated in this study, even those who had connected with White middle- or upper-class mentors in high school, moving to a predominantly White, wealthy institution was a social shock. Moreover, while absorbing this shock, youth had to figure out how to balance their own shifting cultural and social positions within the families they had left behind. The experience was confusing at best and alienating at worst, and yet it further tuned their social consciousness. Youth became more critical, and some more cynical.

Alberto grew up in a small apartment in Houston with his mom and a rotating group of extended family members. His mom worked long hours as a house cleaner, and because she arrived home late at night, he had to learn early on how to take care of himself, do basic household tasks, and also help care for his ailing aunt and grandmother. Everyone in his household was undocumented. Alberto told me that many of his teenage friends lived in similar circumstances. Though Alberto participated in a college pipeline program that guided him through his college application process and introduced him to the world of elite higher education, it did not prepare him for the wealth and privilege of Amherst College. It did not take long for Alberto to realize that Amherst was an unequal community, and that he was at the bottom of the social hierarchy because of his family background.

> I remember for admitted students weekend I was talking to someone . . . and I made the mistake of asking them what their parents did. And it was like, "Oh yeah, my dad's an engineer and my mom is a biochemical researcher." And she was like, "What does your mom do?" And I was like, "Oh, my mom's a housekeeper." . . . So early on, I realized those discrepancies. . . . All of my classmates in Houston were first-generation. All of my classmates' parents were immigrants. All of them were low-income . . . all Latinx. So . . . this is the Whitest place I've ever been.

Angelica recalled a similar experience. Santa Ana, California, the community in Orange County where she grew up, is predominantly working-class and immigrant, though it is currently gentrifying. Like Alberto, all of Angelica's friends and classmates growing up were poor or working-class and Mexican, Central American, or a mix of both. She had never felt that she needed to explain how poverty, or having parents without papers, impacted her life. She just assumed that her peers understood because they were living a similar reality. At Amherst, Angelica came to realize that relatively few people faced legal or resource-based limitations, and that many had grown up with wealth and opportunity. In interactions with her dorm-mates early on, Angelica found it sobering to learn how few students understood her reality.

> We were all in the common room doing work. Eventually we would have a few moments for a study break, and someone would make comments. "Oh, I remember this is how it was like in school for me." I'm like, "Really? Because I never had this." And people would say, "I remember the tutors," or, "I remember the boarding school, living in a dorm." And I'm like, "Nope. I lived at home. I didn't have tutors." . . . Or even people talking about their homes. They'd say, "Yeah, my room is a lot bigger than this." And I'd say, "I have to share a room with five other people." And they're like, "What? Where do you live?" I'm like, "In an apartment." They'd say, "You don't have a house? Why?" I'd have to explain, "Because it's too expensive," . . . So it was just small things like that. . . . And then eventually, it was people saying, "Oh yeah, we're going to go out to eat. Do you want to come?" I'm like, "I don't have money for that." And people saying, "My parents are going to come, they're going to drive up from . . . D.C.," for example. And, I'm like, "Oh no, my parents can't come. They can't even get on a plane. One, because it's expensive, and two, because they're undocumented. They don't have that legality to be able to fly."

The response in these moments after Angelica revealed her parents' undocumented status and financial reality was usually awkward, drawn-out silence. The alienation she felt during such experiences characterized how she often felt throughout her time at Amherst.

Inequality among students also surfaced in students' interactions with college staff, especially dining hall and custodial staff. Like Alberto, many low-income Latino students had parents who worked as custodians or house cleaners or in restaurant or cafeteria kitchens as dishwashers. Being faced with the Amherst staff, some of whom were Latino, doing the same jobs their parents did was a difficult reminder for students that they were now in a social rank above their parents.

Shamus Khan, in his ethnographic study of St. Paul's, one of the top prep schools in the world, found that class-privileged students were often more at ease interacting with low-wage staff than were working-class students, because they had grown up being served by working-class people and had been taught to feel at ease with people from all backgrounds.[6] Learning this ease was part of their informal training in privilege. Khan found that interactions with staff were much more emotionally complicated for working-class students. Similarly, in my research, I noted discomfort among Latino students in their relationships with staff. I also observed frustration. Though privileged students often easily bantered with staff, this ease did not necessarily translate into respect for their work, as low-income Latino youth noted in the overtly disrespectful ways some White wealthy students behaved when staff were not around.

Gaby, for example, found it especially difficult to observe the lack of respect that some students displayed for custodial staff on campus. She remembered accompanying her mom to work cleaning rich people's homes. Some of these memories were happy, but others, such as witnessing her mom being disrespected or unappreciated by her employers, were quite painful. These painful memories emerged in force whenever Gaby observed students leaving huge messes for the dining hall and dorm cleaning staff to deal with. "I'm shocked by how disrespectful some students can be," she said. "For me, it's especially hard because my mom does this kind of work. When I see students disrespecting custodians here, I feel like they are disrespecting my mom. I just think, 'Who are these people? This is not fair. I don't want to be part of this.'"

Gaby wasn't the only one who had this experience. Several participants talked about their shock in seeing the damage done to dormitories and public bathrooms during weekend parties, and the seeming lack of concern of some of their classmates about the time and effort that it would take to clean up the messes. They hated the possibility of being associated with this behavior because it hit close to home.

To be sure, moving away from family into an elite space and suddenly being on the other side of the privilege-subordination divide proved emotionally jarring, presenting a barrier to incorporation. Yet some students were more prepared to confront the emotions of this shift than others. This is to say, students experienced the privilege implicit in an elite institution in different ways depending on the nuanced intersections of their own social position—their race, class, gender, legal status—and the context of their lives and educations growing up. Among the most prominent indicators of how they experienced Amherst, especially initially, was the type of high school they attended and their level of academic preparation.

Jack compellingly argues that not all low-income students enter elite schools with the same level of social, cultural, and educational capital.[7] I noted that students who received a scholarship to a private preparatory school or attended a highly ranked "specialty" public high school (think Boston Latin or Stuyvesant High in New York City) were more emotionally, socially, and academically prepared to navigate Amherst than those who attended an underresourced public school in their home neighborhood. To them, Amherst was less of a shock socially, academically, and culturally than it was for the doubly disadvantaged.

Indeed, those who had gone to a prep school tended to describe Amherst as "just more of the same." They told me that they had accumulated cultural, social, and academic tools in high school that they could draw on to navigate the elite space of Amherst. Specifically, they had received strong academic preparation, and they were better prepared emotionally to confront wealth and Whiteness. By contrast, the doubly disadvantaged, like Gloria, Alberto, Angelica, and Gaby, struggled the most. Their efforts to incorporate themselves into Amherst inevitably made them realize that they had low stores of the social, human, and cultural capital that were assumed in elite spaces, and that they had to devise ways of dealing with the deficit.

Fiona entered Amherst doubly disadvantaged. She spent all but a couple of years of her childhood in a housing project in the South Bronx with her older brother and undocumented Mexican parents. As I detailed in chapter 1, the only time Fiona had left the Bronx was to live temporarily with family in Mexico. She was nine when she returned to the United States from Mexico. She was tracked into English-language learner (ELL) classes, where she remained through most of elementary school; then she was incorporated into the general education track in middle school. For a confluence of reasons—her time spent in Mexico and then in ELL; her return to an overcrowded, underresourced school; and her parents' lack of time and know-how in advocating for her as she got older—Fiona did not have access to the social networks that helped most of her Amherst peers from New York City apply to specialty public high schools. Instead, when it came time to decide which public high school to attend—a decision that required navigating a complicated lottery system—Fiona randomly applied to one in Manhattan that was close to the factory where her father worked, the only area of Manhattan she knew. She was accepted, fulfilling her goal of going to high school outside of the Bronx. Despite the school's overcrowded classrooms, heavy security apparatus, and multiplicity of other distractions, she learned about QuestBridge during a rare meeting with a guidance counselor. She applied and was matched with Amherst.

When Fiona got to Amherst, she expected that there would be other students from a background similar to hers. To be sure, she did meet other low-income Latino students, and she made close friendships with a small group of them. But none of her close friends came from her same level of disadvantage.

I went to houses of other people that I knew who were also QuestBridge scholars, but they lived in a house. I live in an apartment. And it's literally the tiniest apartment. And it's safe in the Bronx, but people still get robbed all the time. And I can't come home late because, like, the last time I got home late, someone had gotten into a knife fight and the police were there. . . .

I've only met one other girl who, I would say, has a similar background. We're both from a similar area in the Bronx, and she went to a normal high school too. She's the only person. . . . A lot of the people I did end up meeting that were from New York, they went to specialized high schools. . . . And my school was just not that.

Fiona felt alone when she arrived at Amherst. She also felt misunderstood, even by other Latino students, because few other Amherst students had experienced her overall level of disadvantage. She quickly realized that she was positioned differently than her Latino classmates who had arrived at Amherst with social know-how about what to expect. Miguel is an example.

Like Fiona, Miguel grew up in a small, subsidized apartment in New York City. Although he loved his vibrant Dominican neighborhood, life was a constant financial struggle. But unlike Fiona, Miguel attended a magnet school during his elementary and middle school years, and he was encouraged by his teachers to apply for Prep for Prep. He did, was accepted, and after matriculating out of the program's summer academic "boot camp," left New York City at the age of fifteen to attend an elite preparatory boarding school in rural New England. Miguel experienced in high school much of what doubly disadvantaged students experience in college. "At my prep school you learn that x and y's parents are the owners of this company, or their dad is a lawyer, or, you know, their parents went to x and y school. My mom's literally a waitress . . . and there was a constant questioning of her belonging."

While Miguel thrived academically in prep school, he struggled with feelings of social exclusion and alienation. Yet he was grateful that he learned how to deal with those feelings then, because when he got to Amherst he was armed and ready to take the school by storm. He felt exceptionally prepared academically, having written long papers, studied Latin, pulled all-nighters, and participated in small seminars in which students were expected to engage in discussion, pose critical questions, and tackle difficult ideas. Perhaps most importantly, Miguel was no longer intimidated by wealth and prestige.

I am grateful, because my prep school did prepare me for being at this place. I walked in here and I was like, "Who cares if these kids are rich and White and wealthy. Whatever! I can lay my claim here because I already did this. I know exactly who these people are." I had it figured out in a way that other people didn't. Like, someone was just telling me she didn't know what an outline was before she came to Amherst. She hadn't gone to office hours because she was afraid to go. That was something I didn't care about. I was going to go if I needed help. I knew what I was doing.

Few students in this project had Miguel's high level of academic and social preparation. There were also only a few who came from the level of disadvantage that Fiona described. And yet, all felt disadvantaged in some ways compared to their wealthier and Whiter Amherst peers.

It was not just social capital that differentiated them but human capital. Miguel had studied Latin and experienced small discussion seminars, but most of those who attended a public high school said that they arrived at Amherst with much lower levels of academic preparation. Kimberly, for example, attended a public high school in Florida. Her parents were U.S. citizens, originally from Panama, and solidly working-class, and she felt that the public schools she attended were "good." And still, when Kimberly arrived at Amherst, she realized that what she had thought was a good public school education was lacking compared to the education most of her peers had received. For example, while she had been schooled in memorization, which enabled her to do well on her high school exams, her professors at Amherst were looking for a different type of thinking and learning than anything she had experienced before.

> Writing is still a struggle. I remember in my freshman seminar, the very first assignment, was a six-page paper. And I had never written more than a page. . . . And I remember thinking, "What can you possibly write about for six pages?" Also, professors kept saying over and over again, "It's not just a summary. I want to know what you think." But in all of my K-12, no one ever asked me what I think. Really the point of my K-12 education was "What did I just say?"

Alberto had a similar experience. Before going to Amherst from his public high school, he considered himself a strong and confident student. Yet early on he began to feel that he was unprepared for the academic expectations of a highly selective college.

> I still feel like I'm at a disadvantage, to be honest. This school is significantly harder for me than public school. And I've heard people . . . that went to, let's say, a prep school in New York, that are even Latinx, being like, "Oh yeah, Amherst is way easier than what I did in high school." And it's like, "Oh shit!" Because for me this is pretty rigorous. . . . I think what was most shocking to me was when my first-year seminar professor asked me, "What do you think about this book?" No one had ever asked me that question. No one ever asked me, "Do you like this book or do you agree with the author?" I was like, "We can disagree?" I didn't know.

For most of the doubly disadvantaged students in this sample, like Alberto and Kimberly, adapting to Amherst did not just entail getting used to the new demographics. It demanded that they scamper up a steep academic learning curve. They had to exert energy to build confidence and to fight against feeling like imposters, while also having to complete an enormous amount of highly challenging academic work. There was nothing easy about their efforts to adapt to Amherst. Many described it as "exhausting."

It is not surprising, therefore, that feeling unprepared for the type of work that Amherst College demanded led many study participants to initially feel discouraged and frustrated. Sandra, for example, had attended Newark, New Jersey, public schools, which had a reputation, she knew, for weak academic preparation; she had believed, however, that her extra-curricular college prep program had filled the deficiency gaps. Yet, despite her high school investment in weekend writing and debate workshops, she still felt unprepared for Amherst.

> I was just angry at a lot of things. Angry at, like, "Why can't I write this paper? Why am I having such a hard time? Why do I have to spend two hours on a problem when the person next to me spends thirty minutes?" That's my anger. It's anger at the system for not giving me the same education that the kid sitting next to me had.

Sandra overcame her initial fear of office hours by forcing herself to go to her professors for help. Still, no matter how hard she worked and strove to make up for what she described as a "Newark-deficit," that first year she still didn't receive the A grades that she saw her peers get without working, she was certain, nearly as hard as she did. Sandra was like many other students whose initial frustrations devolved into a crisis of confidence.

Naomi, for example, told me that almost immediately upon arriving at Amherst she felt like she wasn't smart enough to be there. She was born in the Dominican Republic and had come to the United States on a tourist visa as a young teenager. She and her mom overstayed the visa, becoming undocumented. Naomi attended public high school in a small industrial, immigrant city about an hour outside of Boston. She was one of several students in this project who made her way to Amherst from community college, as a transfer student. Naomi had graduated first in her community college class and was a prominent, award-winning leader in her community, and yet she still felt that she did not have the academic preparation or the confidence necessary to thrive at Amherst.

> My confidence just started going down once I got here. It really did. . . . I kept thinking I don't have the vocabulary, you know, I don't have this, I don't have that. So you start pinpointing the things that you don't have and

you forget about the things that you do have. And also, English is not my first language, and I learned English not so long ago. And I grew up in a very Latino place, so I always spoke Spanish. Coming here, it's like English, that's it. . . . I'm like, "Oh my God, this is so new, so different." . . . I of course had written research papers before, but I never had to write every two weeks a paper. That wasn't something that you actually do at community college, so it was, like, completely different.

Naomi ended up doing very well academically at Amherst. And yet she got choked up as she talked about how out of place she had felt when she first arrived, and how difficult it still was to fight against the feeling of being "less than" her more well-to-do peers.

Not having the right "type" of academic knowledge was another experience that many shared. Arriving at Amherst already "knowing certain things" was not a formal institutional expectation, but an unspoken one that low-income Latino students felt in many of their classes. Kimberly shared one of her experiences with the knowledge mismatch that the doubly disadvantaged commonly confronted.

I remember taking this "History of the Enlightenment" class, and it was the first time I had heard about Adam Smith. . . . And I remember talking to other students, and I was like, "Have you heard of this guy Adam Smith?" And it was totally silent in the room, and people were like, "You've never heard of Adam Smith?" And I was like, "Oh, okay. I was supposed to have heard of Adam Smith somewhere?" Yeah. There was that. But now I feel like, when that happens, rather than feeling there's something wrong with me, there's this sense of anger, where I'm like, fuck you.

Through her social science and humanities classes, Kimberly came to realize the critical difference between intelligence and the ways of being educated that are prized by the elite. She had high levels of the former but was out of sync with many of her wealthy Amherst peers with respect to the latter. As Kimberly developed her critical understanding of a social world in which this subjectively valued difference in preparation was indicative of the vast structural inequalities that cut across the student bodies of contemporary elite institutions, her feelings of intimidation evolved into feelings of anger.

Those structural inequalities became glaringly obvious to many students as they came to realize that they were just as smart, and just as ambitious, as their peers. They simply had more barriers to overcome. But it surprised them to learn that the barriers confronting them were not only structural but also cultural.

NEW CULTURAL SCRIPTS

The types of intellectual knowledge that have historically been valued in elite institutions of higher education are partnered with cultural codes that include ways of speaking, types of vocabulary, and ways of dressing and presenting oneself.[8] Indeed, not only is inequality a structural phenomenon rooted in resource disparities, but it is also experienced culturally as students, depending on their social location and background, become fluent in vastly different sociocultural scripts.

The sociologist Pierre Bourdieu coined the term "habitus" to describe the intimate relationship between individuals' cultural dispositions and the contexts of their daily lives.[9] Implicitly connected to social class, habitus is conditioned by an individual's history of socialization and daily life practices. An individual's habitus can be transformed through social mobility, but Bourdieu maintained that it is more obstinate than fluid. Thus, when individuals experience upward social mobility, they may experience emotional challenges as they navigate between the tastes and preferences they developed in their childhood and the expectations of their new class position and cultural context.[10] For most participants in this study, attending an elite college entailed a major habitus disruption.

The cultural dispositions that most students had developed growing up in low-income immigrant families did not fit at Amherst. Some wanted to make a habitus shift, accepting that upward mobility required it. Others resisted. Most students treaded in the water of cultural uncertainty, feeling socially unprepared, at least initially, to navigate an elite institution. Students sensed that in order to fit in they had to speak differently, use new, often obscure vocabulary words, and present themselves in a novel way. Here again, depending on their background and high school context, students confronted Amherst's cultural milieu in various ways.

As with academic preparation, the privileged poor had a leg up on the doubly disadvantaged in navigating Amherst's cultural terrain. Miguel, for example, had to learn a new cultural script while in prep school, and thus he was able to bring his newfound fluency to Amherst and avoid what he described as the cultural pitfalls that he believed poor students easily fell into when they were new to an elite environment.

If you're from the inner city, New York, or from an ethnic neighborhood or, like, you know, from the Black community, there are certain phrases or things you say. And over time I stopped dropping or saying those because I was like, "This is not how everyone else is talking." . . . It is like you had to adopt these things in order to fit in. And even with your close friends, everyone was doing this. Everyone was complicit in this acting. And, no lie, everyone was acting in the same way in order to fit this mold. It's kind of wild. You know, the whole point of having these diverse students was to have people learning about a different background, but I really had, to some extent, to perform and change some things in order to really fit in.

Miguel continued to change his presentation on his path through Amherst. He also began to gain a more critical view of the process, which empowered him to resist the cultural conformity in other ways. For example, while he kept much of his newly adopted fashion and vocabulary, he began to speak out against the cultural demands of elitism. In this way, his elite education, while the source of the pressure he felt to conform, also provided him with the fuel to resist it by helping him think and reflect more critically. He described grappling with the tension between being complicit in the reproduction of elite cultural norms and owning his authentic self. But what is authentic, he pondered, at this point? He was as much a product of an elite environment as he was of Dominican New York, and he identified with both.

Iván traveled a pathway to Amherst similar to Miguel's, having arrived there as one of the privileged poor. While he was in middle school, he followed in his older brother's footsteps, winning a scholarship to a prestigious New York City day school. Like Miguel, Iván told me that it was there, years before arriving at Amherst, that he learned that if he did not change the way he spoke, he would face total social exclusion. This pressure caused internal angst and led him to question who he really was. Iván's story is not unique. Cultural collisions with elitism commonly tormented students as they struggled to figure out who they really were and who they wanted to be. Iván described this conflict:

One of my earliest memories at prep school was coming from the Bronx and I still spoke in slang and had a heavy Bronx accent. And then one of my peers was like, "Yo, why are you talking so ghetto? Why do you talk like that?" And I was just like, "What do you mean? That's just how I speak." And he was like, "You sound so ghetto." And I was just like, "There's something wrong with, like, the way I speak? What does that mean?"

And so that made me, like, very timid at first. I felt like I couldn't speak up in class discussions. . . . And it still affects me to this day. The school conditioned you, which, now that I'm thinking about it, is kind of problematic. They really push you to be articulate and eloquent. They push you to learn all this vocabulary and sound very sophisticated. Partly through the curriculum, but also the school culture. They condition you to speak like that. So over time I started to lose my Bronx slang. In class, I started to adopt that preppy way of speech. I would still talk in slang with my Latino friends. That's when

I really felt like I was code-switching for the first time. You know, I would change the way I speak with my White peers versus my minority friends. I felt inauthentic in all of those circles, because at that point my identity was becoming blurred. Like, who am I at this point? I'm just like this Bronx kid going to this preppy school, who's still trying to fight the preppy culture, but it's still subconsciously and consciously being adopted. Like really, who am I? Those were the questions I was struggling with.

These questions around authenticity continued to bother Iván throughout his time at Amherst. They also helped him further develop his critical understanding of his place in the world, as he spent a lot of time thinking deeply about how he wanted to manage his self-presentation and what the implications of his choices would be.

Jon was Dominican American and also from New York City. Unlike Iván and Miguel, Jon attended public high school and was not confronted with a new cultural script until he arrived at Amherst. Though it happened in college instead of high school, Jon went through an internal struggle similar to what Iván described. He fought against the pressure to assimilate, to start speaking in a different way and to be more "American," but he also went back and forth between putting up full-on resistance and doing the hard work of learning how to perform being elite. Overlaying all aspects of the struggle was an emotional storm of shame and uncertainty, especially concerning his immigrant and racial identity.

What you hear now was the product of an intense and strenuous effort to speak properly and enunciate. I worked on it for a solid year, probably more. . . . I don't know at what point it stopped being fake and started being just the way I spoke. . . . It feels weird. It feels really fake. But I just feel it's something I have to do. Like, there's no way around it at this point. . . . I've sold out in many ways. . . . I've basically denied aspects of my Dominican-ness and some Blackness. And I feel like in some ways I've permanently lost them.

Jon's sense that assimilation was inevitable if mobility was his goal would have been familiar to many of those who shared their life story for this book. Most students, including Miguel, Iván, and Jon, developed a critical tolerance for the instability inherent in identity and a familiarity with, though never an acceptance of, the inequality at the root of it.

Informal language codes are another cultural element that can reproduce inequality. As the examples cited here suggest, language is not just about the words people use. It is about the way those words are spoken. Heather Curl, Annette Lareau, and Tina Wu have found that a change in language patterns and vocabulary is an important mark of a habitus shift.[11]

Similarly, many students spoke about a particular voice they encountered at Amherst. They described it as a voice that is not too loud, not too emotional, and that radiates confidence and ease. It is learned through practice and consistent immersion in elite spaces. This voice is part of the habitus of students who grew up in upper-class, English-speaking, highly educated spaces. Low-income Latino students noted that not having "the voice" excluded them and marked them as different. Fiona noticed the voice right away. "I couldn't speak the right way. And I still can't. People speak in a weird way. Everyone was so annoying. It's literally an Amherst voice. I can hear it right now, and I can't simulate it because I don't have it."

Isabela similarly realized early on that she not only used the "wrong" vocabulary and sentence structure but spoke too loudly. She told me that to be respected and taken seriously in the Amherst classroom, she had to take on a new persona, starting with a new voice.

> How I talk now is so much different than when I came in. I think it's the vocabulary, but it's also the manner in which you talk. You have to have a certain voice. You have to talk in a more professional way here, whereas I used to be way more lax, and I used to just throw in whatever I wanted. And I try to do that every once in a while, but I have to be very conscious of it, whereas before I would just do it.

What was most frustrating to Isabela, Jon, Miguel, Kimberly, and Fiona was that students who grew up with privilege already seemed to have "the voice" down. It was part of their cultural disposition, part of their habitus; it was the same voice that their parents, siblings, and friends back home used. The voice was one more thing that did not worry them, that they did not have to learn. Students from elite backgrounds did not face new cultural demands when they got to Amherst, and they did not have to code-switch, at least not to the extent to which low-income Latino students did. Growing up with such a habitus is part of the ease of privilege, which is rooted in Whiteness, wealth, and a power structure that, even in progressive spaces, unconsciously expects cultural assimilation from those who aspire to its social ranks.[12]

Assumptions of privilege manifested in other ways as well. Anyone aspiring to belong among the elite must possess special stores of what Bourdieu termed "cultural capital." This is the skill set that equips people to interact in elite society with ease and confidence. These skills are conceptualized as a kind of capital because when employed properly and strategically they can translate into wealth and opportunity. Acting in a way deemed culturally appropriate at a dinner party at the boss's house, for example, might pave the way for a promotion—or a demotion if the boss judges the performance as poor. This is to say, learning the etiquette, tastes, and cultural expectations of elite society might be as important to an individual's mobility chances as getting an A in calculus. Student participants in this project recognized that not only did they have to employ grammatically correct and academically sophisticated English to fit into their new academic world, but they had to learn and adopt the ways of the elite, which never came to feel natural for most of them.

Cesar grew up in Los Angeles. He migrated, undocumented, to the United States from Mexico with his mom when he was in elementary school. He was offered a spot in a well-regarded magnet program when he was in middle school because he had good grades and did well on standardized tests. He went on to participate in a STEM [science, technology, engineering, and math]-focused pipeline program that exposed him to elite colleges and universities while he was in high school. But before going to Amherst, Cesar had never attended a fancy dinner that served multiple courses. He knew nothing about wine or gourmet food, or what was expected of him in certain social situations. When he received an invitation for an etiquette-training dinner his junior year at Amherst, he tentatively accepted, even though he knew he would be uncomfortable.

> They have these things called Pindar dinners, where you're supposed to be able to meet people from other class years and stuff. It's like a formal event, and they demand that you dress in formal attire. I remember the person that's in charge of it sent out a link with etiquette tips . . . like, if the woman leaves a table, all men have to stand. You know, things like that. . . . And I appreciate the idea. But I don't know, it just feels so uncomfortable for me to be in these sorts of situations. I went . . . and it was interesting. The food was nice. The conversations were nice. But it was just like, I don't know. It just feels so bourgeois. And that's when I feel even more of an imposter. I don't know what to do in these situations. I've never been in these situations before. And so, it just feels like a disconnect. Like, I don't belong here.

Although low-income Latino students were not the only ones who had to adjust to these new cultural scripts, for participants like Cesar, moments like these highlighted the tension they felt between their strong drive for upward mobility and the pressure to adopt cultural norms that felt not only radically different from those of their immigrant families and communities but also, for some, like a betrayal. Some participants, like Fiona, adopted an attitude of, "Screw them. I'm not going to play their game." Yet Fiona also acknowledged her fear that her refusal to go along might result in social exclusion by many of her peers and professors that could hinder her future prospects. Ultimately, she figured out that to get the most out of

Amherst she would need to get along with the right people and not ruffle too many feathers.

Some participants decided to take advantage of every cultural lesson offered at Amherst. In their estimation, getting ahead in class and income was what they owed themselves and their immigrant families. As such, they decided to adopt whatever script was necessary in order to make that happen. It is important to note that they were not naive about the unequal social terrain they were navigating, but rather had made a tactical, pragmatic decision after deep thought and contemplation about the stakes of assimilation.

Sandra, for example, concluded early on in her journey through college that learning a new cultural script was a sacrifice she was willing to make. She approached her elite acculturation seriously, as if she were in a training camp. She thought strategically about what to study, what activities to join, who she would make the effort to meet on campus, and what experiences would boost her confidence and ease. Her ultimate goal was to land a high-paying job in finance that would allow her to support her mom so that she could stop cleaning houses and move out of the Newark housing project in which they had lived since Sandra was a toddler. When I first interviewed Sandra, she had decided to major in economics and was doing well, but she knew that to land her dream job on Wall Street she needed more than straight As.

> I knew that I needed to find a way to bond with the interviewers. I could say all the right answers, but if they don't like me, they're not going to hire me. So, it was like, what are the chances that I have something in common with these interviewers? And I was like, zero. So I was like, how do I increase my chances? I did want to be in crew before even thinking about these things, so I was like, okay, let me try this. I kept going with crew because I knew that it would help me interview better. Because what rich White boy from Princeton doesn't row? You know what I mean? At Goldman, that's the kind of people you're going to get. There is a good chance I'm going to get someone that did crew, that rowed. So I said, okay, let me do this, because I need to find something in common. . . . I also felt that I needed to train myself to be more comfortable around rich White people. I knew that I could get the technicals okay because I've studied them, but what was more important was having them like me. So I knew that I couldn't have them like me if I felt really tense in their interview, if I was uncomfortable. So I made a big effort to feel very relaxed, to smile a lot, to laugh. But to do that I knew that I needed to be comfortable with those kinds of people. So I started talking more to people on campus that are similar, that are rich, White. . . . Whenever I would go out on a Saturday night, I would try to go to spaces around those people,

even though I was desperately uncomfortable. I was like, let me just go for a little bit to train myself.

Ultimately, Sandra got her dream job.

Sandra's commitment to learning what she called the "rich, White script" stands out in the life stories I collected because of how unapologetically she crafted her plan and how disciplined she was in seeing it through. She was strategic and savvy. Sandra was on to something. In her sociological study of elite job recruitment, Lauren Rivera found that those who demonstrated comfort in elite spaces and knew the elite script were more likely to get high-status jobs in finance and consulting.[13]

Most participants admitted to feeling ambivalent about whether and how to play "the game," but everyone knew the game existed. Julia, who was preparing for graduation and then heading straight into law school when I interviewed her, joked that the only thing she hadn't taken advantage of at Amherst was the chance to make friends with rich White students. "I know my life moving forward would be easier if all my friends weren't poor and brown like me. Yeah, I should have schmoozed with more rich White folks," she sarcastically noted with a grin. Indeed, part of the hidden curriculum of elite schools is the lesson that cultural and social capital are often as important to future opportunities as academic performance, if not more important.[14] Most study participants said that their Amherst experience hammered that point home.

PLACE MATTERS TOO

Confronting inequality and navigating new cultural scripts were not the only shocks that Latino youth had to absorb when they arrived at Amherst. They also had to adapt to the material environment of the campus, which for most of them was radically different from the places of their childhood. In other words, it was not just their cultural habitus that was disrupted, but also their geographic habitus.

By geographic habitus I mean the disposition that participants developed through their relationships with the natural landscapes, built environments, and sensual contexts of their lives leading up to Amherst.[15] Building from Bourdieu's concept of habitus, I propose that individuals' geographic habitus is greatly influenced by the context of their childhood and coming of age and shaped by social class. Thus, if a young adult moves to a place that geographically approximates home or the places they visited during their childhood, their geographic habitus is reinforced. Yet the opposite is also true. Moving to a place that is geographically and environmentally different from what they know can be jarring and alienating. The majority of those

I interviewed had the latter experience. Amherst was not only a different social world but also a different material world, one in which it was hard for them to feel at home.

The majority of the youth who participated in this study grew up in a densely populated immigrant neighborhood in a large city. They seldom found themselves in quiet spaces or on empty streets. Their relationship with nature was limited to time spent in city parks, which did not happen very often. Additionally, most had never traveled to places that were different from their home neighborhood or city. Thus, transitioning into a small-town campus in a semi-rural part of Massachusetts was a shock for which most participants were not prepared. They had spent time and mental energy before coming to Amherst preparing for the academic challenges they knew they would face, and they had thought about how they would meet new friends and create community, but none had considered what it would be like to live in a place whose natural and built world was so different from home.

Fiona, for example, was caught off guard by what she perceived to be the rurality of Amherst, which added to her sense of loneliness and unease after she left her home in the Bronx.

> When I got to Amherst, I was like, this is honestly the most trees I've seen. It is just so green. I don't know what they do. It's like witchcraft. And I hated the birds! Freshman year I remember going into my dorm and the first night I was like, what is all that noise? I am in hell. It was so annoying. I literally, I couldn't deal with it. And then the cicadas. I was like, what are they? I hate them. Loud music or like cars honking was what was normal to me.

Fiona never came to appreciate the birds, trees, or cicadas. In her mind, they were the natural props of suburban youth, of the world of the White and wealthy. Instead of symbolizing the rural idyll of New England, they were yet another example of inequality and served as barriers to her incorporation.

For Isabela, it was the dark and the cold that were most difficult. Having lived all of her life in urban southern California, the New England winters hit her hard. Isabela's travels had been limited to a trip to Mexico when she was a child. She most certainly had never experienced a northern climate or snow. Although she thought the first snowfall was "magical," the novelty wore off quickly, and Isabela found herself fighting against what she now realized was season-based low energy and mild depression. "I don't know what it is, but the air and sun are just different here. Yeah, even the sun feels different. When I go back to California, I love the way the sun feels on my skin. I don't know, but even when the sun is out in Amherst and it's warm, it doesn't feel the same." Isabela worked hard to learn to appreciate the change of seasons and the different sensual experiences that Amherst offered, yet she never truly felt at home. In her homesickness, she missed not only her family and friends but also the air and warmth of southern California.

Although students struggled with the dark, the cold, and the quiet of a rural campus, they also came to appreciate the security they felt there. For most, a sense of safety on campus was a welcome change from what they were used to at home. And yet, even their appreciation for the security provided by Amherst reminded them of how far they had moved from their family's reality. Many spoke of their parents' lack of understanding that they felt free to roam around campus and town late at night without feeling afraid. Because many parents did not have the financial means or legal security to visit Amherst, they had no sense of the environment in which their child was living. Cesar explained his experience:

> I think my mom thinks it's a lot bigger than it is. . . . Like, I would call her and be like, "Oh, I just got home from work," or whatever, and it's like 2:00 in the morning. And she's like, "Why are you up? Why are you walking around this late?" And I don't think she understands, because we're from L.A., like a big city. And I think she's gotten used to that big city. So she doesn't understand like how small Amherst is. I think, someone said this and I really agree with it: I've never been in a place where I felt safer than Amherst, like just overall walking around or just in general, just like a really safe place. Yeah, I think she underestimates how small it is. I don't know. Because they haven't seen it either, so I think, yeah, they don't know exactly what to expect.

Cesar appreciated the security and tranquility of Amherst. As he said, it felt like the safest place he had ever been. And yet his mother's lack of understanding that the safeness of the campus was part of his college reality was yet another reminder of how different their worlds were, and how difficult it was to bridge them.

Although the disruption in geographic habitus was most obvious for those students who came to Amherst from large cities, students from suburban areas, small towns, and remote or rural areas experienced it too. For some, the built structure of the campus and the density of the town center felt foreign. Many of the participants from cities did not know how to drive, but almost all participants from more remote areas did. The latter were used to navigating large expanses between places, though instead of quaint town centers they were more familiar with stand-alone strip malls and big-box stores. For them, Amherst did not feel rural, but it did feel dense and unfamiliar.

Antonio, who grew up in a town whose culinary offerings included a mix of mom-and-pop Mexican restaurants and fast-food joints, was put off by the limited fast-food offerings in the Amherst area. When he pooled resources with friends his second month at Amherst to rent a car and drive to Boston so that they could get their Five Guys burger fix, Antonio didn't flinch at driving ninety miles for the occasion. Indeed, a Five Guys burger was the antidote he needed for his homesickness first semester.

Similarly, few students from remote areas had been exposed to residential campuses before. For them the brick and stone buildings, manicured lawns, and obvious geographic division between town and gown were all new. Most urban youth, to the contrary, had been exposed to college campuses, because their cities were home to so many of them. What most often generated geographic habitus disruption for all participants, both urban and rural, was a lack of previous exposure to or familiarity with places that privileged students might have gained through travel, summer camp, or other opportunities to occupy different types of natural and built environments.

WRITING A NEW SCRIPT

The youth I interviewed came to understand that educational mobility mandated learning how to survive in a new and structurally unequal world that assumed particular cultural and social scripts and familiarities. Some, like Sandra, approached this challenge pragmatically, doing whatever they felt was necessary to move ahead without compromising too much. For everyone, the dance between incorporating themselves into a new environment and maintaining what several students termed "authenticity" was difficult and often emotionally painful. Several students stood out for how they coped with the demands of mobility by utilizing every educational and social resource at their disposal to rewrite the script. These youth used their Amherst education to build new communities away from home, to better understand their own and their family's struggles and the roots of the inequality they were experiencing, and then to employ their knowledge to challenge the institution to be better.

A common way in which participants found community and support at Amherst was through affinity groups, mostly race- or gender-based, that met regularly to discuss everything from politics to culture to social justice issues on campus and beyond. Groups also organized social events, cultural presentations, and celebrations and invited speakers to campus. It was often through affinity groups, participants told me, that they connected with others from similar immigrant and social class backgrounds with whom they could relate over the intangible things they missed about home.

Participants described feeling immediately lighter entering the spaces of their affinity groups, because there they could just be themselves, and because in these spaces they realized they were not alone.

Affinity groups also formed the base for leadership opportunities on campus; students were able to draw from their own experiences as first-generation Latino college students to help younger students who were just matriculating. Noel, for example, was one of several participants who worked as a counselor for the Summer Bridge program during his sophomore and junior summers. In this job he was able to mentor other low-income students about confronting wealth without falling into the imposter syndrome and adapting to a new environment without falling prey to assimilation pressures. Noel told me that working for Summer Bridge "was one of the most meaningful parts of my Amherst experience. It's where I felt like I really made a difference." Leo also participated in Summer Bridge. It was there, he told me, that he first found community at Amherst, and where he met his best friends. These were the friends who "helped me through the hard times at Amherst, because they got it." Like Noel, Leo dedicated his sophomore and junior year summers to working as a Summer Bridge counselor so he could pay back and pay forward the community and support he himself had found in the program.

While many participants credited affinity groups or special programs for low-income youth for their social survival on campus, others cited specific academic courses as the source of newfound confidence and knowledge that helped them better understand their place in the world and their family's. Silvia's story is one example. She grew up in New Jersey in a low-income, medium-sized city about an hour outside of New York City, and she attended public schools. Silvia's initial transition to Amherst was both enthralling and discouraging. She was motivated by every opportunity the school presented, especially the community of Black and brown students who shared her academic passions and aspirations. But she also struggled to find her voice in the classroom. She felt intimidated by the many students around her, most of whom were non-Latino Whites; others, however, were Latino and Black and seemed at ease academically and socially. After not participating in class discussions her freshman year, Silvia made a commitment to herself to get out of the rut of silence and intimidation. She signed up for a political science class that was focused on urban poverty and inequality, a class that she hoped would speak to her reality and give her the knowledge to better understand her own background.

It was an incredible class. And I remember that class changed everything for me in that I started seeing structures. . . . Oh my goodness, when I read *Being Black, Living in the Red*, it blew my mind. It documented wealth accumulation, and it compared African American wealth accumulation with White American families, and just going through the policies that inhibited wealth accumulation, analyzing data numerically and qualitatively. And that blew my mind. I was like, you can do this? I talked to the professor, and I was like, I didn't know academia cared about poor people. That was the first time I had seen the study of systems in that way. . . . That, I think, really contributed to my understanding of why my neighborhood was the way it was, but it also helped me understand how my parents were responsible for some things, but also, they weren't responsible for other things.

After taking that class, Silvia felt a new sense of passion and power. She started to talk in class. Most importantly, she started to carve out a course schedule and an Amherst life that supported her newfound belief that she could contribute to changing structures of inequality.

I'm doing things now that I might have done before, but [now I'm doing them] for the right reasons. It took coming here to do that. Now I'm doing more stats and econ, not because it looks good and because it's what you do if you're smart, but because it's important to have that understanding in order to change things. I also took Black studies, and I was like, "Wow, this is amazing history." I've never learned this before.

Silvia also, like many other students in this study, made it a point to nurture relationships with faculty and staff of color, especially those who were Black and/or Latino. She talked openly with them about her struggles and her dreams, and she was amazed by the support and care that she received.

I talked to a professor about my struggles my first two years here, and she always told me . . . "You have to let go of your identities at the door," because I was so aware of being a woman and like being Latina, being Black, and being low-income. It was good that I was aware of it, but it was to the point where I was so aware that I was like, these are barriers. And I was so obsessed with that almost. And I remember her telling me, like joking, but also not, being like, pretend you're a White man when you're sitting in class.

Silvia became an important leader on campus. By the end of her four years at Amherst, she did not need to pretend she was anyone other than who she was. She embraced her identity—her Dominican-ness, her Blackness, and her *latinidad*—and she worked hard to ease the path for future students. She was a core member of the group of faculty and students who created a new major in Latinx and Latin American studies. She protested and she collaborated and she moved the college to do more to support low-income Latino students and to teach them early on about the importance of finding mentors and utilizing the college's resources.

Alberto also made the decision to utilize the resources at his disposal to deepen his understanding of his life, his family's struggles, and his place in the larger social world. He knew that being undocumented put limitations on his life that he could not control. But he wanted to learn why those limitations were in place, and more importantly, he wanted to learn how to better navigate the limitations psychologically and emotionally. Although he had always assumed that he would major in a STEM discipline, he began to eye classes in the humanities as a means to this goal.

> I wanted to understand inequality. And sadly, you know, I understand it now. And it's pretty depressing. But it's okay, because I need to understand the reality of it. . . . I took "Revolutionary History" . . . and it's one of my favorite classes I've taken here. It was so great. I started reading more philosophy, and that really impacted my thinking about religion and nihilism, atheism, all these different things. So I found myself really liking humanities classes. . . . And then I took "Intro to Sociology," and that also impacted my thinking about education. I read *The Diversity Bargain*. I also read *The Big Test*. And I just started thinking about how from very early on, students are taught very differently. I realize now that the reason I felt so stagnant in high school was because the education system was designed to be that way. . . . I'm not really intended to go to a school like this, so they don't prepare me for that. They don't prepare me to question authority. I've come to the conclusion that it's not my fault that this place has been hard.

Alberto's realization that it was not individual intelligence or effort alone that determined who thrived helped him regain confidence in himself as a student. He stopped blaming himself and instead put more effort toward advocating for policy changes. He partnered his schoolwork with activism in a community organization that focused on immigrant rights, joined efforts at Amherst to foster greater equity and inclusion, and made close friendships with other activism-minded Latino students. Although his efforts neither erased all of his struggles and suffering nor shifted his reality of being poor and undocumented, they erased the shame he initially felt about his place at Amherst and in the world. And his new understanding of the social world enhanced his appreciation for his own survival as well as that of his family and community.

Gloria too chose to write a new script. She started by returning to the questions that had emerged during her first days on campus: Why did she have to come to college alone while most students had parents who could support them directly? Why was she sitting in her room alone while her roommate was going out for a fancy dinner with her parents? Gloria sought out classes that would help her better understand her parents' immigration story and her family's reality. She found other students in many of these classes who were seeking the same understanding. She enrolled in economics, sociology, American studies, and history classes that focused on immigration. According to Gloria, these classes "gave Latinx students the space to recognize that everyone was going through it, and so it was like, I'm not by myself, and it's okay. I can now contextualize my experiences." In these classes, Gloria found a haven where she didn't have to worry about how she sounded or whether or not she used the right words. Free to bring in her full self, she felt like her lived experiences were valued as a critical source of knowledge. Gloria came to understand the policies and laws that were at the base of her parents' undocumented status, and she came to understand the "ways undocumented labor contributes to the economy, that the economy would struggle without it." This knowledge was empowering, and she came to appreciate that more important than adopting a sophisticated way of speaking was the know-how and confidence she had gained to talk about immigration and inequality with depth and nuance.

Gloria also came to appreciate the many important skills she had gained by growing up poor and with undocumented parents who needed to be savvy to survive.

> I am resilient. I had to seek resources. I know where financial aid is. I've used so many resources throughout my time here due to medical illnesses, due to mental illnesses, due to so many things. Part of me thanks my parents for putting me in certain situations, because now things don't scare me, and I know where to look and I know how to look. I know how to ask for help, which some students don't want to, or they feel weird asking. Whereas I'm like, "No, like I'm going to go seek all the resources I can."

It was in classes that sharpened her critical understanding of the social world that Gloria discovered her passion. She utilized a career center program to fund an internship at an immigration law firm in Chicago. Through that internship she was able to learn more about the process for helping her parents, and others like them, move toward citizenship. Ultimately, as difficult as it was to learn how to survive at Amherst, it gave her the means to know herself, her family, and her community better.

Slowly but surely, students' resistance efforts, partnered with allyship from faculty, staff, and students, are changing the culture of Amherst. Students I interviewed in 2020 and 2021, for example, seemed to have had a better time than those I interviewed in 2016 and 2017. Between the time when I started and finished this project, Amherst ended legacy admissions, opened the Office of Diversity, Equity and Inclusion, the Center for Restorative Practices, and an immigration office, and it initiated a program to secure internships and summer experiences for low-income students (see chapter 7 for more details). So even if this chapter is replete with evidence of the obstinance of elitism, it should also be read as a record of student resilience and the strength and effectiveness of their leadership and activism. Although it is unjust that youth from marginalized backgrounds have to adapt, endure, and cope in ways that privileged students do not, it is those who face marginalization head-on who have been most effective at inspiring and pushing the institution to be better.

BRIDGING TWO WORLDS

The youth in this study told me that because they spent so much time and energy, for so many years, focused on getting to a school like Amherst, they were caught off guard by how difficult it was to move in and through their new elite environment. For most of them, their worlds of home and school had been radically different. Most participants described home as immigrant, Black or Brown, and Spanish-speaking, and as a place of collective struggle and survival. School, on the other hand, was wealthy, White, English-speaking, and individualistic.

With their diverging cultural and social norms and expectations, participants' worlds of home and school were vastly unequal. It was this inequality, and their intimacy with it, that made youth's educational mobility experiences most challenging. For the doubly disadvantaged in particular, their arrival at Amherst was the first time they had experienced this inequality up close and in person. And so it was the first time they saw their own lives through a comparative lens as they took in how different were the lives of their wealthy, mostly White classmates. By developing a comparative perspective, students also gained a more critical understanding of the social world.

Because I had the opportunity to spend time with nine of the families of the youth in this study, I got a small glimpse into what it must have been like for them to move between the different worlds of home and school. I was indelibly marked, for example, by my visit with Gloria's family in Chicago. As we sat around their kitchen table on a steamy July day in 2018, the World Cup buzzing on a small television in the background, I was struck by the material differences between Gloria's small house and Amherst's dormitories and academic buildings. I journaled about the ease with which we talked in Spanish, noting that it was Gloria who kept the conversation flowing, gracefully and without a blip, as she translated whenever a phrase or word was used that was new to me. Of course, this was a role—that of translator—that she had filled for a long time. I was also struck by how little Gloria's parents knew about Amherst. Sitting with them in their kitchen, I understood more easily how hard it must have been for them to say goodbye when she flew off to a place they literally could not envision and would never see. It became clear to me that day that Gloria, after four years of living a time zone away from her family, experienced her life from a dual frame of reference, having developed a critical consciousness about why her family's circumstances diverged so radically from her life in Amherst.

It never became easy for them, but Gloria and the other youth in this study learned to move between home and school. Most, though not all, told me that they eventually learned how to overcome the imposter syndrome they felt when they first arrived. They found support and strength through building relationships with each other and finding spaces on campus where they could "just be," with no need to explain their family's struggles with poverty or illegality. They identified allies on campus and found ways to influence Amherst policies and the curriculum to make the experience better for future Latino youth. Indeed, the participants in this study became powerful agents, leaders, and advocates for social change.

Many learned how to not just survive but thrive at Amherst by coming to understand the structural and systemic inequalities that framed both the campus and their families' lives. They strategically either adopted or disregarded the elite cultural scripts that were assumed to be the norm, and some fought to deconstruct these scripts and rewrite them. In all cases, I found that they acted with intent, finding a way to move through Amherst on their own terms. This is not to say that it was easy. For most of the participants in this study, getting through Amherst was really hard. Some vowed after graduation that they would never go back. Still others told me that they had slowly gained an appreciation for the college and its malleability; they had come to see it as a place that wanted to change, had changed, and would continue to change in large part because of their presence and perspectives and the life experiences they had brought to campus life. One of these experiences was the familial price that Latino youth had to pay to achieve exceptional educational mobility. The next chapter tells this story.

Chapter 3 | The Price of Mobility

What preoccupies me is immediate: the separation I endure with my parents in loss. This is what matters to me: the story of a scholarship boy who returns home one summer from college to discover bewildering silence, facing his parents.

Richard Rodriguez, *Hunger of Memory* (1982), 4

IN HIS NOW classic memoir *Hunger of Memory*, Richard Rodriguez reflects on his extraordinary upward educational trajectory and its impact on his relationship with his working-class Mexican immigrant parents. His narrative highlights the hidden complexities of mobility. Rodriguez credits education for giving him the intellectual tools to think critically about the world, as well as to understand his place in it and his family's. He touts the benefits of the intellectual passions and skills he has come to possess, the networks to which he has gained access, and the prized placement he has achieved among the academic elite. And yet, in Rodriguez' reflections, these joys and privileges are eclipsed by the losses they have implied. For Rodriguez, loss was an intimate partner to mobility's gains.

Rodriguez was still a primary school student when he came to believe that language was power, and that English was situated above Spanish on the U.S. language hierarchy. He determined that a sophisticated command of English was necessary if he was to become an "educated man." And becoming an educated man was indeed his goal. In powerful prose, Rodriguez describes how, as he gained competence and confidence in English, his second language—and in his estimation the language of assimilation— he began to move emotionally and intellectually away from his Spanish-speaking parents. This move was inevitable, he argues, as the educated person he was becoming was being formed by a language that his parents did not understand well. The gap widened between Rodriguez and his parents as his intellectual growth drew nutrients from words, ideas, and sources to which his parents did not have access. In the process, his world and the world of his parents drifted further apart; his reality became less comprehensible to his parents, as did theirs to him. Ultimately, Rodriguez realized that in fulfilling his American Dream, he had ironically sacrificed the close family bond that had formed the original base of his aspiration. "In singing the praise of my lower-class past, I remind myself of my separation from that past, bringing memory to silence. I turn to consider the boy I once was in order, finally, to describe the man I am now. I remember what was so grievously lost to define what was necessarily gained."[1]

I have taught Rodriguez's memoir a few times in my upper-division seminar "Immigration and the New Latino Second Generation." This class tends to draw mostly low-income Latino students who are searching for a sociological understanding of their family's immigration story. My students' initial reaction to *Hunger of Memory* is almost always negative. They scorn Rodriguez's critique of bilingual education, in which he argues that English is the only public language of the United States, and thus that it should be the only language of formal education. To deny this reality, he argues, is to further disadvantage the most disadvantaged. My students also tend to get riled by his critical account of affirmative action, which, he argues, privileges well-to-do and upwardly mobile students of color over those marginalized by poverty. In his estimation, affirmative action policies ignore social class to the detriment of those who most deserve a boost. He uses himself as an example. The recipient of an elite education, Rodriguez no longer considers himself marginalized, despite his race.

To be sure, there is much to discuss about Rodriguez's controversial and quite radical critiques of bilingual education and affirmative action. Yet my students typically do not want to pause on these topics for long. For even the staunchest critics of Rodriguez's policy stances tend to find that his narrative about the high familial cost of educational mobility resonates. Powerfully. This theme—the initial feelings of loss or change implicit in educational mobility—is what my students have the most to say about. And at semester's end it is typically *Hunger of Memory*, more than any other book, that my students cite in their final essays, in which I prompt them to put a piece of their own life experience into conversation with a text from the course.

Like the students in my "Immigration and the New Latino Second Generation" seminar, the youth I interviewed for this book spoke at length about the loss implicit in their own experiences of educational mobility and the change in their relationships to family and to home after they came to Amherst. Their narratives about loss and change in no way diminished the many joys they attributed to their opportunities and accomplishments. Like Rodriguez, they prized the exciting new ideas and questions that their classes and college experiences had generated and the close friendships they had made away from home. And they rejoiced over the incredible opportunities and resources that an elite education had given them—for some, being able to travel to new and faraway places, and for all, being able to nurture their creativity and stoke their aspirations. Many also said that higher education had exposed them to social, cultural, and economic contexts from which they had acquired a new and more critical lens on the world. What they had not anticipated, however, was that through this new lens many of them would come to see their community and their family differently, and that their relationships with family and with home would change.

NEW KNOWLEDGE, NEW PERSPECTIVES, AND NEW UNDERSTANDING GAPS

For the vast majority of youth who participated in this study, attending college entailed a move away from home—often far away. Moves can be measured in miles. They can also be measured in new experiences and knowledge stores. As I have already suggested, geographic and educational mobility tend to go hand in hand, as do the tangible and metaphorical distances they represent. As the students I interviewed engaged in studies across the social sciences, humanities, and STEM disciplines, they accumulated knowledge that they came to realize typically made sense only to those who were, or who had been, immersed in similar educational contexts, or who had access to the same academic language and tools they did. Student after student told me that their thinking about the world had been revolutionized by the classes they were taking, the relationships they were forming, and the experiences they were having, but that they found themselves struggling to translate what they were learning to their family and kin back home. They found themselves compelled to sort out a slew of complicated emotions—passion and enthusiasm partnered with shame, frustration, guilt, and sadness.

Iván was exceptionally close to his mom when he was young. When his brother started to hang "with the wrong crowd" and get in trouble in high school, Iván's bond with his mom grew even tighter. Their connection was based on their shared goal of social mobility, which they both believed was dependent on his academic success. Yet when Iván began to leave the Bronx each day to attend an elite preparatory high school, and especially when he moved from New York to Amherst, he found his relationship with his mom growing more distant.

When I started at Prep, that's when I really started, like, to lose that intimacy and personal connection I had with her, because I couldn't talk to her about classes. . . . [At Amherst] it's even more of that sense of loss. . . . This is the time where I started to pick up a genuine interest in academics. I'm starting to choose my classes. . . . But I can't share that with my mom because she wouldn't understand, right? Like, she doesn't have that background. Like, if I talked to her about philosophy, what is she going to know about that, right? So it's weird. It became almost a bureaucratic relationship, which is a weird way to describe a parent/child relationship.

As Iván moved deeper into his education, his conversations with his mom shifted to the mundane—what he had eaten that day, what the weather was like, how their extended family was doing. A connection remained between them, to be sure, but it had changed. Iván grieved that he had lost something meaningful in the shift, and he became resentful of the students who were not experiencing the same understanding gap with their parents.

I remember for freshman year when I'd call my mom and be like, "How are you doing?" And she'd be like, you know, "I paid the bills today," "This is how the weather is," . . . or whatever. But it was just not very personal; like, no storytelling, no really intimate conversation. Whereas, like hearing my friends FaceTime and Skype their parents and they're like, "Yo, I'm taking this class. I just wrote an essay on this." Or there were even some of my peers who would send essays to their parents to proofread for them. . . . I think me becoming very close to my peers here, and realizing the amount of students whose parents come from educated backgrounds, and who are a lot more involved with their child's lives and whatnot, I think that really exacerbated the sense of loss that I felt.

Iván recognized that the change he had experienced in his relationship with his mom was a product of their different positions in the social opportunity structure. But his more privileged peers did not seem to experience with their families the kind of distancing he did as he moved away from his mother socially and culturally and felt his perspective shifting, along with his tastes and interests.

Kimberly experienced a similar sense of distancing. She had already started to drift away from her parents in high school. When she got to Amherst, she spent a lot of angst-ridden time and energy trying to figure out how to share her college experience with them and close the divide. It was a difficult task. In the past, language had been the most explicit experiential barrier between them. Although Kimberly spoke Spanish, she had come to live most of her life in English. As such, there were many experiences she could not share with her parents. As Kimberly moved deeper into her college life, she came to realize that English was no longer the only barrier. Within her first year at Amherst, she noted, an intellectual divide had also developed. When Kimberly was a child, she had at times felt embarrassed by her parents' lack of English fluency and inability to navigate U.S. society with ease. As she settled into her Amherst life, her emotions shifted from shame to sadness about the gap that was growing between them.

> When I got here, this thing about being embarrassed of my parents was actually replaced by just feeling really sad. There's this really big gulf between us now. I mean, my mom cannot imagine what I do here. She just can't. Like, you know, in this class, I'm reading *The Communist Manifesto*. My mom was like, "Oh, what are you learning?" And I'm like, "Oh, it's actually kind of exciting, Mom. I just read *The Communist Manifesto* by Karl Marx." And she's like, "I don't know—what is that?" . . . I used to think it was about it being in English or, oh, these are American things. But I remember taking a class on *[One] Hundred Years of Solitude*, which changed my life, and she asked me, "What are you learning?" And I was like, "Mom, I read *[One] Hundred Years of Solitude*," and she doesn't know what that is. It's sad. It used to be embarrassing, but now it just breaks my heart.

A full immersion in a residential college in which attending class, studying, and discussing ideas with their peers were part of daily life was a new and different experience for all of these youth except those who had attended prep school. The intensity of the experience made it all the more difficult for Kimberly when she could not share what she was learning with her family, such as the classic of Latin American literature *One Hundred Years of Solitude*. The knowledge she was acquiring was completely changing Kimberly's life perspective, but it was foreign to her parents.

Not only was it difficult for students to explain *what* they were learning to their parents, but it was also hard, as many told me, to explain *why* they were choosing to study certain topics. Their diverging life experiences had shaped different expectations, strategies, and decisions. Heidi, for example, was drawn to sociology because these classes gave her a framework to understand inequality and immigration. Both of Heidi's parents were undocumented, and she wanted to learn about the social forces at the base of their migration from Mexico, her father's deportation, and the mismatch between how hard her parents worked and how little they had to show for it materially. But Heidi's mother did not see education as a forum for thinking about one's place in the world. For her, the goal of education, short and simple, was to get the credentials and skills to get a good job. When Heidi told her mom that she wanted to major in sociology, her mom pushed back. Despite Heidi's efforts to explain it, her mom never grasped what sociology entailed, and because of the discipline's relative obscurity outside of the academy, she believed that sociology would not add value to her daughter's future. Heidi had many challenging conversations with her mother. Over time she shifted her strategy from trying to explain what she was studying and learning to simply trying to gain her mom's trust in the classes and major she chose. In the process, however, they drifted further apart.

> I still can't fully explain to my mom what sociology is, and what I can do with it, and it's hard for me to explain the type of research I'm doing. . . . I'll be like, "I'm really interested in immigrant rights. I took this class, and I learned so much, and it's just opened my eyes to something that I'm truly interested in." And my mom is like, "Why did you choose that? Why are you interested in that?" And it's a hard thing for me. I'm like, "What do you mean, why am I interested in this? Because of us, because of what we've gone through, because of what you've gone through."

I have spent many hours in my office talking with low-income Latino students like Heidi about how to navigate the gap between their parents' belief that they should study whatever will best help them get good jobs and their own intellectual passions, which they often bring to areas that their parents have never encountered—such as film studies, American studies, philosophy, sociology, or art history. From the moment they set foot on the Amherst campus, students are told that the liberal arts mission is to support them in developing their intellectual passions and curiosities. Academic advisers, myself included, encourage students to explore the open curriculum and to take intellectual risks in their learning paths. But such exploration is foreign to students' immigrant parents, who have had very little opportunity in their lives for intellectual pursuits or for nurturing their passions or curiosities. For most of them, life—and immigration specifically—has been about survival and a shot at upward mobility. Intellectual pleasure was absent from the immigration narratives of all the parents I met in the course of this study.

Noel's mom, Suzy, wanted to become a teacher. Isabela's mom, Victoria, wanted to be a nurse. In my interviews with these mothers, they gave me similar versions of "I loved school and had dreams of studying more, but I had to go to work." Indeed, all the parents I interviewed told me that they would have chosen to study more. But early on they had to put intellectual curiosity aside so that they could work and support their families. Their intellectual aspirations were limited by the harsh material reality of their lives. And so, even now, though all the parents I interviewed told me that their children's education was their top priority, they also made clear their belief that education, first and foremost, would lead to social mobility. Their difficult material circumstances continued to limit their ability to center intellectual curiosity.

And so it should not be surprising that tensions commonly developed between parents and students when parents' stress on practicality and survivability—born of their own childhood and migratory experiences—clashed with their children's newfound scholarly passions and aspirations. Samantha, for example, ended up majoring in French and physics, after contemplating math. Like Heidi, she found herself at a loss when trying to explain to her parents, who were from rural Puebla in southern Mexico and lived in New York City, why she was studying something that was not going to lead directly to a career path that they understood as upwardly mobile. For her mom, who worked as a nanny, and her dad, who worked in a deli kitchen, the formula for upward mobility was simple; go into a well-known, highly regarded profession like medicine, law, or business. Samantha did not want to work in any of these fields.

> They know that school is a lot of work, and they know that I am doing the work. But every time they ask me about the degree or my major, my mom is always like, "You are going to be a doctor, right?" Or, "You're going to be a lawyer, right?" And I'm like, "No, I'm not going to be either of those things." Or I just don't respond, because, no, I'm not going to be a doctor. I'm not going to be a lawyer. Or my dad is like, "What are you studying?" And I'm like, "It's math." And he's like, "No, don't study math. That is not where the money is at. You should study computer science or something." And I don't want to study that!

Even though Samantha realized that her parents only wanted the best for her so that she "would not have to struggle like they did," tensions ensued that were never fully resolved during her college career.

Distance and loss were also generated when students' political perspectives shifted in a direction away from those of their parents. This was the change that Silvia found to be the most difficult. Through classes in gender studies and Black studies, Silvia came to identify as a feminist and an advocate for gay rights, neither of which resonated readily with her more conservative-minded, Catholic Dominican parents.

> I don't think I actively thought to myself, "I know more than my parents," but I actively thought to myself, "If only they knew these types of things," like feminism and all that stuff. . . . Like, with my mom, whenever we would get into a discussion about these things, we would always get into an argument. And I was just really tired of getting into an argument. Like, we would talk about gay rights and always butt heads.

Silvia coped by putting strict boundaries in place. She rarely went home after her first year, and when she did, she did not share much with her parents. In her view at the time, distance was "better than the alternative, better than getting into altercations." But the self-imposed distance also signified a change in their relationship, a loss that might never be recovered.

Cesar experienced a similar political dissonance with his mom. They were both undocumented, a shared social position that had reinforced the bond between them as they strategized together on how to navigate the world and work toward upward mobility. Cesar assumed that his mom's experience of living as an undocumented immigrant in the United States would make her empathetic toward other minority groups and give her a critical understanding of the injustice of their shared marginalization. Yet, in his estimation, that did not happen; indeed, he felt like she just "didn't get it."

> We try to talk, but it's difficult. Like, I remember I was trying to explain to her gender, and how gender's now thought of as different from sex and things like that. And she didn't understand these concepts. She wasn't even open. She was just like, "No . . . that's not how things work." A lot of times she has a more traditional view on things. . . . Right now, she's working as a home-health aide, and so she'd be telling me things that happened to her at work. And, it's just like, "Mom, that's paternalism!" But how do you get that across? . . . It's just kind of weird.

Edith too found that as she delved into humanities and social science courses and got more deeply involved in race- and gender-based affinity groups on campus, her perspectives on the world were becoming radically different from those of her Venezuelan parents, especially when it came to race. She was one of several students I interviewed whose studies, close friendships with other Latino students, and engagement with college-based affinity groups had changed the way they thought about their own racial identity.[2] As Edith's identity evolved, she came to see her parents as "kind of racist" and became frustrated and uncertain about how to confront them about their attitudes. Edith had dark eyes and dark hair but could present as White. In Venezuela, her parents were middle-class; when she was growing up, they socialized her to believe that a middle- or high-class status in Venezuela and having one grandparent from Europe equated with Whiteness, even though her other grandparents were dark-skinned. It was not until she was progressing through her classes at Amherst that she began to embrace a non-White Latina identity.

I remember I was in the Queer Resource Center my freshman year, and there was an event for queer people of color, and I asked the director, "Am I a person of color? Can I come to this?" And I just feel like that's hilarious now. I used to think I was one of you [White]! I'm so different now. But people from home are still not there. And I don't feel like I'm better than anyone, I just think we've been exposed to such different experiences. The way that I see things now is very different than it would have been if I stayed in Florida for the past four years. I mean, if my parents were filling out a form, absolutely they would be like, "Oh yeah, she's White." They're not going to write anything else. My sister and I talk about it, and it makes me happy that we can have these conversations. She'll be like, "Oh my God, our family is so racist." I'm like, "Yeah, you're right." I feel there's just a lot of stuff that they need to unlearn, but it's so hard, you know? Like, we went to this soul food place and my mom was like, "Ugh, I don't like this food. This is Black people food." And I was like, "Okay, educational moment." And we had a conversation. And we've actually had conversations where I tell them that I don't want them to be racist.

Several students, like Edith, said that through their coursework they had come to see that racism, specifically anti-Blackness, was not just "a White people problem" but was embedded in their own parents' views of the world. These were painful realizations. Most said that they tried to change their parents' views but found this difficult because their parents did not have access to the same information they did, or had "never met a Black person," as was the case for some of the non-Black Latino parents, and were not open to changing their views.

The students who expressed the most frustration were those who had come to identify racially in a way that their parents didn't approve of. This happened most often among Dominican students who came to identify as Afro-Latino/a/x. They had grown up with narratives of anti-Blackness, rooted in the historical tensions between the Dominican Republic and Haiti. Francia, a Dominican from New York, talked in depth about her mom's refusal to accept her Blackness. "Haitians are Black," her mom would insist. "You are Dominican. You are different." Francia felt liberated by and proud of her new identity, even though it upset her mom. She finally understood the history that had produced her family's struggles and led them to migrate, but she also came to understand their complicity in the system that had marginalized them. As Francia refused to cave to her mom's adamant anti-Blackness, a wedge developed between them, spurring grief and frustration.

The new knowledge stores, critical lenses, and identities that students talked about were products of their college education. Students understood the irony. They were beginning to see the world differently in large part because they had access to knowledge and learning that was unavailable to their parents. Their new ways of seeing the world were also moving them further away from the people they cared about most. What frustrated them, students said, was that, as much as they were pained by the loss and discombobulation, they did not see a solution.

Gaby was well aware that she had gained privileges and knowledge through her education that her parents, through no fault of their own, would never have. And yet, despite knowing that their differences were rooted in inequality, Gaby still could not help but be bothered by the political and moral differences she started noticing between herself and her parents.

> We'd have these discussions, and like, seeing them not get it, but then also trying to understand that it's not their fault. Like, these are conversations I'm constantly having, and I'm literally taking courses explaining this. And I have the time and the space to do it and they don't. It's like, that's already a huge difference. But now my political views are different from theirs. Like, my moral views are different from theirs. And like, we haven't had time to explore that because I'm not home often. I'm mostly here. And then when I go home I feel like I'm in a cage, and I feel like I'm the Gaby that I'm not. And like, it's weird because they don't know me anymore. . . . Like, I guess it just happens when you live your life, when you grow up outside of the home. But it's just hard. . . . I didn't realize why there's so much tension between us and why I couldn't talk to them about things and why I still felt shame for certain things, and why I felt guilty for certain things. And so, I had a conversation with my professor [also Latina] and she literally looked at me, and she's like, "Nanna, something that you need to recognize is that you are a different social class from them now." And she's like, "You have been presented with opportunities that they don't have. And you're being shaped to be a different person that they were not expecting and that you were not expecting." And I, literally I sat back and I was like, oh my gosh. It was a revelation for me. I was like, wow. But they are still my family.

Ultimately, as Gaby concluded, "they're still my family." Because of the strong ties generated by immigrant life, and the sacrifices that parents made for their children, it is no surprise that not one student I interviewed said that they were going to cut ties because of the distance that had developed between them and their parents. Instead, students tended to sit in the discomfort and try to figure out how to deal with the loss, to come to peace with the change in their relationships.

Adding to the challenges that came with students' feelings of loss and distance was the judgment they felt when family members and friends asserted, "You've changed." Students interpreted "you've changed" to mean that their family and friends now found them to be uppity or elitist. The irony is that student after student with whom I talked felt alienated by the educational elitism of Amherst, and most wanted to have nothing to do with it. To be associated with what they themselves despised was tough.

Luna remembered how excited she was to see her family after being away from them her first year of college. But almost immediately upon reuniting with them at the airport, she sensed that they were judging her. Her family had celebrated her acceptance to Amherst, putting her on a hero's pedestal, but now Luna sensed resentment. Trying to make sense of it, she wondered whether "they might see me as elitist because of where I go and what I've learned and because of the people I'm around here. . . . My aunt told me when I got off the plane, because I think I was talking more and differently than I usually do . . . 'Oh, you changed.'" Luna responded by returning to her quieter ways. But not all students were able to shrug off what they perceived as judgment from their family.

For example, Diego admitted that he was pushing back on his parents because his views had changed while he was at Amherst. He was okay with the back-and-forth of their discussions, and with the disagreement. But he was not okay with his parents' claim that because he was going to college he now thought he was superior to them.

> With my family it's definitely a lot of demonizing. At home a lot of times I get into arguments with my parents, my dad in particular. Every time I get into a conversation with him he's like, "You just think you're smarter than me because you go to the good school. . . . Every time I talk to you, there's just some air about you, like you think you're better than me." And I'm like, "No, that's actually the opposite." And so, it's just really interesting to see that dynamic. Oftentimes when I go home, my parents will try to discredit a lot of the things that I've learned at Amherst.

Several students, like Diego, said that the most maddening thing was that there seemed to be no solution to these disagreements with their family. They felt "damned if you do, damned if you don't." Change was inevitable, and both parents and students wanted it. But when students embraced their newfound confidence and spoke out about racism or sexism, they were often labeled as elitist by family members.

Cesar was philosophical about the impact of his movement between home and school: he realized that even as he had been personally transformed by his education, that experience had also created a trap. Like Diego, he knew he had changed, and with that change his relationships with family members at home had become more complicated. He understood and accepted the complexity, but was frustrated that there seemed to be no way to untangle it.

> [Going home,] it feels like everything is different, but then you realize that everything's the same; you're the one that's different. I don't know. It's sort of like you're in a different place than where you were before, and it's weird to come back. It's like coming back to the past, but you're someone else, someone different. . . . I remember I was talking to one of my cousins . . . and she's older than me, like late twenties. And this was like two years ago when the whole, like, the Black Lives Matter movement was really starting to gain momentum. And she was just, like, "Yeah, I don't understand these Blacks. Like, they're just always causing trouble. . . ." And it's just so uncomfortable. And I just want to be like, "Here are some books you can read," you know? It's just weird. It's also difficult because whenever you do try to explain something to someone or say, like, "Oh, maybe you can try looking at it this way," I feel like, even if you're not meaning it to, they sort of take it as condescending. Like, "Just because you go to school you think you're so much better," or whatever.

Cesar was not alone in feeling stumped by these changes. There just did not seem a way for youth to share what they were learning or how their views had changed without coming off as boasting or asserting superiority. Thus, tension and distancing ensued.

Students did not just experience this struggle with family. Friendships from home also became strained for some. Several talked about returning home and being cast out by those they had considered their best friends. Zaida found herself in this situation when she returned to Miami one Christmas break. While out with a close group of friends, she decided, after much hesitation, to call out one of their jokes as sexist. The friend pushed back. After this incident, home became more complicated.

> Home still feels like home. The heat, the good food, but it's just funny, because now when I'm home, I, like, pick up on different things that would be considered problematic here [at Amherst], that I would have never picked up on before, like sexist or *machista* jokes. . . . Sometimes I say things and sometimes I just hold back. And the times I do say something, my friends are like, "Zaida, this is just college getting you all high-minded and stuff." And I have two guys that I consider brothers—one of them I haven't spoken to now for about a year because we had a falling-out. It started off with him saying, "Zaida thinks she's better than us. Now she goes to

college. . . . College has changed her." And that hurt, because I don't feel like I've changed.

Like many students, Zaida felt torn between the person she had been at home and the person she had become through her education.

> I feel like I'm always at a point of conflict. Like, yes, I want to continue with my educational career and learning and associating myself with these great people [at Amherst]. But at the same time . . . I also like the communities in Miami, even though it's not, I guess not as educated. I don't know if that's, like, the best word. But I feel like, now there is some sort of disconnect. . . . Like, my conversations with my friends here [at Amherst] are very political, very informative. . . . Whereas at home, it's just very, like, let's have a good time, or it's very personal. Like, if you're going through something, you share it with them. So it's very different, the types of conversation, the environments that I'm in. It's really weird.

As communication and knowledge sharing became more difficult and confrontations followed, students said that they felt themselves moving further away from their family and kin at home and closer to friends at school or those from home who were attending similar schools or studying similar subjects. They experienced the emerging distance from home as a loss that went deeper than different ways of knowing, or divergent perspectives on politics and social issues. Students also found that people back home—their parents in particular—could not imagine what it was like to live in the elite space of Amherst College. Getting to college had always been the goal. Now that these students had achieved it, how could they possibly explain that the challenge had not ended and in some ways life felt even more difficult?

"THEY JUST DON'T GET WHAT'S HARD ABOUT THIS PLACE"

While students expressed deep respect for their parents' sacrifices and tremendous appreciation for the wealth of resources and opportunities that Amherst offered them, they said that Amherst could nevertheless be a difficult place. Their ongoing labor on behalf of their families at home added to the strain. Yet they found it hard to complain. This is one of the untold burdens of the immigrant bargain: students felt that they had to keep their struggles to themselves.

Fiona came to Amherst with the goal of attending medical school. She was exceptionally smart, but her college grades, which included Cs, Ds,

and Fs, never reflected her intellectual potential. She formed close friendships, which became her support base, but friendships alone were not
enough to alleviate her suffering and loneliness. Her experience at Amherst
was not complicated. It was simply, in her words, "awful." Instead of
gearing up for medical school her senior year, she barely graduated.

Fiona's childhood had been hard. She had lived most of her life in the
same "tiny" Bronx apartment with her parents and older brother, but
did not feel emotionally close to them. It was not just her education and
experiences that drove a wedge between them but also trauma. Fiona had
survived two sexual assaults—one from an uncle in Mexico when she was
eight and one from a high school classmate in the United States. When she
was nine, she was separated from her parents after they were detained
trying to cross the border to return from Mexico. Fiona had also long been
troubled by her father's heavy drinking. The scars from these experiences
had generated family coping mechanisms rooted in silence. Thus, when
Fiona started spiraling into depression during her first year at Amherst in
2014, she kept her suffering to herself. She did not know whom to ask for
help, or how to ask for help, but more importantly, Fiona did not want to
burden her parents with mental health struggles that she did not think
they would understand.

> It can get lonely. . . . I think I just repressed a lot of stuff up to that point.
> And I don't know if my body was just, like, oh it's a new place. . . . I don't
> know what it was. I'm still not sure to this day. . . . And it just all fell apart.
> Everything started coming back. And I had to deal with it. . . . When I was a
> kid, I was a robot. I just did what I had to do. But at Amherst it didn't work
> anymore. For the first time I started oversleeping or undersleeping. I couldn't
> wake up on time, and I would always be tired in class. . . . I literally stopped
> going to classes, and I just stopped talking to professors. It was just terrible. . . .
> But, like, who am I going to talk to? And so, I wasn't talking to professors
> and I wasn't talking to the counseling center and I wasn't talking to my
> dean, because [at the time] I didn't know you could. . . . Also, I think there's
> a shame element. It's like, everyone is so smart, and it sucks finding out that
> you can't do it. I failed classes. Literally, I just didn't hand in stuff. Honestly,
> something in me just snapped. I don't know. I was just going through stuff,
> and I couldn't name the process. And it was so exhausting. . . .
>
> And I never told my parents. I was always just, like, "Yeah, I'm okay,
> I'm fine." And they just took my word for it. I was going through rough times,
> but I didn't want to make them worry. So it was me trying to protect them.
> That's when I got academic probation. You have to leave for a year once that
> happens. I just said I'm taking a break. And they didn't probe. I was so sad,
> and I was crying all the time. And I wanted to die. . . . I would just tell them

that it was really White, and that it was hard on me. But . . . they knew that it was a good school, so when I would complain, my mom would be like, "Why are you complaining? You're in a good place. I don't know why you're complaining." And so, being here was compared to having to work or having to pay for my own education and stuff. And I get what she's saying, but that's not how I felt. And so, it just became difficult to talk to them about it. And they also don't believe in depression, so it was just like, "What am I going to talk to you about if what I would talk to you about you don't take seriously?" And so, I just couldn't tell them stuff. And I couldn't tell them that I was flunking out of school, not doing good in classes. And it was just a mess.

Fiona, while frustrated with her parents' inability to understand her suffering, also felt empathy for them. In her view, they were doing their best with the stores of knowledge and experiences they had to draw from. She knew that they were struggling too.

As Fiona fought through her depression, she mustered the energy to fulfill her responsibilities at home, like dealing with the building supervisor when there was a problem in the apartment and making sure the landlord knew if the rent was going to be late. This was the kind of work she had been doing since she was a child, because her parents did not speak English and did not have the legal documentation to feel secure engaging with others in public. She did not blame her parents for their expectations, and she did not complain about the work she had to do for the family. This was just "life."

It's stressful for them too, because I think they've always, like, really bought into this whole [idea]. . . . Like, my mom still says it all the time: "School is the only thing that's going to get you out." And it's like, that's not true. You know, it's not necessarily true. And I think she, she thinks that once you go to school and you do all these things, that you should be able to get out of poverty and stuff. And I do know that I was privileged in, like, a lot of ways. But I am also dealing with an illness, which they don't understand. . . . I think everyone's just frustrated because we're poor. So it's rough. Because they want to understand, they want to be supportive, but at the same time they just don't understand.

Although Fiona felt empathy for her parents, she was also frustrated by how little they understood the challenges in her life. Her parents still believed that she had punched her ticket to social mobility when she was accepted to Amherst, but she had come to believe that such mobility was uncertain, unlikely even. The hard time she had at Amherst made Fiona feel like she would never be able to pull herself out of poverty and depression, even with an Amherst degree in hand. Her view of the world had become more critical and cynical, and she believed that her eyes-wide-open approach to dealing with her life had contributed to her depression. Fiona assumed that her parents' unwavering belief in education as the key to mobility blocked them from understanding and sympathizing with her despair.

Kimberly also struggled mightily at Amherst. While she loved her classes and never lost her passion for learning, she became anxious and depressed and felt like an imposter who would never fit in with her classmates. Kimberly took two extended academic leaves over the course of her Amherst career. She graduated by the skin of her teeth, in large part because, in her estimation, a couple of professors took pity on her and passed her when she should have failed their classes. One of the most difficult aspects of her time at Amherst was her parents' belief that she had no legitimate grounds for suffering. "They don't really get what's hard about this place. Because I think, from my mom's perspective, she's like, 'Well, you just do your homework and you do what your teachers tell you.' And I'm just like, 'It's not that easy!'" Kimberly found solace in a group of friends she met through a job with a food justice organization while on academic leave. These friends shared her social justice–oriented view of the world and were open about their own mental health struggles. As Kimberly got closer to this group of friends, she turned further away from her parents.

The mental health difficulties spurred by being in an elite space often caught students by surprise. When Angelica got to Amherst, her initial feeling was one of liberation. As I detailed in chapter 1, it had not been easy to convince her parents to let her leave California and move across the country to go to school. They let her go only when she promised that she would return home every summer and that she would move back after graduation. She also promised her parents that if they disapproved of how things were going, she would move home after sophomore year and go to the local state university.

Angelica's feelings of liberation were short-lived. After only a couple of months at Amherst, she found herself exhausted, lonely, and "incredibly stressed out." Not only was she working harder than she ever had in school growing up, but she was continuing to manage her family's household, albeit from three time zones away. Rarely a day passed that she did not interrupt her studies to fulfill a task for one of her parents. Because she was a citizen and her parents were both undocumented, and because she was the oldest daughter, her parents assumed that she should be the one to take on the household duties that required English and citizenship.

Until very recently, all of the household utilities, as well as the leases for the apartment and car, were in her name.

> My mom will be like, "Okay, you know the electricity bill is due. Can you pay it?" "The gas bill is due. Can you pay it?" . . . There are a few things that I don't have to do, but everything else they are like, "Can you do it for me?" I'm like, "Okay, I'll do that as soon as I'm done with work."

The family responsibilities Angelica continued to fulfill and the conditions her parents had placed on her made it hard for her to be honest with them about her challenges.

To make matters worse, Angelica's parents did not consider school stress-worthy. She understood their viewpoint that life was supposed to be hard and that school was much easier than other things she could have been doing, like low-wage manual labor. They had both grown up in an impoverished rural community, one in Mexico and the other in Guatemala, and had been doing hard physical labor their whole lives. In their minds, Angelica had it easy. And family came first, always. As such, Angelica had no reason to complain.

> I feel like they have a very warped understanding. . . . At first, I would talk to them about the stress and that it's not what I'm used to. And they're like, "But it's school. It's not that difficult. You don't have a job. You're not [physically] tired." I would tell them, "But I'm mentally tired. That's a different thing. It's mental health." But that's not a conversation we have. That's not something that exists. [In my family], you're not allowed to be mentally tired. That's not a thing. You just push through it. That's why I stopped telling them about how stressed I am. Or, I just say, "Oh, I'm busy. I'm doing homework. I'm studying for an exam." Because that's the only acceptable answer. Anything else they either invalidate or they just can't wrap their head around it.

As Angelica kept quiet about her struggles, she found her resentment growing along with the distance she felt from family and home.

Gloria too struggled with high levels of stress during her first couple of years at Amherst. Like Angelica and Fiona, she was on call as a translator for her parents as well as a tutor for her younger brothers, for whom she was "like a second mother." The stress manifested in an eating disorder. She believed that the seeds for the disorder had been planted long before she went to Amherst, generated by her long-standing anxiety about her family's economic insecurity and her parents' undocumented status. She had never gotten used to living with the constant fear that they could be deported. For as long as she could remember, Gloria had felt a lack of control in her life. In her assessment, denying herself food became a weapon with which she could exert control.

> I have always had certain anxieties and coping mechanisms. But they have just skyrocketed here. For example, I recall instances where I experienced trauma or anxiety where I kept thinking to myself, "This is going to go away. In a couple of hours this fear or this thing is going to go away." But now I'm super-anxious. I think, definitely, my eating disorder, definitely my anxiety, has been a product of being here. Like, it's been there; it didn't come out of nowhere. But I feel like this place definitely caused it to come up.
>
> But then this place has also helped me. I thank Amherst the most for my eating disorder recovery. I would not have been able to afford treatment. And it wasn't just treatment, it was a nutritionist, it was therapy, it was so much that they gave me. I literally don't know what I would have done if I had gone through an eating disorder at home and not had that. So that's the biggest thing. And now with my anxiety, I finally realized that I actually need help, so I just started medication, and it's already starting to help.

While Gloria blamed Amherst in part for her suffering, she also credited Amherst for her recovery. How she could be both resentful and grateful, however, was hard to fully convey to her family.

With guidance from a college therapist, Gloria told her mom about her eating disorder while she was back in Chicago during a summer vacation. It meant the world to Gloria that her mom responded with support and love. She recovered from her eating disorder that summer. But after she returned to campus, anxiety sometimes crept back in. In these moments, Gloria found that she could not figure out how to communicate the complexity of her emotional state to her parents.

> How do I convey the passion that I have and tell you that I'm okay because I really like it here? Or how do I explain things that I don't like? How do I tell you I'm suffering, without you worrying and telling me to come home? How do I convey that to you? How do I explain things in a way where you give me the support I need, without burdening you?

Gloria decided that while she was away from home, she would stay quiet about her struggles. Her parents had enough to worry about, and if Gloria herself did not fully understand how she was feeling, she did not think she could effectively communicate her emotional state to her parents.

Like Gloria, Noel found the transition into Amherst difficult. The week before school started, his mom, Suzy, got into legal trouble for not revealing on a food stamp application that her husband, Noel's stepfather, lived with them. In her mind, this was a legitimate omission because he was not contributing anything financially to the family. Noel was with her when she was confronted by the police, and he was the one who connected her with an attorney. The experience hovered in the background like a heavy storm cloud his first year at Amherst. He called home daily to make sure everything was all right, typically taking on new logistical tasks with each conversation, like talking with the attorney, trying to renegotiate his financial aid package so he could send more money home, and supporting his younger brothers, who were living with the stress firsthand. That few of his peers or teachers knew what was happening behind the scenes contributed to Noel's feelings of loneliness.

Yet life was not all bad. Though struggling to manage the crisis at home, Noel also really liked his college life. He was enjoying his classes, had started to use the gym, was attending a church group, and had joined the jazz band. When he was not missing home and worrying about his family, he was feeling guilty about the privileges he now had that his family did not, and about how difficult it was to explain these complex feelings to his mom. He felt deeply and utterly confused and even considered transferring to a public college closer to home. It was a conversation with an adviser, also a first-generation college student from a Mexican immigrant family, that transformed his perspective.

> I was always worried about needing to be there to support the family. I had to learn that there's only so much I can do. . . . One of the big things that really helped me out was when I had a conversation with my adviser my first year. . . . [And he said], "You know, if you go back, the help that you can provide is only going to be temporary. If you stay here, in the long run you're going to be able to provide permanent help." So it's just a matter of sticking through it, and eventually hopefully getting with it.

Noel heeded his adviser's advice and stuck with it at Amherst, but it was not easy. He talked at length about the ups and downs of trying to maintain close family ties and offering his mom the support she needed while also taking care of himself and prioritizing his studies. In a follow-up conversation after his mom had finally put her legal troubles behind her and he had found his stride at Amherst, Noel shared a reflection. He had come to a place of peace in the realization that even if his mom could never understand his life at Amherst, he could never fully understand her life either. No matter their vast experiential differences, however, they needed each other.

MISUNDERSTANDINGS FLOW BOTH WAYS

Noel was on to something important. In my conversations with the parents of nine of my participants, I learned that it was not just parents who could not understand their children's lives. Having been born in the United States or come of age here, their children were hard-pressed to grasp the reality of their parents' lives and experiences. The sociologist Cecilia Menjívar and her colleagues have analyzed the often diverging perspectives of different generations in immigrant families, shaped by where they came of age.[3] The parents in many contemporary immigrant families have a transnational perspective that their children do not share.

The parents of the youth in this study were born in countries with difficult material and political conditions that pushed them to leave. Most told me that they grew up poor, in rural areas with weak physical infrastructures—some lacked running water or electricity—and, as I have already detailed, with little opportunity to pursue school beyond high school and, for some, beyond primary school. Immigrant parents experienced the United States and viewed their children's opportunities through this lens. Although they might have struggled with financial insecurity in the United States, all now had a roof over their heads. They had water, electricity, and access to food and emergency health care. Relatively speaking, life in the United States, while difficult, was pretty good. Most importantly, in the United States their children had access to school, which they all celebrated. Many youth said that they had a basic idea of what their parents' childhoods had been like, but few had a detailed understanding of just how hard life had been for their parents. I came to realize that students were not the only ones keeping things to themselves.

Fiona's mom, Nayalea, was born in the sierras of rural Oaxaca, one of the poorest states in Mexico. It is also one of the states with the largest indigenous population. Her town, home to fewer than a hundred people when she was a child, was majority-Zapotec. Most homes lacked running water and electricity. In Nayalea's words, "It wasn't easy. It was very different than the life my children have. I never had the possibility to focus on school." Instead, Nayalea worked in the fields with the cows and at home helping her mother. When she was only eight years old, she started looking after her older sister's young children.

> Everyone worked so much and so hard. . . . We were grateful if we had a plate of food.
>
> When I was ten years old, I was taking care of many children. . . . I didn't have any other opportunities. My job was to work and take care of the house. No one cared about my education. . . . My life was to work and to

help my family. . . . And then I got a job selling cakes in the town. . . . I didn't go to school.

When Nayalea was fourteen, she went with another girl to the Mexican capital, Distrito Federal (D.F.), to work. She found a job cleaning the house of a rich family and taking care of their babies. When they asked her how old she was, she lied and told them she was twenty. She worked for this family for two years, sending money home to help support her family. Nayalea described the work as "unjust." Indeed, living in an upscale neighborhood and seeing how rich people lived, she came to realize how little she was earning for how hard she was working. After two years in D.F., she returned to her village. "When I returned to the *campo* [countryside], I still didn't have enough money to buy even a pair of shoes for my mom. The prices kept going up. I was depressed. . . . I was sad. . . . I knew there was no future there. . . . And I got the idea to cross to the United States."

As I listened to Nayalea, I was surprised to hear her say that the difficulty of her life had made her "sad" and "depressed." Indeed, she understood depression, because she had experienced it. She had endured hardship, fear, and frustration. Yet she had also come of age in a context in which there was little room for reflection or healing, and no resources to help those who were struggling materially or emotionally. Through it all, Nayalea learned how to survive, a lesson she had passed down to Fiona.

Most of the parents I interviewed had similar stories. Their childhoods were extraordinarily difficult materially and emotionally. Yet they did not have the vocabulary or the space to talk about the difficulty. Isabela's mom, Victoria, also grew up in rural Mexico, in a place that was poor, rural, and remote. She described it as "the most beautiful place," but she also said that there was no opportunity there to better one's life. Her experience growing up there shaped her perspective on her children's opportunities in the United States.

We were twelve children, but one died. . . . I was the fifth. . . . I started to work when I was about six years old. . . . We lived in a *rancho* [a small agricultural village]. . . . My father had some cows and land, and we planted and harvested crops. The women woke up at 3:00 AM and started to prepare the lunch for the men to go work in the fields. We made tortillas. We ground the corn and prepared the masa, and we cooked the food for the whole family. . . . We traveled on horses and donkeys, no cars. . . . Things were difficult for our family. . . . All of the children had to work. I first went to the city with my mom to work and to go to school. I was eight years old. When I left school every day, I would go to work selling *refrescas* [homemade cold drinks] for a woman. . . . I prepared the *aguas* [flavored waters] and juices and sold them from a cart. . . . I was so little. I remember one time the cart tipped over and I lost everything, and so I didn't get paid, and I had to go back and tell my mom. It was terrible. . . . I did this until I finished the fourth grade, and then I started to work with an older woman who had a small *tienda* [store] selling clothes. I would go right after school to help the woman . . . and then later, after work, I would be able to eat something and then I would do my homework. . . . When I started to go to high school, I met someone who told me about how to come to the United States. And I thought about the difficult situation of my family. I thought about studying and trying to have a career, but everyone was in bad shape economically. This was the case for many families in the area . . . not just my family. I was sixteen years old, and I knew I had to do more to help my family economically.

Victoria, like all of the other parents I interviewed, never forgot the struggles and dreams that motivated her migration to the United States. Most parents in the study had risked everything, and some made dangerous border crossings. Transitioning to life in the United States was difficult for all of them.

Omar's dad, Pablo, migrated from Guanajuato, Mexico, to Los Angeles when he was a young man and had to live in his car for three months while working in the fields picking fruit. He told me, through tears, that he had never told his children about this experience. It was his suffering and shame during that time that made him so invested in their education and that continued to motivate him to work hard every day, even knowing that he was not being paid fairly. His experience had also made him grateful for the one-bedroom basement apartment shared by all five family members. Other parents also told me that they had not shared very many details with their children of their most difficult times. For Pablo, I got the sense that it was just too difficult to talk about. I also intuited that he did not want to burden his children with the emotions he still had surrounding that time in his life.

Every parent I interviewed told me that parenthood had been life-giving and life-changing for them. And every parent told me that the hardships they had endured and the risks they had taken to come to the United States were "worth it." Thus, they were confused when their children told them that they were beginning to have doubts about the promise of the American Dream and the assumed link between educational and social mobility.

Nayalea, for example, in reflecting on Fiona's struggles in the United States, told me, "I love this country because it gave me the opportunity and gave my children the opportunity to study. . . . It has its ugly things, but it's not this country, it's that there are bad people. . . . I know there are difficulties here . . . but I am so grateful for this country." Indeed, the gap between how parents understood the opportunity structure of the United States and how their children had come to understand it had caused tension in many families. But I do not think that their parents were as starry-eyed as some of these youth thought they were. Nayalea told me, "Fiona is *bien inteligente* [very smart], and she worked so hard. . . . But life is harder for her than for her brother. It's always harder for women." Indeed, Nayalea recognized that Fiona's struggles with depression were rooted, at least in part, in gender inequality. She told me, "It's been hard for her. . . . But she is very strong. . . . I want her to know that she will never be alone, that I will always support her. . . . She is struggling day by day, but I know she will be okay."

I got the sense from all the parents I interviewed that they did understand how difficult life could be for their children, even if they did not understand what their children were studying or what it was like to attend an elite school. That said, they had survived their own hardships by accepting that life was difficult and doing what they had to do to stay afloat and strive to get ahead. From their perspective, by attending Amherst their children had entered a space of unique privilege and opportunity and should be grateful for the experience.

Parents also believed that they had fulfilled their end of the immigrant bargain by working long hours, often at taxing jobs, so that their children could pursue their education. They now expected their children to fulfill their end of the bargain by doing well in school and taking advantage of every opportunity available.[4] Most parents also expected their children to continue helping with family tasks that could be done from afar, like translating, helping younger siblings with schoolwork, and serving as the family liaison with the public sphere. They did not see these expectations as unreasonable, because family was the only survival tool they had. Ultimately, and perhaps ironically, the tensions that developed between children and their parents as the former became more critically minded were rooted in love and respect for each other and a shared understanding that family was central to how their lives had unfolded and would continue to unfold in the future.

BRIDGING THE GAPS

In *Hunger of Memory*, Rodriguez never strays from his conclusion that individual social mobility inevitably entails loss within familial relationships. Yet throughout the memoir he seems to be moving toward a tenuous peace with the change in his familial relationships. "I came home. After the year in England, I spent three summer months living with my mother and father, relieved by how easy it was to be home. It no longer seemed very important to me that we had little to say. I felt easy sitting and eating and walking with them."[5]

Rodriguez's enlightenment was spurred by the new and unexpected loneliness he experienced in his elite academic and intellectual life. While he was sitting in the British Museum working on his dissertation, nostalgia beckoned. He missed his parents. After deep reflection, he realized that, while his education had changed his relationships with his parents and he had experienced this change as loss, education had also given him the capacity to understand both the change and the loss. With that realization, he saw that he had achieved the true gift of his education—the ability to speak about and understand the ways in which he had grown culturally separated from his parents.

> My need to think so much and so abstractly about my parents and our relationship was in itself an indication of my long education. My father and mother did not pass their time thinking about the cultural meanings of their experience. It was I who described their daily lives with airy ideas. And yet, *positively*: The ability to consider experience so abstractly allowed me to shape into desire what would otherwise have remained indefinite, meaningless longing.[6]

Many of the students I interviewed did not readily accept the loss that mobility initially entailed. Instead, they struggled to find ways to bridge the gaps that had developed between them and their parents or other family and kin. Several students stood out because of the ways in which they had used the space, time, and skills they gained from their education to reflect and to come up with new ways of being at peace with their parents, despite their differences, and to appreciate them.

Iván was one example. He took my "Immigration and the New Latino Second Generation" class a year before I interviewed him. He was one of the students on whom *Hunger of Memory* had a huge impact. Iván found comfort in sharing with Rodriguez the same experience of loss. Perhaps most importantly, the book ultimately inspired him to reconnect with his mom:

> This year I've made a much more concerted effort to kind of reconnect with my mom. . . . It's a learning process for both of us. I made the concerted effort to be more open with her. And I think she's starting to slowly accept that. . . . It's strange to think this is something novel for a nineteen-year-old, but . . . I haven't been close to her since my middle school years. And so, here at college, I'm a lot more mature, and I think that, like, I'm starting to realize, I need to appreciate my mom and make that invested effort. . . .

I'm starting to call more often and just be more open. . . . You know that scene in *Hunger of Memory* when Richard Rodriguez comes back and has dinner with his family and all his siblings are there, and his parents are, like, quiet for the most part? Aren't really engaged in the conversation? Like, all the siblings are talking about what they're doing, and there's that disconnect? That's what I'm trying to avoid. I want my mom to be a part of that and be comfortable and know what's going on. I can't tell her about what I'm studying and whatnot, but I can tell her, "These are the internships I'm looking at." You know, "This is what I'm doing in school. These are my friends. This is what I do, blah, blah, blah." It's just a learning curve. It's a learning process.

As Iván strove to regain closeness with his mother, he took advantage of a study abroad opportunity in Puerto Rico, his father's homeland. There he met cousins and aunts and uncles for the first time. The experience was "life-changing," and it deepened the connection he felt with his family. Ultimately, Iván's abstract critique of his family's situation combined with his deep reflection to pave the way for renewed love and appreciation for them.

For many students, the pathway to closeness to their family and appreciation for them was emotionally painful. When Miguel first left his family to attend prep school, he was exuberant. Though he was close to his mom, stepdad, and siblings, as well as his grandfather, with whom they shared their small apartment, he felt constrained by their constant monitoring. He longed to see more of the world. Miguel ended up both loving and hating prep school. He loved it for the world of opportunity it opened up to him. But he hated feeling poor and "other" in a sea of wealthy White students. His resentment spilled over into his relationships with his family, spurring negative feelings about home. His relationships became strained, and distance developed.

Going back home, it was just like, we're in such a small apartment and everyone is so uneducated here. No one can talk or speak about things. . . . And I really internalized these feelings about my family being stupid because of the way the school built me up to think about them. And it was so bad. And that was also a point of contention with my mom for a long time, because I started kind of acting uppity. I was thinking I was better than my family in many ways. . . . And my mom was like, "You're trying to act so American now! Like, what's wrong, like, what's happening, why are you doing this? You're acting like someone you're not!"

His mom's words stung, and Miguel thought about these accusations for a long time. When he got to Amherst a few years later, Miguel took classes that changed the way he viewed his family. He started to realize that they were not the problem; he had failed to see the context in which his family was struggling. Ultimately he concluded that he was the one who needed to do the work to mend the broken relationship.

> And it wasn't until I got to Amherst where that changed. I'm not so uppity anymore about things or pretentious about stuff. And like, I understand things. I think taking classes, honestly, and being able to understand, you know, how systems work, and the way things work in this world, that I understand where my feelings were coming from and where my mom's feelings [were coming from], and the way this world is. . . . Whereas before, I just hated being home, because I felt so poor and I felt so limited in the way that my classmates were not.

Miguel did a lot of work to reconnect with his mom. He reflected that, as a college senior, he now had a relationship with her that was stronger than it had ever been. When I spent the afternoon with Miguel and his mom a year after Miguel's graduation, in the summer of 2018, I was touched by the closeness and trust that I saw between them. At the end of our visit, as Miguel walked me to the subway, he told me how happy he was that his feelings of shame and resentment had been replaced by feelings of pride for all that his mom and his family had accomplished and overcome.

For the students who were able to grow their relationship with their parents, the road to renewal was typically complicated. It entailed deep reflection and critical thought about their family's position in the world. Their heightened social consciousness also helped them understand the inevitable inequalities that had developed within their families as a result of their own educational mobility. Finally came acceptance—the realization that, while their relationships had changed and inequalities had developed, they were still family.

For example, as Jon got closer to achieving his goal of becoming a financial analyst and living free from money worries, he began to see the reality of his parents' survival strategies more clearly. That clarity triggered sadness and anger. While he was confident that one day he would live a life of meaningful work but also have time for pleasure, leisure, and adventure, he came to see that his parents had never had that opportunity, and never would. It was a devastating realization, but one that ultimately allowed him to accept their divergent realities and to become closer to them.

> Something that I've tried to correct more recently is to be more, like, interested in the lives of my parents. To be fair, though—I'm going to feel bad saying

this, but— . . . my parents' lives, like on the day-to-day . . . I feel like poverty doesn't let you lead a particularly interesting life. . . . Not like you can't have an interesting background or something like that, but I just feel like my dad has woken up every day for, like, the past twenty years at 4:30 in the morning and has worked eight hours as a fucking busboy. So when I ask him, like, "What did you do today?" like, I know what he did today. . . . I remember one time I was home for the weekend . . . sitting there and looking at my parents living their lives, and how many times I'd see the exact [same] motions. And I . . . almost started crying . . . because I was like . . . this is the most depressing thing. . . . It just kills me to see. Like, this fucking sucks. And it's like I'm on a *Flowers for Algernon* trip, where I'm, like, I couldn't do that; I would go insane if I had to do the same shit every day. . . . And that just makes me sad to think. Like, he's just been working to put food in people's mouths, that's just been his thing. . . . But obviously people can derive meaning from that. . . . And so I try to be invested in my parents' lives and be like, "Yo, what are you up to?" And now that my mom . . . goes to church sometimes, she goes to English classes and stuff like that. And I try to be like, "How's your English class going?" and stuff like that.

Jon's honesty revealed what could be interpreted as a condescending view of his parents' lives. Yet ultimately he came to respect the strength and resilience necessary to do hard labor, day in and day out, and to understand that their class, race, and immigration status compelled his parents to live this way. They were doing what they had to do to survive and to support their family as best they could. As he explained, "I just couldn't do it . . . but it must drive them crazy sometimes too. But they still get it done." Jon also came to realize that his parents found meaning in the ability to provide for their children and to give them the opportunities they never had. To be sure, it was his parents' work, day in and day out, that had made his educational mobility possible. He was grateful. Once he was able to move away from only feeling sorry for his parents to realizing the meaning in their lives and the impact on their opportunities of larger social forces, he was better able to connect with them.

In sum, whereas educational mobility entails loss, it can also give students a hard-earned ability to put that loss into context, thus further enabling them to bridge gaps in understanding and to strengthen relationships. I end this section with the words of Silvia, who, after painful ruptures in her relationship with her mother, had an epiphany: she needed to embrace their relationship in its inevitable new context. It was a transformative realization. Silvia's relationship with her mom was still not easy, but it was much less angst-ridden than it used to be because Silvia no longer expected her mom to be someone she was not. Through her educational mobility, Silvia had also gained a new sense of humility when it came to her family—and with that, a deeper feeling of love and appreciation.

> I think a turning point for our relationship was maybe my junior year. We had a really bad argument where she said things and I said things and, like, both of us made good points, and then both of us also made really bad points. There were things that I said that were hurtful and things that she said that were hurtful. And like, it was not a good time. And she was really, really hurt. And it was kind of up to me to mend everything. And I think that was the point when I was like, okay, I need to find a way to get past everything and let some things go and, like, pick my battles and just reflect more. Now, even though our relationship is still strained a little bit . . . they [her parents] have more respect for me, and I have more respect for them. And I understand where they're coming from more. And so I'm not as presumptuous. I try to understand where they're coming from and then respond, and not necessarily be like, "That's wrong!" So I think I'm more nuanced. I try not to assume that I know everything anymore. . . . I think that's what Tess Frenzel, one of the student graduation speakers here, captured really well . . . that "the only thing that I know from coming out of Amherst is that I don't know anything." . . . I think I'd rather know that I know nothing than the alternative—thinking that I know everything.

ACKNOWLEDGING THE PRICE OF MOBILITY

Whereas the glossy veneer of educational mobility highlights success and celebration, my conversations with students suggest that beneath the surface lies another story—a story of familial distancing and change. Almost every student I interviewed talked about the challenges they faced as their educational pathway moved them culturally and socially away from family and kin. What made this experience especially complicated was that they gave the most credit to family and community for their own motivation and success. A seldom talked about aspect of the immigrant bargain is that "paying it back" inevitably entails change in family relationships, which feels to many like loss.

I don't think this story is unique to Latino second-generation youth. Social distancing from parents is not only a part of educational mobility but part of growing up. Although I am White and middle-class, I relate to the grief that comes from being the first to move away from home to attend school and developing a new bank of critical knowledge about the world that doesn't jive with the perspectives of many family and community members. My own educational mobility led me to see home differently. Just like my research participants, I found that it was not just acquiring new knowledge and experiences that changed my perspective but having the geographic distance to process and develop independent thoughts. And yet the immigrant experience adds a nuanced layer to the narrative of mobility and loss that I never experienced.

To be sure, immigrant parents draw not only from their experiences in the United States but from their childhood in their home country, where the institutions, norms, expectations, and material conditions were different. Thus, place matters here too, in that it contextualizes opportunities and norms differently for parents and youth. Few parents in this study had any experience with higher education, and those who did had experienced it outside of the United States. When their children left home to attend Amherst, these parents were watching them cross into a world that they did not have the background to understand. At the same time, these youth lacked the interpretive skills to understand their parents' childhoods and experiences. I believe it is this lack of shared knowledge and experience that is at the base of the loss that participants described.

I wrote this chapter not only because the themes of familial change and loss were prominent in my data but also in response to participants' critique of the typically simplistic portrayals of educational mobility. In their view, the celebration of educational mobility and diversity that tends to be highlighted in college brochures and marketing material is superficial. They yearned for more analysis of the complexities of educational mobility. "Yes," they would say in so many words, "we are so glad that we are here and that we are making good on our parents' sacrifices. But nothing about this is easy! Our families may have more security because of our educational mobility, but our relationships have also been changed by it, and with this change comes loss. And loss hurts."

My research participants had to pay a price for their mobility that arose from the inequalities that structure the broader society and marginalize immigrant families and communities. Social inequalities, in turn, have generated new inequalities within families as educational and social policies pave divergent opportunity pathways for individual family members. If we are to best support high-performing upwardly mobile students, we have to be better attuned to the ways in which family and community shape their experiences.

Rodriguez beautifully set the stage for a discussion about the diverging mobility pathways of immigrant parents and their children, but much less has been written about the diverging pathways of siblings. The next chapter takes up this issue.

Chapter 4 | Siblings

My brother was in ESL up until graduation from high school, and he technically didn't graduate on time. He got his diploma two years after graduation because he had to take the comprehensive test to prove that he was competent enough in English, and he failed it. He took it every year after third grade and never passed. . . . He could speak it fine. He can speak it fine now. But he just never had a good foundation. Fourth grade was rough for him, when I think about it. But there's nothing I could have done for him. I was six. . . . One thing that I know is that my dad did actively try to help. During summers he would buy us both workbooks. My brother got five books: one math, two English, one science, and I forget what the fifth one was. But I only got three. . . . It was an attempt by my dad to get him up to speed, and I just got the benefits of it because I got more exposure to knowledge when I was younger. . . . But he never caught up (*Jon*).

LIKE ALL SOCIAL institutions, families are structured by inequality. Indeed, half of all socioeconomic inequality in the United States is located within families, driven in large part by economic inequalities between adult siblings.[1] Yet, despite this striking statistic, little sociological research has focused on sibling inequality. Dalton Conley's award-winning book *The Pecking Order* is an important exception.[2] Drawing from a large sample of quantitative and qualitative data, Conley concludes that the shifting social contexts in which families are immersed, and the parenting responses to those shifting contexts, are more important than genes or birth order to sibling inequality. As such, parents invest in their children differently and consequently form a hierarchy—a "pecking order" among the siblings.

Sibling inequality is likely to be most pronounced in poor families. Conley argues that when resources are limited, parents are likely to hedge their bets on which of their children is most likely to overcome the family's difficult circumstances and manage to succeed. And yet, as Jon's story here suggests—and as Conley's research confirms—there is no universal parenting formula. Jon's dad, for example, invested disproportionately in Jon's academically struggling brother to help him catch up. And yet, perhaps unbeknownst to Jon's dad, Jon ended up benefiting most from that strategy, as he was exposed to more challenging academic material at a younger age than he would have been otherwise. Despite the best efforts of Jon's dad, his brother continued to lag academically.

Other scholars, while not specifically focused on sibling inequality, suggest that family context and behavior are not enough to prompt individual mobility. Instead, they argue, a "constellation of support" is typically at work.[3] Building from Conley's findings, we can assume that siblings might not only receive different levels of parental support but have different levels of access to extrafamilial support, like support from mentors, teachers, or community members.

Not surprisingly, sibling inequality was common within my sample. Of the fifty-six students for whom I have detailed sibling information, twenty-four had a sibling who had graduated from college or was attending college at the time of our interview. Of those twenty-four, sixteen had a sibling who was attending a state school or a school that these participants characterized as of low to medium selectivity. Only eight had a sibling who was attending a highly selective college or university. Twenty-one students out of the fifty-six had a sibling who did not attend college at all or had dropped out of college. Finally, four had two or more siblings who were on diverging paths from each other. For example, one sibling was in community college while the other did not go to college. Or they had one sibling at a highly selective school and another attending a community college. Eight of the fifty-six either had no siblings or had siblings who were too young to know yet if they would attend college.

These statistics are critically important to understanding the mobility experiences of the families in this study. Research shows that college attendance is an important predictor of not only financial stability and well-being but also mobility.[4] Yet which college an individual attends matters too. The mobility pathway of a low-income student who attends a highly selective school, for example, is steeper than the pathway of a student who attends a lower-status school. This is to say, the payouts from elite schools are higher than the payouts from other institutions.[5] Thus, even when all the siblings in a family have graduated from college, inequality is still likely to compound over time if they attended schools with different selectivity levels. As such, the majority of students in this sample were on a path to increasing inequality over time within their families, relative not only to their parents but also to their siblings.

That is the statistical story. But how do siblings experience this inequality? And how do the unique contexts of immigrant families shape the meanings that siblings attach to family inequality and educational mobility? Recent research on the inequalities that arise in mixed-status immigrant families is instructive. In the mixed-status families that Abrego studied, U.S. citizen youth were hyperconscious of the privileges they had that their undocumented siblings did not have.[6] This awareness, in turn, influenced how they experienced those privileges. Similarly, the life histories I collected suggest that those whose mobility prospects were significantly better than those of their siblings often felt guilty for having opportunities that their siblings did not, and some were also frustrated that their siblings' talents had not been recognized in the ways that their own had been. As Jon stated later in his interview, "My brother is not stupid, and I love my brother. So when I got placed in a magnet program and he stayed in ESL . . . it was a weird conflict."

The students I interviewed who were on a mobility path different from that of their siblings yearned for equality within their family and were motivated to succeed in large part by a desire to pull their parents and their siblings up with them. They told me that they shared information, strategies, and resources with their siblings and did what they could to support their well-being. For their part, the siblings I talked to expressed a mix of resentment toward and gratitude for their more successful sibling. To be sure, some sibling relationships were strained. But most were strong in spite of their diverging pathways. Of course, we can imagine that gender and birth order matter too. Although the sample is not large enough to analyze for these impacts, I pay close attention to them in the narratives that structure this chapter.

In the sections that follow, I draw from family constellation interviews to highlight three pairs of siblings. All were from Mexican immigrant families, but grew up in different places. The first set of siblings, Lisa and Jose, grew up in a Black and Latino area of a small working-class city in Maryland. The second pair, Isabela and Cristina, grew up in Santa Ana, a working-class, predominantly Latino and Vietnamese immigrant city in Orange County, California. The third pair, Leo and Abel, grew up in Edinburg, Texas, a small city near the U.S.-Mexican border that is almost entirely Mexican and Mexican American. I was able to interview in person two of the siblings who did not attend Amherst, Jose and Cristina, while I was visiting their families and homes. I interviewed Abel, Leo's brother, over Zoom during the COVID lockdown.

Two sibling pairs, Lisa-Jose and Isabela-Cristina, were on vastly different educational and social trajectories. The siblings Leo and Abel, on the contrary, were rising together. I have tried to bring the voices and experiences of these siblings into conversation with each other in order to show the complexity of feelings and tensions—and also the bonds—within aspiring immigrant families. The following narratives show the critical ways in which sibling relationships shape youth's experiences of and perspectives on educational mobility and its future promise.

JOSE AND LISA

Both Jose and Lisa were born and grew up in a densely populated sub-urban community about an hour outside of Washington, D.C. I visited them and their mom, Leona, in the summer of 2018. Lisa had recently graduated from Amherst College, and Jose had just finished his sophomore year in high school. The long subway ride I took to meet up with them was telling. Their community is on one of D.C.'s main train lines, but theirs is the last stop. Lisa described her community as strangely proximate to and yet isolated from the capital and its web of magnet schools, programs, and resources. As the train moved farther from the tourist center of D.C., where I was staying, White faces were replaced with brown and Black faces and the fancy briefcases and shoulder bags carried by passengers were replaced with backpacks and paper and plastic bags, confirming, as she had told me, the racial and class segregation of Lisa's community.

Lisa and Jose had spent most of their school years living in a nondescript, medium-sized apartment building characteristic of the bulk of the area's housing stock. Their cousins lived on the floor above them, and other family and kin were down the hall. Only a few weeks before my visit, Lisa, Jose, and Leona had moved from their apartment to the main floor of a small ranch house several blocks away. The freshly painted exterior and well-kept lawn signaled to me that the move was a step up from the apartment. When I shared this observation with Lisa, she quickly corrected me. The only reason they left their apartment was an increase in the building's parking fee that made it unaffordable. They had moved, Lisa explained, because of encroaching "gentrification." "Starbucks and Whole Foods moved in one neighborhood over, and the fees went up." They were sad to lose the close proximity to their extended family. On the bright side, however, the move had taken them farther away from the "rough part of town," where violence and crime were more common.

In Lisa and Jose's small house, the living room was bare save for a television and a side table on which were perched a pot of brightly colored artificial flowers and a statue of the Virgin Mary. When we arrived, Leona was in the kitchen making *quesadillas*. The air was filled with the aroma of homemade *tortillas*, fresh *quesillo* (Oaxacan cheese), herbs, and sautéed mushrooms. A beautiful pitcher of water infused with cucumber slices, orange sections, and mint sat atop their new dining table, the store tag still connected to one of the table's legs. "Little by little we're getting furniture," Lisa explained.

Lisa and Jose were both U.S. citizens. Leona was undocumented. They all told me that not a day went by that they did not contemplate the risks of Leona's legal status. Fear, frustration, and anger had become familiar emotions to them after they exhausted every possible pathway to Leona's legalization. For example, as a survivor of domestic abuse from her former husband, Leona might have been eligible for a visa for victims of criminal abuse. But because she never reported the violence, there was no record of it, and so she was not eligible to apply for that visa. Through tears, Leona explained why she failed to report the violence: "If I would have filed the report with the police, he would have told them I didn't have papers. . . . I was afraid they would deport me."

Legal sponsorship by her oldest child, Lisa, a U.S. citizen, once she turned twenty-one, had been another potential avenue. Yet because Leona had been caught crossing the border following a visit to Mexico for her dad's funeral, current bars to admission had made her ineligible unless she returned to Mexico for ten years first. Applying through DAPA (Deferred Action for Parents of Americans), an executive order issued by President Barack Obama in 2014, had been their last hope. Lisa vividly remembered holding her breath as she awaited the Supreme Court's ruling on DAPA in the summer of 2016. It ended in a 4–4 tie. The missing ninth vote would have belonged to Justice Scalia before his untimely death, or to Obama's replacement for Scalia, which Republicans had blocked. And so that was that. Leona's undocumented status and the roller-coaster of the family's efforts to change it had profoundly shaped her children's coming of age, as well as their hopes for the future.

I had many interactions with Lisa before my visit to her home and heard from her about her mother and brother, but I had never met Jose or Leona in person. Jose was a subtly handsome young man, with a stocky build and neatly coiffed hair. His dark washed jeans and bright collared shirt suggested a keen fashion sense. I immediately sensed an intensity about him, and even a sadness. Leona was young and beautiful, though there was a weariness in her eyes that betrayed years of hard labor and the stress of mothering without papers.

During lunch, Leona spoke about her aspiration to someday have her own restaurant. Lisa interjected often, adding details about her mom's cooking prowess. I did not need convincing, as the food Leona had prepared was phenomenal. Throughout lunch Jose was noticeably quiet. In some ways he seemed not even to be there, his voice and his experiences absent from the conversation. I therefore expected my interview with him later that day to be stilted. Instead, it was much the opposite.

Following lunch and a neighborhood tour, Jose and I found a table at the local public library to talk. During our conversation, Jose was deeply thoughtful and reflective, as well as witty and, at times, gently sarcastic. I found it hard to imagine him navigating a gang-ridden high school, although Lisa had navigated the same school. I also found it hard to believe that he was not on track to follow in Lisa's academic footsteps to attend an elite college. His intelligence and insight were striking. And yet, Lisa had told me, Jose had always struggled in school, and also struggled in life. While Lisa had just graduated summa cum laude from Amherst and had her sights set on graduate school, Jose was contemplating community college or vocational school. He was working hard to identify and then follow his own dreams and forge his own path, but he was clearly having a difficult time of it.

Lisa and Jose had the same mom, but they had different biological fathers; neither had been consistently engaged in their lives. Only seven years old when Jose was born, Lisa was Leona's coparent, taking care of Jose while Leona was at work. She changed his diapers, gave him a bottle, and put him down for naps. Lisa and Jose now both realized how young Lisa was to have carried such adult responsibilities. Jose did not remember details from that time, but he recognized the toll that his care must have taken on Lisa. "She had to take care of me when she was only seven. So, I think, like, I was just a burden to her because she was so little. . . . I feel like that was too much for her. Because again, single mom, no dads; it just feels like I was a burden."

Jose's dad, Lisa's stepdad, was in the picture for a while. Even though Lisa was young when he lived with them, she remembered him well—better than Jose did—and with horror. Her most vivid memories were of being afraid of his physical force and his violence toward her mom, as well as the abuse she endured from him. She also remembered the fear he instilled in all of them, making them afraid that if they resisted he would punish their mom by turning her in to the authorities and getting her deported. Lisa recalled that

he banged the door on her face, and she wanted to call the police. And this is the thing that is really scary, because he threatened her. He was like, "You want to call the police. You know they're going to deport you." He wasn't documented either, but he used that, yeah, to control my mom. Jose was only two, so I don't think he can remember it. But I remember him watching, and being horrified that he had to go through that.

They all survived the nightmare. Soon thereafter, Leona kicked out Jose's dad. Lisa was still in elementary school, and Jose was approaching kindergarten. Afterward, the three of them never talked about what had happened. Yearning to leave the trauma behind, Lisa dove headfirst into school. In her words, "school had always been my escape." With the support of caring and supportive teachers and a close posse of friends, she thrived.

> I would say I was very smart as a child. Like, in kindergarten I went in only speaking Spanish and then by the end of kindergarten I was already speaking English. And by first grade, I remember, they put me in the ESL class for, like, one day, and the teacher was like, "She doesn't have to be here." So that really shifted my trajectory throughout elementary school, because so many of my friends stayed in the ESL class until they were like in fifth grade. . . . I had a lot of support.

School was different for Jose. He struggled from the beginning. As he recalled, all the teachers knew he was Lisa's little brother, and so they had high expectations.

> I wasn't the teacher's favorite, and I wasn't very smart in school. So I would always need help. Lisa, she kind of set the standard high. And sometimes I feel like there's this certain pressure on me because . . . she did so well at school. She has her picture up in the high school! . . . And I see that, and, yeah, it's kind of a reminder that I have to do something great because she went to Amherst and she's doing all these great things. So I just, I feel like it's been a lot for me to live up to, because it's been a lot of pressure. Because they're expecting great things from me too. And it's just like I, I'm not the smartest in school. School really isn't for me. She did really great and, like, I want to do the same, but it's just too much for me sometimes.

No matter how hard he worked, Jose felt that he just could not measure up.

Lisa always tried her best to support Jose in school. Following her mom's orders, she "helped" him with his homework, sometimes just doing it herself, which was often easier. In retrospect, she realized that she was not the most patient or enthusiastic tutor.

> My mom would expect me to help Jose with his homework. But he would frustrate me, because he wasn't getting it as quickly as I wanted him to. But he was only a little kid, and I just didn't have the patience because I was only in middle school. . . . A lot of times I would just help him do the homework quickly. . . . I never, like, sat down and explained things properly to him.

He had so much trouble with math and reading, and it held him back a lot. Even in elementary school he just struggled a lot academically. And I would tell him, "I don't know why it's taking you so long to learn these things when I was able to do it on my own." And now I realize how damaging that was to him. I think he really internalized "I need to be as good as her." . . . I've thought about that a lot. Because of the community we live in, I just really wanted him to be able to succeed so that he isn't left behind. Because that's what ends up happening. . . . Like, these teachers and these mentors come in, and when they see students that are already doing better than the rest, they support them. And my brother, he never had any support from his teachers.

To be sure, Lisa credited wonderful mentors and supportive programming for her upward educational trajectory, neither of which Jose was able to access. Because he never performed well on tests or got top grades, he did not get tracked into special academic programs.

There were other barriers Jose had to navigate as well. As he explained it, in his neighborhood gender expectations were such that boys' pathways to social acceptance were limited to sports or the streets.[7] Outside of his family, he got little encouragement to do well in school and instead faced pressure to eschew his studies. Jose credited his family—mostly Lisa and his cousins—and a neighborhood program for struggling youth for keeping him out of trouble.

I think I was in seventh grade the first time someone offered me weed. It was really scary. . . . I learned, like, to just ignore it, and just not . . . pay attention to anything. I feel like doing that helped me stay away from, like, any violence or anything basically bad. Because a lot of kids in this area were in that situation where they had to either, like, I don't know how to explain it, but a lot of them chose not to go to school anymore and just engage in drugs, and everything like that. . . . My family pulled me away from that situation. I have always had good people around me to guide me not to go on the wrong path. Because it's very easy for someone to choose the wrong path and stay there.

Lisa was Jose's caretaker and guide. Even if she could not help him do well in his studies, she was determined to keep him off the streets.

You see a lot of gang violence, just a lot of, like, children who have no guidance. And so that's what I always tried to instill in him, like, the last thing I want you to do is be a part of a gang or do drugs. And if you do, or are feeling peer pressure to do anything like that, I want you to come to us. Because especially for young guys, there's always that pressure.

Jose faced other barriers too, ones that were rooted in his complicated feelings about his parents. Jose felt abandoned and betrayed by his father and overwhelmed by his mom's stress and emotional needs. Lisa and Jose had both witnessed domestic violence, though Jose was too young to remember it. They had also both observed their mother's resilience when she became a single mother and had to support them by herself after getting out of the dangerous relationship. Gendered expectations along with birth order had turned Lisa into Leona's main support while the violence was occurring, and during that time Lisa had made great efforts to shelter Jose, who was only a toddler, from the stress and the danger. It was also Lisa who for years afterward shepherded her mom through the ongoing aftershocks. When Lisa left home for college, Jose found himself emotionally unprepared to fill his sister's caretaking shoes. "When Lisa left, it put me in the position where I had to, like, shelter my mom, because she was still going through a lot. She was always . . . sad or in a mood." At the same time, Lisa was working hard to adapt to college and the radically different social context of her new life. She realized now that in the midst of managing her own transition she had not been there to support Jose, who was directly confronted with Leona's emotional pain for the first time. "I never talked to him after I first left. It wasn't until I went home on the weekends that we would chat about something, but we barely talked." So Jose was very much on his own.

Things got worse when Leona's mom, Lisa and Jose's *abuelita*, became terminally ill in Mexico. She had been a fixture of love and stability in all of their lives, living with them for a while in the United States when Jose was young. Indeed, Jose and Lisa credited their *abuelita* for motivating Leona to finally kick her abusive partner out of their apartment and out of their lives. Because Leona was undocumented and could not safely travel, when their grandmother became ill, it fell to Lisa and Jose to travel to Mexico and help care for her. Lisa went first. It was the summer before her senior year in college.

> The first thing [my *abuelita*] asked me was, "Vino tu mamá?" [Did your mom come?] Nothing was more difficult than explaining to my *abuelita* that I was not able to help my *mamá* get her papers so that she could come to see her. I spent that week giving my *abuelita* the love and care that I imagined my *mamá* giving her.

Lisa was grateful that she could serve as a bridge between her mom and her dying grandmother, but it was difficult not to mourn what should have been—all of them together at their *abuelita*'s side.

Jose traveled to Mexico later that fall, and it was he who was with their *abuelita* when she passed away. The trip was difficult for Jose. As he recalled,

> I was the one who was there with her when she passed. . . . It is why I have so much resentment towards my mom, because, even after coming back from Mexico, she didn't ask me how I felt. She didn't ask me anything about it. . . . I understand that she was her mom and it was hard for her not to be there, but I was there, and I had to see her go through that, and . . . like, it hurt knowing that she didn't, she didn't talk to me or anything.

Jose felt lonely and abandoned.

Meanwhile, Lisa's life had gained powerful momentum, and she was thriving academically at Amherst. Jose had complicated feelings about how her upward trajectory was changing her, in his view. Jose was happy for her, knowing that change was an inevitable part of going to college, but at the same time he was annoyed, frustrated, and further alienated by her code-switching between her home and school personas.

> I would make fun of her sometimes. . . . I would say that the school is chang-ing her, like, that she's not who she used to be. I just feel . . . like her going to Massachusetts helped her communicate more. . . . I don't know how to say it. But she changed her tone of voice, actually. Because at home she would speak a certain way. It bugged me a lot. But then, at the same time, her going over there [to Amherst] helped her, like, to choose her tone of voice and certain words when she needs to use them. . . . So at work she chooses to use her educated voice. But at home she chooses her different voice, her alter ego. She has two voices. She has two personalities. When she went to Massachusetts, she grew another personality. Yeah. I didn't like it. . . . And she tried different foods and, like, I guess that's good, because, you know, it's good to keep your mind open to new things. And I think that kind of helped her. But, well, certain aspects when she got back kind of bugged me. I would call her *gringa*. She got Whiter.

While Lisa had changed, Jose thought that he had stayed the same, their mom's situation had stayed the same, and their community had stayed the same. It was tough to think that Lisa had found the recipe for leaving it all behind, while he felt stuck.

Still, Jose had his own ambitions. He wanted to grow as a person. He just did not know how to go about it. Although he was doing better academi-cally in high school than he had in middle school and had also joined his high school's lacrosse team and developed close new friendships, he still did not have a clear vision of what he would do next. Maybe college? But he was not confident that he was smart enough. At the time of our interview, his focus was on becoming a mechanic. He told me that he loved cars and thought that if he could someday have his own garage, he could do quite well for himself. As we spoke about his future, I sensed a mix of enthusiasm and fear, ambition and resignation. Jose knew that Lisa was an exception and that he was unlikely to emulate her. He wanted to be realistic. And yet he did not want to give up on his future. "I don't want to stay here for long. I mean, I don't want to be in the area I grew up in. . . . I just don't want to be trapped or stuck in the same place for the rest of my life. Because if I allow myself to do that, I won't be able to grow as a person. I won't be able to do the things I want to do."

While preparing to apply to doctoral programs far from home, Lisa also found herself weighing Jose's future. She understood the reality of their disparate paths, as well as the injustice of the inequality that separated them.

> I think a lot about my brother. I think about taking him in with me and, like, taking care of him, helping him get into college and sort of like guiding him. . . . I still don't know how I got here. . . . I do know that I had mentors through each step of the way that could help me. It still surprises me. I feel like it was almost like at each stage in my life when I needed the most help, someone was there to help me. I only wish that my brother could have had the same.

As of the writing of this book, Lisa was living across the country, enrolled in a top doctoral program. She was thriving. Jose was at home, giving community college a try for the second time. Since the onset of the COVID-19 pandemic, college enrollments have dropped precipitously, especially community college enrollments. Jose was part of this story, stepping back from community college in 2020 and unsure about whether he would return.[8] Panic attacks overwhelmed his ability to focus on his studies. He needed a break. His ambitions never faded, however, and according to Lisa, he is slowly but surely finding his way.

ISABELA AND CRISTINA

Isabela was a year beyond her graduation from Amherst College when I visited her in California. Despite my protests, she graciously picked me up at the airport, and we enjoyed catching up as she patiently and expertly maneuvered her way through L.A.'s traffic to Santa Ana, where she, her younger sister, Cristina, and her mom, Victoria, had just moved into a neighborhood of duplexes. As soon as we pulled up to their small white stucco abode, Cristina and Victoria emerged to greet us. Within minutes we were seated in their cozy, sunlit kitchen, lunching on delicious Mexican food. The conversation flowed easily. As I ate taco after taco, chased by chunks of fresh pineapple, Cristina took the lead in sharing jokes and stories. She was as boisterous as Isabela had described her. Victoria too was open, enthusiastic, and easy to engage in conversation. Isabela had talked a lot about her mom and her sister in the study interviews, and I reveled in the experience of meeting them and seeing their relationships in person.

Only two years apart in age, Isabela and Cristina had always been best friends and confidantes. They shared fond childhood memories of playing outside in the warm southern California sunshine, as well as painful memories of their dad's deportation and, relatedly, the period when they did not have a secure place to live or enough to eat. Being older, Isabela remembered the tough parts more clearly than Cristina did. After two years of living on the edge of homelessness, moving between relatives' homes, Victoria got a job bagging and delivering newspapers. Life got a lot better after that. They moved into a studio apartment in Santa Ana, where Isabela and Cristina were surrounded by many children their age who also spoke Spanish, a nearby truck vendor selling *churros*, and rows of trees with beautiful purple flowers. Isabela and Cristina loved the trees. Victoria, on the other hand, hated them because the flowers would drop on her car, making a mess—just one more thing she had to clean.

Isabela and Cristina's dad returned to Mexico a few times during their childhood, and he was in and out of their lives as they moved through their teenage years. The times when he was around were tumultuous, characterized by fighting, yelling, and a lot of tension. Like her husband, Victoria was undocumented, and her status added to the family's stress. Their illegality had been a source of anxiety in Isabela's and Cristina's lives since they were young.

Isabela was still in elementary school when she learned that, though her parents "didn't have papers," she and Cristina were U.S. citizens. She was shocked to know that because they were born in the United States, they had rights that their parents didn't have. But it was complicated. Victoria told Isabela and Cristina that even though they were citizens, they still had to be careful. If they got in trouble, it could lead to Victoria being taken away from them. Isabela's consciousness was already finely tuned to the intrafamily inequality as a result of their different legal statuses. She remembered questioning how a family that was so tightly bonded could have such different levels of opportunity and protection just because of where each had been born. And she remembered pondering why it was that her citizenship seemed so different than the citizenship of her friends whose parents had papers. These friends never had to be afraid of being separated from their mothers.

> My mom would be like, "You can't do this," or like, "You can't tell your teachers I don't have papers . . . because they're going to take me away and we can't be separated." And that was a very big thing, like, you don't want your mom taken away. . . . So it was very much, like, whenever a cop passed, like, "You have to sit down, you can't do that."

Cristina was still quite young—in second or third grade, as she recalled—when she began to learn the rules about how to act in order to keep the family safe. At first, she questioned why the rules existed and why they could not change them. But even amid her questioning, she knew that it was critically important that the rules be followed. Like Isabela, she was mostly afraid that she could lose her mom. "I remember her talking about immigration. . . . I remember getting scared because she would tell me that they could, like, take us away from each other. . . . I remember being scared of the immigration police."

As the oldest, and as the best English speaker in the family, Isabela carried a disproportionate weight of responsibility, serving as Victoria's main emotional support, translator, and co-strategist, and Cristina's protector and mentor.

> I was the one in charge whenever my parents had to go out and we were alone. My sister didn't have a lot of, like, big responsibilities. . . . I think it was just because I was the older one, and my mom was very much like, "the older one does this." I was always the one called over to translate. Or . . . because I learned how to read first, I just had to read a lot more things for my parents . . . and like, figure out . . . whatever needed to be done . . . like talking with the doctors and the credit card people.

Isabela was not sure if the adult responsibilities she took on as a young child facilitated her quick learning and excellent academic performance, or if it was her ability to learn things quickly that caused her parents to always turn to her for help with logistical tasks. Whatever the case, Isabela felt pressure to support the family, and particularly Cristina, who even at a young age struggled with school.

Cristina interpreted all the attention and responsibility that Victoria gave to Isabela as favoritism. She felt that Isabela was given more responsibility because Victoria had more confidence in her ability and trusted her more. In Cristina's estimation, Isabela was the smart one and the successful one, while she was the problem child. There was a definite hierarchy in the family, and she was at the bottom of it.

When I was smaller . . . I thought my mom preferred my sister over me because Isabela at a younger age was more, like, outstanding in various ways. Like, you could tell Isabela was very smart . . . at a younger age than you could for me. . . . It was two sides of the same coin. I was the side that would, like, underachieve, while she was the side that would overachieve. So in that respect I feel like my mom gave her more attention.

While Isabela was held up at home and at school as an exceptionally smart and responsible child, Cristina was struggling just to get by. Isabela tried to help Cristina however she could. And yet she too would get frustrated when Cristina was slow to pick up a new concept or learn a lesson.

I definitely had to be the one helping Cristina learn her alphabet and her math. And I had to be the one checking her homework. After third grade, my mom was like, "I can't. I don't know what's happening." So I had to be the one checking it. . . . Now that I look back on it, I think very early on, Cristina just took a long time learning how to read, and so people still stuck her in ESL. . . . And at a certain point it was just like the teachers didn't . . . care enough to keep pushing her. . . . And they would, like, actually get . . . mad at her. Once I got called over to the office with my sister because they thought I had done the essay for her. And the teacher looked at me and was like, "You cheated. You had to have done this for her." . . . I think it was just because people, like, the teachers, didn't have faith in my sister that she could do it. And so she ended up just being like, "I can't do it." . . . She just didn't get the same chances that I did. . . . Like, my mom also, like my parents also, would be like, "You're just not trying. You're not focusing." And like, all these people kind of telling her this. It affected her. . . . She would tell me, "You do so well in school. I don't even know why I have to do this, like, I just don't get it." And she would just give up. And it was weird for me. I'd be like, "I just don't understand why you don't get it." Now that I look back, I think that was pretty shitty of me.

Cristina had a similar analysis. She remembered that Isabela was her main support, but also someone who got frustrated with her. Although they had always been close, their relationship had also been complicated. Cristina felt that she could never be as good as Isabela, no matter how hard she tried. As such, Cristina both looked up to Isabela and resented her.

School was very hard for me. It certainly came harder to me than it did to my sister. I was always aware. . . . I would see, she would get a lot more diplomas, she would get a lot more awards, better grades. And I would always tell myself, how is it so easy for her, but it's so hard for me? Like, what does she do that I don't do? It was never really clear to me until later on. I was, like, okay, I guess I'm just, you know . . . I'm just not smart. . . . Now I know I'm just smart in a different way. . . . People who learn the "traditional way" were labeled smart. . . . It was more noticeable when I got to middle school because that's when they introduced the honor system. If you were able to learn in the traditional way, you were put into the honors classes. And Isabela was . . . in honors classes, versus I was always regular CP [college prep], that's what they called it. And then it was even more apparent when we went into high school, because they had the ones that were AP [advanced placement]. They had three tiers: they had CP, they had honors, and then AP. I was always doing CP . . . Isabela was AP. I'm not going to deny it, it was frustrating, and it did take an emotional toll on me for a while. But I guess, you know, we're sisters, not twins. But, you know, you get bent out of shape thinking that you're not as good as your sibling.

As Isabela and Cristina were forging divergent pathways through school, pressure was mounting regarding Victoria's legal status. Since learning that Victoria was undocumented, Isabela and Cristina had known that when Isabela turned twenty-one she might be able to sponsor Victoria for residency and then citizenship. This was a responsibility that Isabela was enthusiastic about taking on. For her part, Cristina remembered feeling envious that Isabela, as the oldest, was the one who could bestow this most precious of gifts.

It was always on Isabela because, obviously, she's oldest. So my mom would be, like, "When Isabela turns twenty-one, she's going to give me my papers." . . . And then, I remember at one point, when my mom was hitting a rough patch with Isabela, and she was, like, "I don't think Isabela's going to want to give me my papers when I get older . . . because she's, like, drifting away from me." And I remember my mom was . . . really scared about this. And I was like, "I mean, you'll always have me. You know, I'm also still alive! I'm going to turn twenty-one too. And I'm a U.S. citizen too!"

When Isabela and Cristina investigated the process for sponsorship by talking with an immigration lawyer, they learned that because of the way Victoria had entered the United States, she was ineligible. The news was heartbreaking. It also put even more pressure on them to do well enough financially to be able to take care of Victoria when she got old, to make up for her lack of Social Security and retirement savings. The realization that she might never get papers seemed to make Victoria lean even more on Isabela, whom she thought of as having the best chance of finding professional success. As Cristina recalled,

She always had the basic goal of us going to college. I remember that. But I feel like she had more specific goals for my sister. She was like, "Oh, your sister, I want her to go to college. . . . She's going to be the one that's going to take care of me when I'm old. She's the one that's going to take care of the family." . . . Like, her hope was my sister.

Isabela took this responsibility seriously. She continued to work hard and to thrive in school while seeking out opportunities for college. After learning about QuestBridge from her counselor, she applied to the summer program. When she was accepted, she began to realize that she "had a shot at going to a really good school." She wanted that for herself, but she also "wanted it for my family." Cristina remembered Isabela doing what seemed like endless amounts of research into schools and scholarships. She was excited for Isabela, but she was also a bit envious.

I was with her when she was doing all her apps, and I remember her, like, looking at all these colleges that are super far away, or, like, are Ivy. . . . She was in the QuestBridge program, so I went with her on the trip where she went to Stanford. It was very, I want to say . . . bittersweet, because I was like, "This is something I would like to do, but this is something I know I can't do, because I'm not smart. . . ." Again, it was bittersweet, because I was like, "That could be me, but it's not for me."

Following the QuestBridge summer program, Isabela applied to the college program and got matched with Amherst. This was when life truly started to change for all of them. Perhaps most strikingly, it marked a separation that would no longer be based only on academic performance or legal status. Soon they would also be separated geographically. Moving up meant moving away. Cristina still remembered how she felt the day Isabela left for Amherst.

I remember the first day that she left, like, when we saw her go on the plane. The whole day. . . . Obviously we were sad because she was leaving. But I was also sad because I'm getting left behind. I'm stuck here now. There's nowhere I can go. I'm forever going to be here, whether it's my choice or not, I'm here. And she has a choice to leave and never come back. . . . I was seeing it as, like, "My wings got clipped." (*tearing up*) It was very hard. I'm still kind of getting emotional thinking about it.

While Isabela transitioned into her new life at Amherst, Cristina tried to turn her attitude around. It was difficult because there was a lot of drama going on at home. Their dad was back in the picture, and their parents were fighting a lot and preparing to split. Cristina felt a mix of emotions during that time—grief, love, resentment, and appreciation.

> I was in the middle of all that, and Isabela didn't have to hear it. I missed her a lot. But I resented her too that first year because I felt trapped. And then after I got over that whole episode of feeling trapped, I was like, "I love my sister." . . . And I realized that there was a lot that she did to help me that I never noticed.

As she started to feel more motivated, Cristina committed to pulling herself up "by the bootstraps." She enrolled in the local community college and started working long hours with her mom.

> But then, I don't know, I started looking at it in a different perspective. I was like, "Okay, yeah, I'm here, but what can I do to make me being here better?" It was like, "No, she didn't clip my wings, I clipped my own wings a long time ago by telling myself I couldn't do it." And I was like, well, "I don't have to stay stuck here. I can fix this. It's going to take me longer, but I can fix it. It's not necessarily a lost cause." . . . I wanted to be a good worker, a good school student.

During this time Isabela and Cristina were both working harder than they ever had before, and they were both having a hard time. Yet neither truly understood the daily reality of the other. The vast geographic distance that separated them and the very different places in which they were living made it even more difficult to comprehend each other's life. Isabela was having a difficult experience adjusting to Amherst, to New England, to the dark and the cold, to a rich, White campus, and to being away from home. Cristina assumed that life at Amherst was all roses. Isabela would try to explain, "Cristina, it's not always easy here. Sometimes it's really hard and I hate it." But Isabela's reality didn't register for Cristina, who was working long hours, managing her parents' drama, and struggling to keep up her grades with no support from anyone. Moreover, having never visited a northern climate, she had no idea what that was like for Isabela. Most importantly, she was still at home, in the same place where she had always struggled.

Isabela now realized that, as difficult as her transition to Amherst had been, she had what Cristina lacked: resources and a supportive group of friends and teachers. Indeed, Cristina, now on her own, was beginning to spiral. Balancing work with studying and trying to support her mom became too much for her. Eventually Cristina crashed.

I was like, "You can't, you can't stop. Keep going, keep going, keep going." . . . And I burned out in the worst way possible. . . . I went from being pretty much a straight A/B student in community college to being an F student in one day. . . . The day of finals I was so tired. All of my finals were online, so I was, like, "Okay, I got this." . . . It was a Friday, and I remember the newspaper on that Friday got there late; it didn't get there until five in the morning. My test was supposed to be at eleven. And then I didn't finish my route until like eight-thirty. So final time rolls around, I'm knocked out. . . . I'm asleep on my computer, logged into the website. And my mom wakes me up at like two, and she's like, "Hey, wake up. You should probably move to your bed." And I was like, "What time is it?" And she's like, "It's two o'clock." And I'm like, "Mom, I missed my finals!" . . . I talked to my teachers to see if I could have another chance, but no luck. I had no option but to bawl my eyes out. . . . I had the overwhelming feeling of, I just let my mom down. I let everybody down. Everybody was depending on me, and I let them down.

Cristina dropped out of community college and started to work longer hours. She added a waitressing job on top of her job bagging and delivering newspapers. It was a dark time for her, and she became depressed. Slowly, over many months, she clawed her way out of what she described as a pit of despair. In her telling of it, when she finally emerged she was stronger and more determined than ever. Then a friend told her about an opening at a nearby pharmacy. Cristina applied and got the job. With a bump in hourly pay, she was able to leave her waitressing job and cut back on her hours with the paper.

When I spent the day with Cristina, Isabela, and Victoria in the summer of 2018, Cristina was enthused about the opportunity she had to get trained as a pharmacy tech. After graduating from Amherst, Isabela was working at a local nonprofit and had her sights set on graduate school. Victoria was back in conversations with a lawyer about a pathway to citizenship. They loved their new rental duplex in a nicer neighborhood. Life was good. Perhaps most importantly, Cristina and Isabela had reunited emotionally and were newly committed to making it as a team. In Cristina's words:

We're like super-teaming this thing. We're going for it. We're going for gold basically. . . . I'm very aware that the clock is racing against me, because every minute that passes my mom is getting older. So I need to kick things into high gear and, like, get myself somewhere semi-stable so I can find my mom her forever home so that she can just, like, you know, relax. And it's something that me and Isabela have talked about. . . . My goals in life . . . have always mainly been centered on family. . . . Because if I wasn't working two jobs, Isabela probably wouldn't even be able to think about going to grad school. We are a team, and I want to keep her unattached . . . so that she can go out and do her things. . . . I'm choosing to stay here. I'm choosing to take the more difficult path so that my sister can trail her own path somewhere else. . . . I feel like we're both going to get our day and we're both going to get our own things that we're both good at. And I feel like Amherst is one of the things that helped Isabela a lot in, like, waking her up to the world. And I'm very happy that she went there because it made a ripple effect onto myself. And it changed some of the things that I didn't think about before now. In a way, Isabela changed the way of thinking for all of us.

As of the writing of this book, things continued to look up for Victoria, Cristina, and Isabela. Victoria was working with a lawyer to get residency via a program to support undocumented women who had been victims of criminal abuse. Cristina was a pharmacy tech, and Isabela was in her fourth year of a doctoral program. Financially, life was still uncertain, and the COVID-19 pandemic had been tough on all of them. What was certain, however, was that they were indeed a team.

LEO AND ABEL

Gloria Anzaldua, in her classic book *Borderlands/La Frontera*, moves between Spanish and English to describe the ways in which geographic borderlands map onto the borderlands of language, identity, and belonging.[9] Growing up as a queer Chicana in Texas near the U.S.-Mexico border, Anzaldua always felt betwixt and between shifting social worlds. When I interviewed Leo in the spring of 2020, he had just read Anzaldua's book. Having also grown up Chicano in the Texas borderlands, he exclaimed, "I read the book, and while there were some parts that didn't resonate or that I didn't agree with, mostly, I was thinking, 'Oh my God, this is my life!'"

According to Leo, the Rio Grande Valley of the Texas Borderlands is a unique place for Latinos to come of age:

It's 85 percent Hispanic, and it's one of the poorest counties in the United States. But it's also really different than places in California that are Hispanic but where White rich people live nearby. Here it's all Hispanic. We don't have proximity to Whiteness. If you live here, you just never see it . . . so you don't see the disparity. There are divides here, but they are by class, not by race.

Much of Leo's new consciousness about the Valley came to him after leaving and then returning with a different social lens. Through it, he saw the poverty more clearly, as well as the segregation and the omnipresence of policing. As he explained, "Immigration policing is everywhere here, not just at the border. It's in McDonald's and in the stores." He had also come to see more clearly the complexity of this policing, and the Border Patrol in particular. His uncle was a Border Patrol agent. His uncle and his dad, Raul, grew up in the same household, but they were born in different countries—his dad in Mexico, his uncle in the United States—just by happenstance. Their birthplaces were determined by where their parents happened to be working at the time and by the different costs involved in giving birth in each place. Such calculations are common among borderland families. "The crazy thing is that people get a job at the Border Patrol and use that job to get U.S. citizenship. . . . The Border Patrol is a big employer here, and everyone I know who works for them is Hispanic. So it's like Hispanics policing each other."

Leo's mom, Sally, was also born and grew up in the borderlands. Both Sally and Raul spoke English and Spanish, though Leo and his siblings grew up speaking only English. Leo was the second oldest of four siblings. I interviewed his older brother, Abel, by Zoom later in the spring of 2020. Abel's description of the Valley was similar to Leo's, as was the new way he had come to see and understand the Valley after leaving and returning. For both brothers, educational mobility had altered their perspective on home. Like Leo, Abel attended an elite school on the East Coast. And as it was for Leo, Abel's relationship with his family and with the Valley was complex. During both of their interviews, they often spoke in terms of "we," as in "Leo and I" or "Abel and I." Indeed, they had traveled similar paths.

Sally and Raul worked a lot during Leo and Abel's childhood. While Raul moved between jobs, Sally was a paragon of job stability, working as a paraprofessional in the local school district for twenty-five years. No matter how much Raul and Sally worked, however, they were always deeply engaged in their children's schooling and activities. They instilled in their children the importance of education from a very young age. Sally used the knowledge she gained by working in the public schools to make decisions about Leo and Abel's schooling. Most notably, she determined which was the best elementary school in the area so that she and Raul could find a house in a zone that would allow their children to attend it. Although money was tight, they managed to buy the house, a decision motivated by their goal to secure the best schooling possible for their children. In the Valley, where one lived shaped opportunity. A few years later, when the town redistricted the neighborhood and assigned it to a weaker school, Sally and Raul registered Leo and Abel for school under a relative's address.

Even though they owned a modest home and worked long hours, Raul and Sally were still poor. Leo and Abel both shared memories and frustrations about the pains to which their parents went to secure their basic needs. Abel remembered that

> my mom always found ways to get the money we needed. There was taking things to the pawn shop or taking out a loan to pay off another loan. And she was part of this thing with other women where they all paid in and then took turns borrowing money. She always had a scheme. . . . It's funny because Leo and I talk about how we grew up thinking we were middle-class. But once we left the Valley, we realized how poor it was, how poor we were.

Leo had similar memories of his mom's schemes. One of the strongest was that of making family visits to the pawn shop.

> My mom was always hustling to get enough money. I have memories of the whole family going to the pawn shop. My mom sold her quinceañera jewelry, and at one point my parents had to sell their wedding bands. It really impacted me. I would be at the counter with her helping her with the process. My little siblings don't remember how hard it was because they were little and always got to pick out a used movie. But for me and for my older brother, it was hard. Sure, we got something from it—the money to do activities, and I got my first calculator. But at what cost?

As hard as it was to be poor, Leo and Abel also agreed that they were blessed with unique opportunities. They felt especially grateful that they had always attended good public schools. They credited their parents' hard work and advocacy for getting them into the "right" elementary school. There they learned how to be students and developed a true love of learning. According to Leo,

> The elementary school we attended was really special. All the teachers were excellent. My mom had built relationships with all of them. The teachers instilled intellectual curiosity. My older brother and I loved school. . . . We really wanted to learn. School was my haven. . . . I just really loved learning. When we got to middle school, the teachers were more hit or miss, but by that time we knew how to learn and we loved learning. Elementary school taught me how to learn.

Abel shared Leo's fond memories and appreciation of elementary school. He also remembered their mom's push to get them into the gifted and talented program, which took only English speakers. He thought that was why his mom and dad never taught them Spanish. In their parents' minds, English was the language of educational mobility. Although both Abel and Leo would grow to regret not learning Spanish when they were young, they also now recognized that being in the gifted and talented program had changed their lives. They had come to consider it a necessary trade-off that they would remedy in college, when they both finally had the chance to learn Spanish.

From the very beginning, starting with testing into the gifted and talented program in kindergarten, Leo and Abel thrived in school. Their academic passions and loves were nurtured at home, where, in Leo's words, "there's always been a culture of intellectual curiosity." Home was also where Leo and Abel began to compete with each other intellectually. The competition was always rooted in love and respect, and it helped move both of them forward academically. Abel shared a strong memory of trying to teach Leo integral calculus when he was a sophomore in high school and Leo was in eighth grade.

> I found it absolutely fascinating when I learned that you could find the area under a curve by finding the integral of two points. So, of course, I wanted to share it with Leo. But he just couldn't get it. And I was so frustrated with him. I remember yelling. That was part of the competition. . . . I think my siblings viewed me as a kind of tyrant because I really pushed them.

Leo brought up the same incident in our interview: "He was so into it and wanted me to learn it, but I didn't get it. He would get so mad at me. But I must have gotten some of it, because when I got to high school, I found advanced math easy to learn; it didn't feel new to me."

Leo and Abel said that they always knew that they would go to college. They did not experience the expectation as pressure, but as motivation. While they both excelled in school and loved to learn, they also knew that college was a way out of poverty and a way out of the Valley. Leo started thinking seriously about his college plans while he was still in middle school.

> Seventh grade is when I started thinking about college seriously. I learned that doctors made a lot of money and anesthesiologists made the most of all. I also learned that the best place to learn how to be an anesthesiologist was Johns Hopkins, so that became my dream school. I wanted to become a doctor and make hella money. I knew that would be my way out.

Abel was also paving his own way toward college, and was also interested in becoming a doctor.

> My parents never really told us that we had to go to college, but they instilled a feeling in me that it was the way out of poverty. It was always my dream to leave the Valley. I remember that my uncle who was a truck driver would tell Leo and me that someday he would take us to New York. He never did, but it planted the seed. . . . My goal since I was young was to pursue medicine. It started when my grandfather went to the emergency room with slurred speech, and because he was diabetic they told him his blood sugar was just low. But then it turns out he had a stroke. And so I decided I wanted to be a neurologist, because there aren't really any specialists in the Valley, only primary care docs, and I wanted to help fill that need.

While Leo and Abel pursued their individual goals and paths, they remained tough competitors. Most of the time the competition was healthy, pushing them both to be smarter and more ambitious. But there came a time when the competition created a temporary wedge between them. Abel was applying for and ultimately deciding where to go to college. According to him:

> Leo and I were always super-competitive with each other. He always wanted to go to Johns Hopkins. So when I was starting to apply to colleges, I added it to my list, along with Harvard and a few other Ivies and Baylor. I really didn't apply to that many schools. I chose Baylor because I knew it was the best med school in Texas. I didn't really understand the other opportunities, but there were always the stories about the one guy who went to Harvard or somewhere like that, so I applied. That impacted us. And then I got into Baylor and then I got into Hopkins. And I got the Gates Millennium scholarship.

While Leo was really proud of Abel, he was also jolted by the realization that Abel was traveling the exact path he had wanted for himself. It was hard on him, and instead of feeling motivated by Abel's success, for the first time Leo felt discouraged.

> When Abel got into Hopkins, I got really insecure. He also got the Gates scholarship. And I didn't want to be compared to him, so I started pulling back from school. My grades went down for a bit, and I decided I'd just apply to Texas schools, like Baylor. It didn't help that I literally had a teacher tell me that I wasn't as smart as Abel. I started prepping my family to be disappointed in me.

Leo remembered that he had to work really hard to pull himself out of the funk and insecurity. In his mind, "Hopkins was my dream school, and Abel took it from me." Ultimately, Leo credited a counselor, who became "a really good friend," for "pushing me and helping me get back on track."

Two years later, when it came time to apply for college, Leo's confidence had recovered. He decided to aim high. When that process did not turn out as he had hoped, a temporary panic set in, but ultimately things turned out okay, and he had no regrets.

> I applied early decision to Johns Hopkins. I also applied to the Gates scholarship. And then I got denied at Hopkins. It was a shock, because I had come to think that I had done as well in high school as Abel, so if they accepted him they would accept me too. And then they didn't! But I hadn't thought seriously about any other schools. So I had like two weeks to figure something out. So I applied to all the Ivies and to Amherst, because I knew it was the best liberal arts school. And I had no one to help me; I was on my own. Amherst was the first notification I got, and I got in. I remember telling my mom and she said, "What's Amherst?" That was hard, but I was set with Amherst. I had watched videos about it and loved it. Then they invited me to visit, and I loved it. And on the plane ride home I learned I got the Gates scholarship. So it all worked out.

While Leo was following his own path to college, Abel was struggling academically and socially at Hopkins. He had always thought that getting into a top school would be the hardest, most stressful part of his educational journey, so he was caught off guard by how difficult life became after he left the Valley. This was the first time he had felt the harsh reality of social inequality, and the first time he started to think deeply about his racial-ethnic identity.

> I wasn't prepared academically for Hopkins. Most students already had research experience. I remember applying for a job in a neuroscience lab, and the professor asked me why I didn't have any research experience in high school. He didn't get that where I came from it wasn't an option. It was super discouraging. It wasn't until my junior year that I started to feel comfortable at Hopkins. I looked for friends in the Latino student group, but I immediately realized that I didn't fit in because I didn't speak Spanish. I never felt Mexican enough. I felt most comfortable with low-income students.

Abel's struggles with his identity were intensified by his homesickness. Although he had always wanted out of the Valley, as he looked at the wealth and Whiteness surrounding him at Hopkins he missed it. And he missed his family.

> While I was first at Hopkins, I missed home a lot. I was the only one in my high school class who left Texas, and so I couldn't share what I was experiencing with anyone. . . . It wasn't just academically hard. . . . One of my roommates got sent a thousand dollars a month to just to practice playing the stock market. And he spent a lot of money on Subway and alcohol. I mean, he was funny and super nice and we were friends, but we just came from such different backgrounds. . . . So, yeah, my first year I was pretty depressed. I didn't get that at the time, but in retrospect I do. I slept all the time and watched movies. And I had a hard time doing work. I didn't share that, though. Then I started going to the counseling center, which helped. And I think because we grew up not sharing a lot of emotion, I couldn't share what I was feeling with my family. I remember that I didn't feel comfortable telling Leo that I missed him.

Raul and Sally had borrowed money to travel to Baltimore to move Abel into Hopkins. In retrospect, Abel thought that they should not have acquired this debt, since it threw them into financial insecurity for the next few years. When it came time for Leo to move to Amherst, they couldn't afford to move him in as they had done for Abel, and Leo had to do it alone. It was a tough way to start his college career, but ironically, there were perks to his solo transition.

Because Raul and Sally were with him when he arrived at Hopkins, Abel had forgone all of the orientation programming in order to spend time with them. On his own, Leo took advantage of all the orientation opportunities. As I wrote in the last chapter, Leo credited Amherst's Summer Bridge program, which provides a special orientation and academic preparation for first-generation college students, for giving him the social and academic support he needed to start Amherst off on the right foot. Students he met in Summer Bridge became his best friends. It was also through Summer Bridge that Leo realized that he could love STEM and the humanities. This early exposure to these disciplines proved especially helpful months down the road when he was struggling in his premed classes and deciding to change course. Instead of framing his move into the humanities as a result of not doing well in STEM, he was able to think of his decision as shifting majors because he felt the most at home and inspired in his humanities classes and with other humanities students.

For a few years when Leo and Abel were in college they did not talk regularly and did not feel close, but ultimately their shared experience of attending an elite school bonded them. They came to recognize their

shared struggles as well as the uniqueness of their Texan-Mexican identities and the place—the Borderlands—where they had grown up. They
both chose to travel to Spain—Leo during college and Abel the year after
graduation—to study Spanish. They both ended up doing well academically, despite their initial struggles. And perhaps most importantly, they
grew to appreciate each other more. Independently, they both told me that
the other was now their best friend, and not because they thought similarly about the world. Indeed, Leo assured me, they argued a lot. For
example, while they agreed that the world was a mess, they disagreed
about how to fix it. Nuanced visions and frequent debate sessions aside,
Leo and Abel shared a perspective on the world, on the Valley, and on
their family that no one else had, and this had bonded them for life. As
Abel put it:

> I think when Leo went to Amherst, he finally understood the transition
> I had gone through at Hopkins. He got it. . . . Leo is my best friend. He's
> always the one I talk to about things. We talk about everything, especially
> now about what's happening in the world. . . . And we appreciate each other
> a lot more now. When we were young, we fought a lot. Now we have hard
> conversations sometimes, but we really appreciate each other.

Leo agreed with his brother:

> I'm really close to my siblings, especially my older brother. We butt heads a
> lot, mostly because we're ideologically different. . . . In our family power
> comes from being smart, and so sometimes we argue just to argue. Just a
> few days ago we were arguing about Audre Lorde. You know how she
> says that "the master's tools can never dismantle the master's house?" Well,
> I believe that. But my brother thinks you have to use the master's tools,
> that it's the only practical way to make real change. . . . We talk all the time.
> We talk about school and our experiences, and we talk about the world.
> We still argue, but we're super close. I stayed with him in Baltimore after
> graduation, and we drove home together. I didn't really get it at the time, but
> we've shared a kind of experience and that helps when we are both at home.

Leo and Abel were continuing to move up the educational ladder at
an impressive and coordinated clip. Abel was still pursuing his love of
medicine: he had finished a master's of public health, and the last time we
spoke he had his eye on medical school. Although he had long thought that
he would return to practice medicine in the Valley, he had grown to love
working with Baltimore's Latino community. Now that he spoke Spanish,
his connection to the community had strengthened immeasurably. At the

time of our last conversation, Leo had graduated with accolades from Amherst, had completed a Fulbright in Spain, and was enrolled in a graduate program at Columbia University. Leo and Abel's younger brother was enrolled in Stanford, also with a Gates scholarship, and their younger sister became a QuestBridge finalist in 2022 and was matched with Emory University.

Having four children make it into elite colleges would be an extraordinary family feat anywhere, but it is even more extraordinary in the Valley, where the vast majority of students are Latino and low-income. And yet Leo and Abel both described growing up in a positive educational environment, starting when they were still in elementary school. It seems that this context, combined with supportive mentors and teachers and a nurturing family for whom education was always the top priority, launched Leo and Abel up the educational ladder despite their remote location. And once launched, their strong sibling relationship helped keep the family price of mobility low.

MAKING SENSE OF THE DIVERGENCES AND PARALLELS

Relationships are complicated and messy in large part because they are framed by larger contexts of familial and social inequalities. The sibling stories I analyzed for this project confirm the importance of looking at the impact of inequalities on close relationships. Even though siblings grow up in the same family network and in the same geographic place, their opportunities and outlooks commonly diverge. Sometimes the divergence is easy to assess. For example, when siblings have different legal statuses, they are afforded vastly different opportunities in the world. And yet, as Abrego argues, family members who have survived by relying on each other develop a consciousness that moves them to pay attention to their siblings' different statuses and opportunities.

Although the first two sibling pairs I have highlighted in this chapter shared the same legal status, they did not share the same opportunities or achievement statuses. There are a few important analytical points to take from the divergent paths traveled by Jose and Lisa and by Isabela and Cristina. First, as Conley concludes, I found that their parents treated them differently, sometimes because of gender or birth order, and sometimes because of their perceptions of each child's potential. For example, I got the sense from both Isabela and Cristina that their mom, Victoria, thought that Isabela had more potential for academic success, and so she placed higher expectations on her older daughter from an early age and asked more from her. The impact on Isabela of being treated this way was not totally clear, as she seemed to just do what she had to do as she carried the bulk of family responsibility and did well in school. But being treated differently by their mother certainly hurt Cristina's confidence and self-esteem. In addition, their mother's differential treatment may have translated into how Cristina and Isabela were treated in school, which is the second point to draw from their example.

Isabela was always a "traditionally" good student. She tested well, did well in all of her classes, was tracked into honors classes, and had the support of teachers and mentors. Living in Santa Ana, in the Los Angeles metro area, she had people in her networks who knew about QuestBridge and need-blind admissions. Thus, Isabela was well positioned to connect with an elite school. Cristina, on the other hand, was "left behind," because her strengths did not line up with the areas the schools deemed most academically important. As a result, her constellation of support was much weaker than Isabela's. While Isabela thrived in reading, writing, and arithmetic, Cristina was an artist and a creative type; she had strengths that her school did not value as much. In this case, being situated in or near a global city was an advantage only for Isabela, who had performed in all the ways deemed important by standard metrics.

Lisa and Jose had a similar story. Lisa was tracked, starting in kindergarten, into classroom environments that gave her extra support, while Jose was left to fend for himself. Although they grew up in the same household and attended the same public high school, Lisa was nurtured toward college while Jose was not. They were from the same place, but place had a very different impact on their educational opportunities because of how they were valued and supported academically by their teachers and school leaders. Gender most likely played a major part in how differently they were treated. Nancy Lopez, in her study of the diverging educational achievements of Caribbean and West Indian second-generation boys and girls, found that girls experienced more positive and encouraging relationships with their teachers than did boys.[10] As a result, girls were more hopeful and optimistic than boys about their educational future. Lopez's findings fit with how Jose and Lisa depicted their educational experiences and outlooks for the future.

Jose and Cristina, though not successful in school like their siblings and not on a path to college graduation, both had a sophisticated analysis of why they had not been able to succeed in the ways their siblings had. In line with my third point, they both had a critical understanding of their own and their family's social position in the world. In other sibling interviews as well, I gleaned that youth in Latino immigrant families, though different in experiences and opportunities, often thought deeply and critically about their siblings' trajectories. Their shared experiences in their immigrant families, especially in facing external and internal threats, seemed to have generated empathy and a keen understanding of the inequalities at work in each other's lives.

Leo and Abel were among the minority of sibling groupings who shared the same path to exceptional educational mobility. Although my sample is too small to generalize about what distinguished them from other sibling pairs, I cannot but notice a few striking characteristics. First, the legal status of both of Leo and Abel's parents, Raul and Sally, was stable. Sally was a U.S. citizen and Raul was a permanent resident, so this family had a general sense of security that the others did not have. Second, Leo and Abel both performed well in the ways that mattered in their school. Indeed, the qualifications for the gifted and talented program matched up with their strengths for both brothers. They might, of course, have been well qualified because they also attended a very good elementary school that their parents knew about because of their mom's job as a paraprofessional in the same school district. Leo and Abel's academic success matches what I found in the rest of my sample: siblings whose education tracked similarly not only performed well according to traditional academic metrics but were also supported by strong family and community networks.

Interestingly, what differentiated Leo and Abel from the other students in the sample who had siblings at elite schools was that they did not grow up in a global city or in a place on the radar screen of elite schools. That said, they did grow up in a geographic area in which they developed a strong in-group identity and had access to well-developed, place-based Latino support networks. Their mom's job connected them, from a young age, with a constellation of support that nurtured their educational aspirations and intellectual curiosity. Although none of their teachers or networks knew much about elite college networks, one of their teachers did know about the Gates Millennium scholarship, which changed their lives. Their story validates the sociological mantra that local context and network access matter a lot to mobility.

Of course, this does not mean that Leo's and Abel's paths were easy. Both struggled a lot at different times in their educational journey. Yet what they had that neither Cristina and Isabela nor Jose and Lisa had was the ability to confide in each other. When they both returned to the Valley after being educated on the East Coast, being able to share their new perspectives and feelings about home made the experience of return much less lonely. And though their academic journeys and life experiences led them to different ideological perspectives, they also were lucky enough to be able to argue with each other about what they had learned and even enjoyed doing so. The price of mobility for Leo and Abel was much lower than it was for those who did not share their educational mobility with a sibling.

What connected all three of the sibling pairs—and indeed, what connected all of the sibling groupings I was able to get to know through this research—was a commitment to family ties despite the inequality and complexity of their lives. Here again I warn against interpreting loyalty as an essentialist cultural trait. Instead, the stories I heard spoke loudly and clearly to the ways in which family is key to survival in contexts of social marginalization. Sibling relationships, just like parent-child relationships, are tools that immigrant families utilize when confronted with social barriers to their well-being.

In times of crisis, relationships become more important than ever to family survival. COVID enters the story in the next chapter, which sheds more light on how burdens, privileges, and the consciousness of how they are distributed are shared across immigrant families.

Chapter 5 | COVID-19 Ruptures

ALBERTO WAS ALREADY struggling emotionally and academically before COVID-19 completely upended his world. Deeply introspective, he was attending mindfulness workshops on campus with the goal of learning how to accept the things over which he had no control—namely, his DACA status and his mom's undocumented status. President Donald Trump had issued an order rescinding DACA only days before Alberto arrived on campus as a first-year student in 2017, and the unease of living with a liminal legal status would follow him throughout his time at Amherst.[1] Now approaching his senior year, he knew that the resources and opportunities made available to him at Amherst were soon to disappear. Though only a little over a year away from graduating from an elite college, Alberto found it hard to be optimistic about his undocumented future.

Then COVID hit and things went from bad to worse. Amherst was a leader in confronting the virus. It was one of the first colleges in the country to announce a shutdown in order to protect students, faculty, and staff from being infected, and college leaders immediately put supports in place to help students and faculty adjust to remote learning. While Alberto appreciated the college's bold leadership and the generous supports it offered, he experienced the shutdown as yet another trauma over which he had no control. Being forced to leave campus felt to him like an "eviction," an experience he had had before, and aroused deep-seated fear and anxiety, especially surrounding deportation. His emotional health "plummeted." Alberto could have applied to stay on campus—an option for students whose home setting was insecure—but he knew that if, as he feared, things got worse with the pandemic, he would be needed at home to help navigate the crisis. As he spiraled into a deeper depression and worried that he would not have the focus or mental stamina to finish out the semester remotely, Alberto went home to his family in Houston.

As he expected, the first few months of the COVID shutdown were incredibly difficult. Alberto did not have the physical or mental space to focus on his remote classes and finish his work. Although his professors were accommodating and his academic adviser offered him extra guidance and support, he felt unmotivated, stressed, and socially isolated. School felt meaningless and obsolete in the context of the larger social crisis. To make matters worse, his family was not taking the virus as seriously as he thought they should, even though Houston at the time was a COVID hotspot, with cases skyrocketing and hospitals overflowing. Deeply religious, Alberto's mom and aunt, who had no choice but to continue leaving the apartment for their work as domestic housekeepers, had decided to "put things in God's hands." Alberto was scared. Following the science and watching the race and class statistical breakdown of infections, he knew everyone in his family was at high risk.

In June, Alberto's aunt, who lived with his family, got sick. Then another aunt got sick. At first, both downplayed their symptoms as those of a cold or flu. Alberto believed otherwise. But testing was expensive and hard to access at that time, so they opted against it. Then Alberto's grandma, who also lived with his family, got sick. When her breathing became labored, he took her to an urgent care clinic, where she was tested and formally diagnosed with COVID. Alberto feared that he would fall ill next. He did. A week later, everyone in Alberto's multigenerational household, except for his mom and cousin, was sick. No one in the family had a primary care doctor. No one except Alberto had health insurance. Looking for what help they could afford, they found a low-cost clinic that Alberto described as "sketch." The clinic, a go-to place for uninsured, low-income Latinos, was set up for telehealth appointments with Spanish-speaking doctors in the Caribbean. A nurse gave them vitamin shots. They just got sicker. Finally, when his grandmother was too sick to be cared for at home, Alberto took her to a hospital emergency room, where she would have to battle the virus without her family present. Five days later, at three o'clock in the morning, a nurse called to tell the family that Alberto's grandmother had asked to be taken off the ventilator. Alberto, quite ill himself at the time, had to translate the call. His grandmother, who was like a second mother to him, died soon after. Alone. His aunt, in the same hospital and in critical condition, passed away a week later.

During this time, no one in Alberto's family was able to work. And because of their undocumented status, no one had access to the federal stimulus money that was distributed to aid working and middle-class families. Extended family members and members of his aunt's church stepped up, providing Alberto's family with money and food. Without their help, Alberto said later, he did not know how they would have survived. Through it all, even as she lost her mom and her sister and nursed Alberto through COVID-induced pneumonia, Alberto's mom "was a rock."

Alberto credited her with preventing him from free-falling into a physical and emotional abyss.

Alberto slowly healed physically, though never completely. As of this writing, his lungs still had not fully recovered and he battled fatigue. He took a medical withdrawal from Amherst for the fall of 2020 in order to stay home with his mom and get a job. And with his energy stores depleted and his mental health in terrible shape, he also needed the academic break. Alberto returned to Amherst in January 2021, determined to graduate but still uncertain about his future. Then, in March 2021, Alberto's uncle, to whom he was very close, died from the virus. Alberto again found it hard to concentrate on school. His grades dropped, and he was placed on academic probation. The setbacks never seemed to cease. He took another leave and invested in trying to heal the mental health wounds that COVID had inflicted. Determined to get back to school to graduate, he started working with a therapist and a psychiatrist. He felt he owed it to his family to make this effort.

For Alberto, COVID had been more than just a temporary disruption. It compounded the traumas of poverty and illegality that had indelibly marked his life. In the process, it intensified his doubts that his educational mobility could protect him outside of the confines of Amherst College. As was true for Alberto's family, most of the families in this study were already stressed in myriad ways before the COVID pandemic. Poverty and marginalization were staples of daily life for most, and precarious legal statuses added to those challenges for many. Then COVID exacerbated their social and economic hardships, hitting the most marginalized the hardest.

To be sure, low-income Latino families have been disproportionately affected by the pandemic. According to the Centers for Disease Control and Prevention (CDC), Latinos are twice as likely to die from COVID than are Whites, and early in the pandemic, when my interviews took place, they were the demographic group most at risk of contracting COVID. At the same time, while overall U.S. unemployment rose to 14.7 percent with the onset of the pandemic, it rose to 19 percent for Latinos.[2] According to the Urban Institute's Health Reform Monitoring Survey, 57 percent of Latinos reported job loss, hours reduction, or income reduction because of COVID, the highest of all demographic groups.[3] Latinos, along with Blacks, were also more likely than non-Hispanic Whites to experience food and housing insecurity because of the virus and less likely to receive government support in the face of those challenges.[4] Many Latinos who maintained their employment were essential workers in low-wage care and service industries and thus were at heightened risk of exposure to the virus.

The Coronavirus Aid, Relief, and Economic Security Act (CARES) Act, passed in March 2020, provided economic relief to most U.S. citizens, including those in this study. The critical support that this money provided was noted by many. Yet for families that were undocumented or had undocumented adult members—like Alberto's family—there was no government support to be had. These families struggled the most.

Aside from not having access to federal economic relief and unemployment benefits, members of undocumented and mixed-status families were discouraged from seeking community supports because of revisions to the public charge rule made by Trump in February 2020, right before the onset of the virus. According to the revised rule, undocumented individuals who applied to public assistance programs, including Medicaid and the Supplemental Nutrition Assistance Program (SNAP), could be barred from future residency or citizenship. Not surprisingly, this rule had a "chilling effect" in immigrant communities, discouraging the undocumented from seeking a broad array of supports.[5] As such, undocumented individuals entered the pandemic not only at greater risk of getting sick and losing income but also unable to access public stimulus supports, hesitant to seek medical care, and fearful that accessing even local or private supports could put their future U.S. residency in jeopardy.

In this chapter, I draw from two waves of in-depth interviews that I conducted in the fall of 2020 and in the spring and summer of 2021 with forty of this study's original sixty participants. Importantly, the majority of the forty had graduated from Amherst by this time. The chapter highlights the main themes that emerged from these interviews—COVID's dire economic and mental health impacts on families, the increased care burdens it placed on youth, and the ways in which their educational mobility had served as a safety net of sorts.

The pandemic added further nuance to how these youth understood the implications of educational mobility. Specifically, they told me that, while they were appreciative of the basic protections offered by their educational mobility—their remote jobs, access to college assistance, and the scientific fluency to understand the true threat of the virus—they also recognized that their families faced dangers from which their individual educational status offered no protection.

The interviews also reveal the evolving ways in which place mattered in the COVID story. During the early phase of the pandemic, families like Alberto's, who lived and worked in global cities, were hit first and hardest. And yet, as the virus spread beyond cities to remote areas, it became clear that community supports and access were more limited there. Indeed, the stories I share here show how the risks and protections associated with geographic context shifted and mutated along with the virus.

COVID'S ECONOMIC IMPACTS

Almost all of the parents of the Latino youth in this study worked in manual labor or low-wage service jobs—economic sectors that provide little to no social or employment protections. Thus, when the virus hit, youth's immediate concerns focused on the job-related risks of getting sick faced by their parents and other family members. But there was a complicated twist to their worries. The only way for their family members to protect themselves was to stop working. But to do that would present the possibly even greater problem of lost income. Work was survival. It was how all of the families in this study met their basic needs.

Jon, who was from New York City, knew that his parents not only had to go to work but had to navigate a city that was overrun with COVID cases in the early months. And they had to do so with no formal protections in place. Jon summed up this conundrum well: "My parents both clean office buildings. My dad is also a busboy at a hotel. . . . I mean, it's this incredible shitty bind that many low-income workers are stuck in, which is, do you starve or do you risk getting a deadly virus?"

Ricardo expressed a similar concern about his parents, both of whom were essential workers in Chicago. The first thing he told me during our interview was how thankful he was that no one in his family had gotten sick and that neither of his parents had lost their job. When the economy shut down in the early months of the virus, Ricardo was certain that his dad's Chicago factory would close. Instead, it was one of the manufacturing sites across the United States that switched to producing protective gear for high-risk workers. Ironically, however, the factory did not have strict protections in place itself. Ricardo, who was working in Seattle at the time, was nervous for his dad; he was following the news and knew that urban factory workers were getting hit hard by the virus. But Ricardo was actually most concerned about his mom, who was working in one of the most dangerous contexts of all.

> My mom works at a rehab center/nursing home. And so, since COVID started she's seen . . . a ton of people at that place get sick. Like everybody was bed-ridden. . . . And she still had to work there. And I was scared because I felt like she was the one most vulnerable. And both my parents are pretty old. . . . My mom is in her late fifties, my dad's in his sixties already. And so I was worried.

Ricardo's fears were realized a few months later when everyone in his family got COVID. Luckily, no one was hospitalized. Still, the virus took a toll physically, emotionally, and, most notably, economically.

To be sure, economic stress increased exponentially when a family member got COVID. In interviews, many of which took place before vaccines were available, youth seemed resigned to the inevitability that their parents would get sick, since many of them were essential workers in large urban hotspots. If it hadn't happened yet, they insinuated, it was "just a matter of time." And when one or more family members did get sick, youth spoke with as much concern about the economic impacts of lost work as they did about the dire risks to their family member's health from the virus.

By the fall of 2020, the virus had expanded beyond its initial urban nodes. At this point, even youth from more remote geographic areas were resigned to the reality that their parents were at high risk of getting COVID. I spoke with Noel in the fall of 2020 while he was studying remotely from West Texas. When the pandemic began to run its course through Houston in the spring and summer of 2020, Noel had held his breath, hoping that it might not make its way into the less densely populated parts of the state. But just as the numbers started going down in Houston, they started surging elsewhere. COVID hit his family soon thereafter.

Noel was almost certain that his mom brought the virus home from the restaurant kitchen where she was working at the time. Luckily, no one in his family got severely ill. COVID did, however, pack a major economic punch when both his parents had to abruptly stop working for a few weeks. They had no savings, no safety net. His mom was eventually able to receive relief payments, but for a period of time they were not sure how they were going to make ends meet. And while large cities were building social infrastructure to support struggling families, Noel's community remained underresourced and completely unprepared for COVID's social fallout.

> Both my mom and stepdad continued to work during COVID, which was really lucky. My stepdad is a truck driver, which is, I guess, a little safer. But my mom, she's a restaurant worker in the kitchen. And two weeks ago, some workers started getting sick. Some were coming in sick. And then . . . my mom was starting to feel a little sick. Then . . . the restaurant had to shut down because all the workers became sick. . . . Then one of my little brothers started to get a fever and feel sick. . . . Mostly, it was an economic factor. Luckily, my mom was able to receive COVID relief pay through her employer. My stepdad, not so much . . . and my stepdad's the main person to bring income. And so, yeah, it's interesting, when the news broke about having COVID, my mom's main concern wasn't the fact that she had the illness. It was, "What are we going to do to pay all these bills that are coming up? What are we going to use to pay rent?" . . . My parents have some debt as well, so it's worrying about all the bills.

Although Suzy's relief payments helped some, they did not cover the loss of income. The family still needed help with food and cash, but no such support was available where they lived.

Government-issued COVID relief and unemployment payments were a lifesaver for many families in this study, but not everyone qualified, and even some who did confronted barriers to access. Rebeca's dad had been working for the same construction company in a rural area outside of Albuquerque, New Mexico, for ten years when COVID shut down the economy. When he lost his job, he was shocked, scared, and ill equipped to navigate the social welfare system in order to access support. "My dad really has had a difficult time with the pandemic. . . . He lost his job in the beginning. . . . He was trying to navigate unemployment, but he can't really read or write English very well. So he was having a hard time going through the bureaucracy of it."

With no community supports to help him navigate the system, and being reluctant to seek help from Rebeca, with whom his relationship was strained at the time, her dad searched for another job, which he readily found. His troubles did not end there, however. In his next job he soon got COVID, had to stop working, and once again missed out on getting unemployment support because he did not know how to apply for it. And out of concern about racism and anti-immigrant attitudes, he also resisted seeking medical care.

> Then he got a job cement-laying for this company that does roads and buildings and things like that. So that was good. But at his job they don't wear masks; they don't take precautions. . . . And he caught COVID. . . . It was really difficult for him. He doesn't have a form of transportation. And I was worried for him, because he's not the type of person who goes to the hospital. I think . . . he's internalized this feeling of, "I'm very visibly brown, and they're not going to take care of me well, and they might not believe that I have my green card." . . . He just worried about any sort of negative interaction. And so that's kind of always been his stance on the hospital. And so . . . the combination of being low-income and having missed out on . . . government support, because he is not able to understand the bureaucracy, just made his experience of having COVID and navigating it a lot harder.

The experience of Rebeca's dad was not uncommon. Immigrant parents I interviewed before COVID talked about how difficult it was to understand the social welfare system and specifically their eligibility. Navigating this system was especially difficult for those who did not live in a major city. COVID added yet another barrier to access to health care—with dire economic consequences.

Workers did not have to get sick to experience the negative economic consequences of COVID. Amanda's mom was working at a New York City restaurant when COVID struck. As was the case for restaurants across the country, her workplace shut down temporarily. Amanda's dad, who also worked at a restaurant, was furloughed at the same time. When they both got invited back to work, they were relieved, yet anxious that another shutdown was right around the corner. They responded by taking on extra hours, trying to save money, and making sure their bosses knew they were willing to do anything to keep their jobs. In Amanda's estimation, their anxiety about economic insecurity served as "a form of social control" that made them more "exploitable" than ever. Amanda shared her story right after her parents returned to work.

> At first [her mom's] restaurant had to close down, and that was really stressful for her. . . . And then she had abbreviated hours. . . . And now they both have been working extremely long hours because they feel anxious about potentially losing their jobs. So if the employer asks anything from them, they go above and beyond, just because they're trying to make sure that their job is secure. . . . Right now my mom is working outside in an extremely cold, rainy environment because of the New York policies around dining. And I understand the thought process behind [the policies], but the people who are passing these regulations don't understand that in these little huts that restaurants are building, there's really poor air ventilation, it's really hard to disinfect, and it's . . . putting the servers in a really difficult situation.

Amanda, who was well versed in sociology, theorized that because low-wage servers were so fearful of job loss, they were unlikely to say anything about poor working conditions, even if they knew they were in danger.

While few families in this study remained unscathed economically by the pandemic, families with undocumented members fared the worst. Not eligible for stimulus payments or unemployment, they were the least likely to stay home from work if they were ill or to seek private community supports if they lost their jobs or got sick. The economic toll of the virus on these families was devastating.

Both of Heidi's parents were undocumented. Her dad was a taxi driver in New Jersey, about thirty miles outside of New York City, and her mom worked at home taking care of her severely disabled younger brother. Even before COVID, Heidi felt a lot of responsibility for the financial well-being of her parents and brother. It seemed like the family was always on the brink of bankruptcy and losing their home. COVID made everything worse, adding to the pressure she felt to ensure her family's financial survival.

> All four of my family members got sick. . . . My dad got it the worst. I started a Go Fund Me page because I was so stressed. Thank the Lord he didn't have to go to the hospital. He was having really bad breathing problems, and it was scary to the point where he almost did go to the hospital. . . . He was able to stay home from work for a little bit because I ended up raising some money. . . . There just weren't many other supports. He had to work. There was no other option. . . . My dad's a taxi driver, so he was really hard hit because no one was wanting a taxi. It was hard being a taxi driver even before COVID because of Uber. . . . So it was really hard to pay rent. It was really hard to pay bills. Financially there was no support. The only support was from the Go Fund Me and the Amherst Emergency Fund.

Only a few months away from graduation, Heidi contemplated taking an academic leave so that she could work full-time and help her family. Ultimately, she decided it was in everyone's best interest for her to finish school and get a "real" job, which she did. In the interim, Heidi was grateful that Amherst gave her emergency funds, some portion of which she could send home. This was an important bandage at the time, but she was stressed to realize that she would not have that support in the future.

As Heidi's story shows, it was not only undocumented individuals who suffered from the COVID-magnified stresses of illegality. U.S. citizen family members were negatively impacted too, as in families, like Heidi's, with undocumented parents and U.S. citizen children. Laura Enriquez argues that the U.S. citizen children of undocumented parents experience the harms connected to illegality as a form of "multigenerational punishment."[6] Children embody their parents' marginalization.[7] COVID made things worse, as child credits were embedded in the stimulus bill. Thus, parents who could not apply for stimulus supports because they were undocumented were also unable to access supports for their citizen children.

For example, though Lisa and her brother Jose were U.S. citizens, the undocumented status of Leona, their mom, impacted the supports they could access. COVID shut down the laundromat where Leona worked, but she had no safety net. Because Jose was still a dependent, he lost out on support as well. Lisa, who had recently graduated from Amherst and was working full-time, was the only one in the household who received any form of COVID relief.

> I never checked to see if she was eligible. I just assumed that she wouldn't be eligible for it because she is undocumented. So she didn't apply for anything.

I got my stimulus check. . . . But then we were realizing that people getting their stimulus checks . . . were getting an additional credit for any children in the household. So we weren't able to get the credit for my brother, because my mom couldn't file.

Lisa devised a family austerity plan. She stopped putting money into savings, using it instead for rent and household expenses, and she identified places where they could cut back their spending. Ultimately, they were able to squeak by until Leona was able to resume reduced hours at the laundromat where she had worked for many years.

Lisa's family was not alone in their struggles. Angelica's dad was also undocumented. Though her mom had recently gotten her green card, both of her parents were ineligible for COVID-related government supports because of how they had filed their taxes. The policy limitations placed on her parents also hurt their youngest children, Angelica's siblings.

They don't get the stimulus payments because my dad's undocumented. Even though my mom now has her green card, because she filed taxes with my dad, who's undocumented and he's down as the head of household and main income earner . . . she doesn't get money. So even though my siblings are U.S. citizens, they don't get anything. And so my dad's, like, "What am I going to do?"

Angelica encouraged her parents to tap into the supports available in Santa Ana, which she had heard were quite generous, but her dad refused, fearing that getting help would reveal his undocumented status and hurt his chances of getting residency in the future. In Angelica's estimation, his *machista* stubbornness also got in the way.

My dad doesn't trust [the system]. He's like, "I don't want them to know." And I'm like, "But can they take down your information?" He's like, "I don't know, but I don't want to risk it. . . . I need to stay under the radar. . . . I don't want to be in anyone's line of sight." . . . And, you know, all of them are just very prideful. They're like, "I came to this country on my own, I'm going to handle this on my own. I don't need handouts." I'm like, "That's not what this is. This is you looking for help because you have kids now. It's not just you." Yeah, but again, it comes back to, they don't know how to ask for help. And it's very much seen as a sign of weakness if you do . . . and it's also that fear of "what if they ask me for some identifying information?"

Angelica was confident that her family would survive this difficult time. They had been through far worse, and she knew that if it got bad enough, her parents would have to take advantage of local support programs. Still, she knew that it would not be easy and that even armed with a college degree, she wasn't in a position to provide the level of financial help they needed.

COVID'S MENTAL HEALTH IMPACTS

For many families, the financial stress accentuated by COVID was accompanied by mental health struggles. In a long-standing societal pattern, mental health stress often accompanies financial stress, especially for the most socially disadvantaged, and COVID only exacerbated this pattern.[8] Indeed, according to a 2020 Pew Research Center survey, lower-income individuals were more likely to suffer from COVID-related mental health struggles than higher-income individuals, and Blacks and Latinos more likely to have mental health challenges than non-Latino Whites.[9] Jonathan Purtle has found that Latinos' disproportionate rates of mental health struggles were likely to be due to financial stress as well as high COVID morbidity rates within the Latino community.[10] My data concur with these findings, while adding a precarious immigration status as a factor that weighed heavily on individual and family emotional well-being. Notably, participants in this study experienced additional stress from worries about family members living outside of the United States as well as the stresses connected to remote schooling. Whatever the roots of their mental health struggles, participants experienced them relationally. Even if they were doing okay individually, they felt an obligation to care for their family members who were not okay.

All of the youth in this study had to bear the burden of class, race, and immigration-related COVID stresses, along with the basic stresses of isolation and loneliness from living far away from their families, as reported across income and racial-ethnic categories. Heidi decided to take advantage of an Amherst program that allowed students without secure home lives to stay on campus during the initial shutdown. It was not an easy decision. She felt impelled to be with her family, but she also recognized that the "chaos" and cramped quarters at home would make it nearly impossible to do her coursework. She was in a no-win situation.

Oh, it was so lonely, man. . . . I didn't expect it to be that lonely. . . . The good thing is I had a lot of friends to video-chat with all the time. But sometimes I really felt like not talking to people. . . . I still see my decision to stay on campus as better than going back home. But it was still a little rough. You have your give-and-takes. But yeah, it was very lonely, and I gained so much weight because I just was not eating well and not taking care of myself, plus not having a support system close to me. . . . That wasn't great.

Heidi told me several times how grateful she was for Amherst's support. Yet even generous support from the college could not address the root of her mental health struggles: the poverty and legal insecurity of her family.

Rebeca also stayed in Amherst. Having recently graduated, she had her own place to live and a job that she loved at the college farm. But when the farm was forced to stop all but basic operations and she had to work remotely from her small apartment, her mental health plummeted. She struggled to find the motivation to do anything. Rebeca had fought depression during her time as a student at Amherst, but with counseling and a lot of hard work she had moved beyond it, or so she thought. The shutdown brought it all back.

> When we went into shutdown, we weren't in person at all. I was doing tasks online, working from home. But I had no experience with doing that and didn't know how to do it. It really felt like I was regressing . . . feeling like I had no motivation, or like, always saying, "I'm going to do it later." And then, at 6:00 PM, I'm like, "I can't work now." I got into a spiral of, "I didn't work yesterday, I really need to work today," and then not working. And then just feeling that tension. I was definitely not meeting the time quota that I was supposed to be meeting. . . . It was such a stressful experience.

Rebeca thought about returning home to New Mexico but ultimately decided that it would be better for her and her family if she stayed in Amherst, where she had a secure job and a place to live. She also realized that going home to the insecurity of her family might make her mental health worse.

Rebeca was not the only one who talked about her complicated relationship with home. Although all of the participants I interviewed who were still students at the time the pandemic hit would probably have qualified to remain on campus after the shutdown, the majority chose to return home to be with family. Going home, however, brought its own set of challenges. For example, while Teresa was close to her family, some in her inner family circle struggled with addiction, and the family's financial insecurity was omnipresent. As such, having to confront her family's challenges while trying to finish the school year remotely was hard. "I was really nervous . . . in a very anxious state. . . . Home isn't the most pleasant experience for me. . . . I didn't have the best time in my childhood here, so I'm . . . just very anxious. I was very anxious back in March and through May." Teresa's experience was representative of the experiences of several in my sample who felt an obligation and muted desire to be home and with family even though home was not always a supportive place for them.

Noel also decided to return home. Knowing that he would have no private or quiet space to attend class or begin work on his senior thesis, he used part of the housing stipend he recouped from Amherst to rent a studio apartment, which was affordable because of the low rents in his remote Texas town. Theoretically, renting an apartment around the block from his family seemed like the perfect solution. Being so close to his family, he could help out and see them often, but he would also have his own space, which would allow him to keep up with his work and have some distance from his stepfather, who was a difficult person in his life. So he was surprised when he started to feel lonely and unmotivated.

> There would be moments where I would get tired of doing work in my apartment. . . . At Amherst, if I was tired of being in my dorm, I could go to the library or I could go to the Student Center with friends and . . . have that motivation from being around other people. Here I would just be working in my apartment and so . . . motivation was much harder to produce. . . . I guess it kind of affected my performance. . . . It was the fatigue of being in this place and on Zoom as well. . . . Sometimes I'd be like, "Okay, I'm just going to do the bare minimum and that's it."

Compounding the challenges for students of going home, often to houses or apartments that did not have space to accommodate them, was losing access to the mental health supports that they had on campus. Students especially missed having access to free college counseling after they moved home, since therapists licensed only in Massachusetts were prohibited by law from treating students who were residing in other states. So not having the option of seeing his therapist made Noel's struggle with low motivation and loneliness especially difficult.

> The mental aspect has been the hardest. . . . Amherst was like, because of the rules established by Massachusetts, you can't do counseling sessions outside of the state. So it was like, "Do I want to get a counselor here for the time being, and get reimbursed, or just wait until next semester?" And I felt like, "Okay, I'll just wait for next semester," because I didn't see the point in getting someone for a couple months. . . . That's been the hardest.

For those, like Noel, who lived in remote areas, finding a local therapist was no easy feat. Few had ready access to local mental health networks that they could tap for support until they returned to campus.

Recent graduates also mentioned having mental health challenges, many of them related to their families. A common theme I heard from participants was that, while they were struggling themselves, they knew that family members were struggling more, but with fewer resources and supports in place to help them. Just as legal status and mobility are experienced relationally, I found that mental health struggles were also experienced relationally. I was reminded of the saying that a good friend shared with me: "Parents are only as happy as their least happy child." In socially marginalized immigrant families in which survival has long been a family affair, I found this saying to be particularly apt, but with an important caveat. Because of the obligation and genuine desire that study participants felt to pay back their parents' sacrifices, they took on their parents' stresses as their own, flipping the parent-child pattern of responsibility. Students suggested in their interviews that they were only as happy as their least happy family member. During the COVID pandemic, that least happy member was usually a parent, though it also could be a sibling or other relative.

Isabela was three years beyond graduation and thriving in a doctoral program when COVID struck. Though her graduate stipend was modest, she made ends meet by having a roommate and living frugally. It helped that she was going to school in the Midwest, where rents were much lower than at home in southern California. With both Isabela's mom, Victoria, and her sister, Cristina, working full-time, some of the family's financial pressure was relieved. But within the first couple of months of the pandemic, Victoria's hours were cut back. Since she was undocumented, Victoria had no access to stimulus money, and she became depressed. Not knowing how to lift her mom out of her funk made Isabela feel guilt and grief. At the same time, she felt the responsibility to fill the financial gaps. We spoke in the midst of this situation.

> She's been having a lot of lows recently. I mean, I'm not a professional, so I don't know where that would be, but she's been a lot more frustrated and has had more mood swings. . . . And she is also frustrated and sad about her job. . . . It's been a tough time for her. It is stressful because I just don't know how to help. . . . Because, even if she works, she can't get more money. And I can only earn so much money. As a graduate student, even though I'm getting a raise, I don't know what stuff is going to look like . . . so I'm just trying to keep my head on straight with school and doing the work so I can actually send some money back . . . And also, [it's hard] just not being there to support her, right?

Later adding to Isabela's stress was her falling quite ill with COVID, which made it hard for her to work and to stay focused on school. At the time she got sick, she was teaching her first class. She was thankful that the class was remote. Somehow Isabela kept it together, finished the semester, and was able to fulfill her goal of sending money to her mom until she was able to start working full-time again.

Amanda also worried about her mom. As I detailed in the previous section, when Amanda's mom went back to work after losing her restaurant job, she took on extra hours because she was worried that the next shutdown was right around the corner. Being in New York City, the epicenter of the virus at the time, magnified her worry. Having struggled with anxiety herself, Amanda sensed that her mom was having a serious mental health episode, but she did not know how to broach the subject or what to do to help.

> At the beginning she [her mom] would call me a lot. . . . I have anxiety myself, so I could pick up on the symptoms pretty quickly. She was experiencing very high-end anxiety. My sister was hesitant to leave the house for groceries and stuff, so she [her mom] was the main person leaving the house, and she didn't really know how to navigate it. . . . I could just tell in her voice that she was very overwhelmed by the situation. . . . And it's very hard for her to get testing because the lines in New York are ridiculously long. . . . And she's misinformed and completely suspicious of the vaccine. So it's just been a very anxiety-ridden time for her. She is becoming increasingly religious. . . . She basically sees COVID as the end of the world . . . and like, you have to kind of turn to God more. . . . It's clear she's living in increased anxiety, but she's not self-aware that that's what's happening.

Having been on a campus where mental health issues were talked about openly and mostly without stigma, students and recent graduates found it difficult to watch family members struggle without access to the supports and resources necessary to help or, in some cases, to know that their family member did not accept their mental health challenges as real.

Both Lisa's mom, Leona, and brother, Jose, struggled with their mental health during the first months of the pandemic. For Leona, the biggest stress came from losing her job and not having access to unemployment or stimulus money. For Jose, it was remote learning that nearly pushed him over the edge. Always having struggled in school, he learned quickly that without the structure of in-person classes and access to a regular teacher, he was lost. Jose was in his senior year of high school, and with the disruptions caused by the virus adding to the uncertainty he felt about his future, his mental health suffered. While Lisa could alleviate some of her mom's stress by taking over the rent for a few months, she found it more difficult to find the solution for Jose's travails.

> My brother was looking forward to prom and all the other activities that seniors get to do. But all of those things were cut short. . . . He really struggled a lot with virtual learning. Already my brother had challenges. . . . He's very smart and he's very capable, but he gets really distracted. So the whole virtual thing for high school was tough. He started second-guessing whether he wanted to do community college or not. I think he was really nervous. . . . He started to have panic attacks, more anxiety, to the point where we had to take him to the doctor. And they were able to prescribe some medication for that. But there's been a lot of shifts in his life during this time, and I see that it's been taking a really big emotional toll on him.

Jose trusted Lisa to take him to the doctor, and he was open to taking medication to help alleviate his panic attacks. While his struggles did not subside completely, he was doing okay when we talked. But for many participants in this study, having mental health struggles that were considered taboo in their family complicated efforts to get help.

Julia grew up in San Diego, California, in a multigenerational Mexican immigrant household. Though she stayed on the East Coast after her graduation from Amherst in 2016 to attend law school and is now working in Boston as a lawyer, she had remained extremely close to her family, talking to them most days. Julia was surprised when it was her grandmother who took the biggest COVID-induced mental health hit in her family. She was even more surprised when her grandmother opened up about it and sought help, going against the cultural norms around mental health with which Julia had been raised.

> In terms of the emotional toll that the pandemic has had on people, therapy isn't something that . . . would be a solution for my family, you know? They don't think of that as a step or a possibility. My grandma suffered from really bad depression at the beginning of the pandemic. Her doctor diagnosed her and tried to convince her to maybe take medication, maybe talk to somebody, go to therapy. . . . She did end up going on antidepressants. . . . To hear that my grandma had been officially diagnosed with depression and experiencing symptoms of depression—that was so wild to me.

Julia shared with her grandmother that she too had dealt with mental health struggles and had taken medication for anxiety and depression.

She hoped that a silver lining of the pandemic for her family might be the realization that "it's kind of good to open up these conversations" and that maybe a shift in cultural norms would result.

Those who were undocumented were in the least advantageous position to alleviate or heal the mental health traumas magnified by COVID. It is instructive to reflect on Alberto's story, which opened this chapter. COVID intensified the fear he had of deportation and about his uncertain future. Because of their undocumented status, his mom and aunt were in jobs that put them at high risk for COVID, and with no access to health insurance, stimulus support, and unemployment, they had no safety net. They had to work. When they got sick and family members died, even more emotional trauma ensued.

Cesar had a similar experience. He already lived with continuous stress because of the uncertainties of his DACA status. Would Trump succeed in ending DACA? If so, would he get deported? If he did, what would he do in Mexico? And how would he survive being separated from his siblings who were U.S. citizens? COVID only added to his uncertainties. At the same time, Cesar was grateful that he had graduated from Amherst before COVID and that he had a good job that allowed him to work remotely. His mom, however, was not so lucky. She had to go to work every day as a cleaner and care worker in Los Angeles, where the virus was surging. He summed up the family's life under COVID: "I just constantly stress about my citizenship status, my mom's citizenship status, and now I stress about my mom getting sick."

Carlos's stress was also rooted in his and his mom's precarious legal status. In reflecting on his undocumented mom's struggles with anxiety, he said that he had looked for a therapist for her, but couldn't find one who "speaks Spanish and has knowledge about being undocumented or having DACA." He and his family lived in a small city, about an hour and a half outside of Boston, where the social infrastructure, while generally strong, was not easily accessible for undocumented, non-English speakers. Carlos paused to gather his emotions after sharing his frustration and then said, "The stress of COVID, it's like trauma that contributes to making everything else worse." A week after I interviewed Carlos, he called to tell me that his stepfather had died from the virus. His mom and grandma had also gotten sick. Though a college graduate and knowledgeable about the virus and the social and health supports in his area, he could do nothing to shield them from the pandemic. Through tears he asked me to let people know how terrible it was not to be able to protect one's family. Without a doubt, Carlos had been emotionally retraumatized by COVID and the intimate violence and loss that it had brought into his world.

CARE IN THE TIME OF COVID

Although COVID added exponentially to the burdens of daily life for low-income Latino youth and their families, my interviews revealed a pattern of resilience and commitment to collective well-being. Family members stepped up and took care of each other. In a pattern that had fallen into place before COVID, much of the caretaking responsibility fell on the shoulders of the second generation, who were the most educated and financially stable in their families. In pre-COVID interviews, the vast majority of participants told me that they were committed to doing whatever they had to do to ensure the well-being of their family. This often invisible labor typically entailed taking time away from work or studies to translate documents, pay bills, or negotiate with a landlord for an extension on rent. Their care work also included sending money home to supplement family wages or fill gaps left by unemployment. To help their families survive COVID and the economic crisis that accompanied it, participants had to continue with their regular care-work duties as well as take on new tasks, such as helping younger siblings with remote school, sharing information about the virus—especially with non-English-speaking family members—and coordinating financial support for struggling relatives outside of the United States.

Navigating COVID also demanded interacting with federal and state governmental bureaucracies. Social supports were available for U.S. citizens and residents, but as Rebeca's dad's situation revealed, accessing those supports was not always straightforward. Thus, youth in this study, because they were fluent in English, educated about basic governmental processes, and, perhaps most importantly, practiced in advocating for themselves and their families, typically took the lead in filling out applications and figuring out eligibility for different types of relief.

Only a few parents in this sample spoke English; those who did not faced a major barrier to navigating U.S. governmental programs, and their children had to step in as application translators. Amanda's experience was typical for many in this sample. She had to help her mom with an unemployment application after her New York City workplace temporarily shut down. Amanda's task extended beyond figuring out the logistics of the application to finding a way to explain to her curious and nervous mom what she was doing each step along the way. Adding to the challenge, Amanda was living outside of New York at the time, so they went through the process over the phone.

> The first stimulus check, for some reason, was very delayed for her, as with the current one. And so she doesn't understand what's happening,

and it usually falls on my sister and me to try to figure out what's happening. I had to help her fill out her unemployment application because she couldn't really do it herself and I had to explain to her. I had to help her apply for food stamps from a distance as well.

Julia also had to help her family deal with the COVID bureaucracy from afar, as well as make sure that her family members knew what the COVID risk level was in their San Diego community. Family care work was not new for Julia, but it took on added urgency and seriousness during the pandemic.

Because my mom speaks English but doesn't feel very confident with it and my grandparents don't speak English, I usually end up making phone calls for them, doing research for them, finding things that they need online, and showing them where to find them. I've also now kind of extended to some other people in the family. I tend to be their translator when they do appointments now in COVID. They'll dial me, and I'll translate doctor's appointments. . . . Or like section 8 sent us this letter, and they'll just send me pictures and, you know, I walk them through the steps of whatever that is. This has been my job since I was young, so it makes sense to not stop that. . . . Now I've taken it upon myself to be in the know about COVID restrictions in California.

The care work that participants were doing in order to help family members navigate the COVID bureaucracy and make sure their basic needs were met was not new, but the economic crisis accompanying COVID, several said, had brought new financial caretaking responsibilities. Participants had sent money home once in a while before COVID, but rarely had they felt that, without their support, their family's basic security would be at risk. Lisa, for example, had to step up to cover her mom's rent.

In March, my mom realized that she wouldn't be able to pay rent. And so, you know, for me it wasn't even a question, I just said, "Of course . . . ," like, "I will step up and I will pay whatever amount we need to pay." . . . When everything was shutting down, there was a lot of eviction protection . . . but my landlord . . . never told us these things. We were just under the assumption that we would have to pay. And fortunately, I was still getting paid from my job. . . . We just felt this pressure, like, "Okay, we have to make sure that we're paying the rent because we don't want to be evicted."

Lisa was in a position to help her family in large part because she had a job with benefits, a product of her Amherst degree and Amherst networks. In this important way, educational mobility helped her take care of her family and helped them survive. What it did not allow her to do, however, was to erase all of her family's hardships and vulnerability. And while she was helping her family survive, Lisa had to spend the savings she had put aside to help herself get ahead.

Heidi also had to step up her financial support for her family. The money she raised from starting a Go Fund Me page for her parents when her dad got COVID and could no longer work turned out to be only a stopgap measure in the midst of a much larger problem. Luckily, she was able not only to work full-time during the summer before her senior year but to take on extra hours in her campus job once the semester started and apply for emergency funding from Amherst. She sent home everything she could from these sources. "During the pandemic, I gave a lot more money . . . I probably gave, like, around $1,000 and $2,000 during the summer to my family. And then during this semester . . . I gave about $1,000 to them." After Heidi graduated in December 2020, she immediately went to work full-time so that she could continue supplementing her parents' income. Like Lisa, Heidi was able to help her family survive COVID, but doing so required sacrificing her own plans and ambitions, including renting her own apartment.

The care work that students did often extended to family who lived outside of the United States, for most of whom COVID had compounded other social ills in their family's home country, like poverty, unemployment, violence, and insecurity. Zaida's mom was from a small community in the north of Honduras. Even when times were good, her family in Honduras struggled financially. Indeed, it was their poverty and insecurity that motivated Zaida's mom to leave Honduras in the first place. Her mom had wanted out, but just as important was her desire to be able to send money home to help those who stayed behind, which was most of her family. Now a young adult herself, Zaida had taken on the transnational caretaking responsibilities that her mom had shouldered since she was a new immigrant to the United States.

In the fall and winter of 2020, Honduras was hit by two devastating hurricanes—Hurricane Eta followed two weeks later by Iota. Already reeling from COVID, a long-standing economic crisis, and high levels of political and vigilante violence, the storms pushed many poor and working-class Honduran families to the brink of ruin, Zaida's family included. Zaida took the lead in rallying financial and material support. She knew that she was privileged to have networks of Amherst friends who could give a lot more relative to anyone else in her immediate family's network. So she tapped into her social capital and launched a fundraising campaign.

My uncle is there with my two cousins. They all got COVID apparently, but luckily, they recovered. But then they were severely hit by the storms.

So I did a lot of outreach on Instagram. And people sent a bunch of donations, like item donations. Then a lot of my friends from Amherst sent money donations. So I was able to raise $800 that helped us pay for the boxes that we sent. . . . It's stressful. But we still felt good that we were providing items for our family and everyone in the immediate community.

Like Zaida, Carlos was Honduran and had family there. When COVID struck, Carlos was especially worried about his elderly grandmother. He intimately knew the insecurity that encased her life because he had lived it with her until he migrated to the United States as a young teenager. Although he had seen and experienced hard times in Honduras, he knew that things had gotten much worse since he left. Luckily, Carlos's uncle, a U.S. citizen, was able to get Carlos's grandma a tourist visa. She came to the United States and was living with Carlos and his mom at the time of our interview. Carlos was thankful that she was safe for now, but he knew that the dire situation in Honduras threatened her future security.

My grandma is here now. . . . Because over there, I mean, she has my uncle, but it's really hard to find a job and be able to survive . . . and having to deal with the violence. . . . And these gang members started asking her for money, "rent" they call it. And initially they asked for $1,000 cash. They threatened that they were going to kill my grandma and my cousin, who's only eleven. We had to keep sending money. . . . My grandma always says we've been displaced multiple times, starting with the war. If it's not the war, earthquakes, it's gang violence. And then COVID.

Carlos's story provides further evidence that COVID not only initiated new trauma but magnified the preexisting traumas and stresses experienced by many families and highlighted the transnational context in which they take care of each other.

Emily was also part of a tight-knit transnational family. She was born and spent much of her childhood in rural Ecuador. She still considered Ecuador home, and most of her extended family was still there. Ecuador has been struggling economically and politically for a long time, and COVID only exacerbated these challenges. Most critically, in Emily's estimation, COVID made the already dire employment landscape "hopeless," directly impacting her family. Emily was a couple of years beyond graduation when I talked to her about the impacts of COVID on her life, and she had an excellent job doing public health research for the City of New York. This job was preparing her for medical school and also providing her with the financial stability to help support needy family members in both the United States and Ecuador. She was partnering with her aunt, who also had a stable job, to make sure money was flowing home whenever it was needed.

> We've been sending a lot of money back to Ecuador because nobody has an income there. All of our family members have no income . . . so when we provide them a little bit of money, it seems like a lot of money. So we've been sending a lot of money back home. Um, but, fortunately nobody has had COVID and everybody has been safe.

Emily credited her strong educational credentials for putting her in a place to help her family. At the same time, the "little bit" of money she was able to send was not enough to make their lives truly secure.

Whereas helping family members in the United States navigate the government bureaucracy and stepping up to provide financial support for family both inside the United States and in their home country were the themes that dominated my COVID-focused interviews, another theme garnered almost as much stage time. Those with younger siblings found themselves putting a lot of time and energy into supporting remote schooling. For participants who were at home, being on sibling duty almost full-time while attending school remotely themselves made it challenging to stay on top of their own work. Yet, they told me, there was no other way. Most of their parents didn't speak English, and many had little formal education. Parents were therefore simply not positioned to play the role of remote-school teacher. Even if they had been capable linguistically and academically, inflexible work schedules would have made it impossible for most. As excellent students themselves and also technologically savvy, participants were the best suited in their family networks to support remote schooling.

Antonio returned home to his small town in southern New Jersey as soon as the Amherst campus shut down. He knew he would be needed to help out with his younger sister. His mom and stepdad worked long hours, and his mom, while a strong advocate for education, had not completed high school. Antonio knew that if he did not step up, his sister would lose a year of schooling. While Antonio had always thrived academically, his sister had encountered many learning challenges. Even while attending school in-person, she had a hard time focusing and learning new concepts. She needed a lot of extra help, which was not always available at their underresourced public school. When the school shut down and shifted to remote learning, there were literally no school-based resources available to support his sister.

> They basically gave her a packet of work. I guess if you're a super-smart first-grader who's very self-directed . . . you could do that by yourself, but

it's basically the parent who becomes the teacher. In my case, I was the teacher, because my mom is really busy and she didn't even finish her formal education. . . . From the beginning, I just knew that I had to do it, because it was very difficult for my mom to help her, and then my dad was always at work too. So I just took that upon myself because I feel like I didn't want to see her get behind any more than she already was.

It was difficult, but Antonio managed to finish the semester while simultaneously helping his little sister over the finish line. When I spoke with Antonio two years into the pandemic, his investment of time and energy had seemingly paid off. He told me that his sister was doing much better in school, had developed more confidence, and had taken on responsibilities within the family. He was thrilled. It is easy to see how it was that many young kids who had no sibling or other family member who was able to step in and pinch-hit quickly fell through the cracks when schools closed down in the pandemic.

Lisa also felt a strong sense of responsibility for her brother Jose's educational success. As I detailed earlier, Jose struggled to finish his senior year remotely and fell into a pattern of anxiety and panic attacks. Suspecting that Jose's mental health problems were closely entangled with his school struggles, Lisa committed herself to tackling both, hoping that success in one area would facilitate success in the other. Jose managed to graduate from high school, and to Lisa's delight, he applied for and was accepted into the local community college. Still living at home during this time, Lisa accompanied him through his first college semester.

I definitely have been very involved with his education. I think something he struggled with a lot going into college was . . . time management and how to even do assignments. . . . The high school we went to was severely underresourced. The teachers didn't give us much guidance. And so we had to learn to do a lot of these things on our own. And one thing I realized is that my brother didn't know how to construct an essay. Like, he had all the thoughts, great ideas, but he didn't know how to write.

So Lisa became Jose's English and writing teacher.

Through this experience, Lisa realized how the inequalities that had framed secondary schooling for her and Jose were now impacting his ability to do community college work remotely. While Amherst College faculty received stipends to get training in remote pedagogies and on how to support students in a remote context, faculty at Jose's community college were left to figure things out on their own. Most of Jose's classes ended up being asynchronous, meaning he listened to taped lectures and then had to do assignments on his own, leaving little room for him to establish any kind of connection with his teachers and providing no opportunities to ask for help. He was lost. Lisa tried to pick up the slack.

> So he never got to talk to his teacher. It was all virtual discussion boards and only doing readings and then having to write the assignments, and so I really had to guide him step by step. It was really difficult for me. . . . I just felt like . . . he has not been prepared for this at all. And he would get really frustrated. . . . He's really hard on himself. And I think when he realizes that he's not able to do something, that takes a toll on his self-esteem. And so . . . I would take time out of my weekends to really spend the day with him and say, "Okay, we're going to do these assignments."

En route to a doctoral program when COVID hit, Lisa was interested and skilled in teaching. And so she was confident that she could guide Jose through his courses. She was successful. The next time around, however, she knew he would have to manage on his own.

Sony (who used "they"/"them" pronouns) also had a younger sister who struggled academically. Though overwhelmed with their own schoolwork, Sony felt that they owed it to their sister and to their parents to step in to help. Their feelings of obligation were genuine, rooted in knowing that while school had always come easily for them and they had reason to be optimistic about their academic future beyond Amherst, their sister had always had a hard time, and she would probably never have the same opportunities. This had taken a toll on her self-esteem as well as on her mental health. As Sony set their sights on graduate school, they were determined to help get their sister through a remote semester of community college. When I interviewed Sony, they were in the thick of it.

> My sister asked me to help her with some of her schoolwork. . . . I'm already stressed out with having to write all these papers myself . . . and I feel really stressed all the time having to help my sister. . . . She had, in prior semesters, basically flunked out. . . . So I really wanted to help her . . . with this English course, to at least pass that course, which she did. . . . She basically passed all her classes. I was like, "Woohoo!" . . . And she had a lot of emotions, so sometimes I'd be like, "Hey it's going to be okay."

Sony's work paid off. Not only did their sister pass her class, but Sony felt like the two of them got closer in the process. Of course, she had a long road ahead to graduation and then into a career, but Sony felt that she had built some momentum. No matter how much pressure and work it had put on Sony, they would not have done things any other way. As Sony said reflectively, what good would their own success be if their sister failed out of school?

EDUCATIONAL MOBILITY AS BASIC PROTECTION

While life during COVID proved difficult for youth and their families, it would have been a lot worse, most concluded, without the protections provided by their educational credentials and connections to Amherst College. These protections came in the form of direct cash and resource support from the college for those who were still students and well-paying remote jobs for recent graduates. Participants also talked about the leverage that their educational training gave them when confronting dangerous mis-information about the virus and vaccines that was circulating in many of their families and communities.

When COVID caused the campus to shut down in March 2020, Amherst reimbursed students for the room and board that they were not using that spring. Everyone I interviewed who was still a student during COVID said that they used that money to shore up their family's finances. Then, when fall came, Amherst gave students the choice of studying remotely and, for those on full financial aid, receiving a generous financial credit for not utilizing the room-and-board portion of their scholarships. A few students told me that while they wanted to return to campus in the fall, they could not in good conscience pass up the money that the college was offering if they stayed home. For many of the families in this study, this financial support from the college proved to be a lifeline.

Noel was one of the students who chose to take the housing stipend and stay home for the fall semester of his senior year. The money provided a safety net when family members got COVID and his parents couldn't work.

Since we got COVID, I've been able to help with some bills and stuff like that. . . . I was wanting to go back to campus, but the thing that held me back the most was that I was afraid that something was going to happen to my family, like potentially getting sick, which happened, and that I wasn't going to be able to do much to help out if I was all the way at Amherst. And I wouldn't have had the extra money to help either. . . . Financially, the emergency fund has been able to provide that protection, like for emergency bills. That's been a huge boost that's been felt by my family. And yeah, and like, it's little things where I see the impact of having Amherst ties. . . . Whether it be certain friends from Amherst or professors or mentors . . . it's impactful to know I have a base of support that can help us out as a family. . . . So far, what the institution has done, I respect and admire. Like being able to provide stipends for those who were going to be doing remote work, being able to have the Student Emergency Fund established. Or simply, you know, like taking off the work-study requirement and giving a grant to cover that.

Noel's narrative revealed not only the benefits of direct material support but also the psychological and emotional comfort of knowing that there was a safety net in place, as well as a strong network of committed faculty and peers who would help if needed.

The college's financial supports for students extended beyond cash pay-outs. It also paid for the technology necessary to make remote learning feasible and rewarding, including new laptops and hot spots for those who did not have internet services at home. Sony expressed deep gratitude for the technological support they received, crediting it for allowing them to finish the semester strongly while sharing the perks with their sister, whose community college was unable to offer any support.

> I feel very lucky actually. I feel very supported. Because we got sent back home and then the COVID emergency fund sprouted. I actually got a new laptop from the fund. I was like, "Hey, I need a new laptop." And I got it, no questions asked, which to me was very surprising. No loans, so I was like, "Whoa!" So definitely it has helped me in that regard, because one, I got a newer and faster laptop, which is great for school, and two, I was actually able to pass down the old slow laptop I had before to my sister, because she was working on a really old Chromebook. So I think highly of the school, especially with its response to COVID-19. Especially when I look around to, like, other colleges and, like, their response, I'm very grateful that I'm at Amherst.

Similarly, while Heidi felt increased pressure to keep her family finan-cially afloat during COVID, she felt like she had a partner in the college, which, when her family needed her in the fall of 2020, provided needed money as well as the technological support to continue school from home.

> Um, yeah, so I have gotten a range of financial supports, like access to internet, having a place to live for a little bit [in the spring of 2020]. . . . And I definitely think . . . the financial support has been crazy. Because, like, first of all, the CARES Act paycheck. . . . I also got another $1,000—I don't remember if it's $1,000, $1,500, but around that—because I needed extra money for rent. And then towards the end I needed to move out, and I needed money for gas and someone from the college came and slipped money under my door. . . . I was like, thank the Lord! So financially, my family has

definitely benefited because, like I told you, I gave a good chunk of the money that I [received] for rent to them.

Many of the students who participated in this study had already graduated by the time COVID hit, and my interviews with them gave me a glimpse into how their educational mobility was impacting their lives off campus and beyond college. Although alumni did not have access to the Amherst Emergency Fund or the CARES Act payments that the college distributed, almost all credited their Amherst education for putting them in secure, well-paying jobs that allowed them to work remotely and thus take off some of the financial pressure for family members who lost wages.

Gloria was almost two years beyond graduation when COVID arrived. She was working as a paralegal in Chicago and had her eye on shifting to a larger, more prestigious, and better-resourced firm. She got the job, which she credited with easing the way for her and her family through the worst of the pandemic.

> I have a strong feeling that they . . . saw that I went to Amherst College and they recognized that. So that alone helped me have this job where I have income stability and have the opportunity to work from home. . . . I think also, I've always been independent, but I feel like I grew even more independent while at Amherst. So I've been able to use what I learned. I've used those skills to help my family through this.

Gloria's higher salary and ability to work remotely were all the more important because one of her younger brothers was immunocompromised. The fewer the number of people in their home who had to venture out into the world the better. And when her dad was temporarily laid off from his factory job, her salary helped keep them afloat.

Julia was thriving before COVID. She was living in an apartment that she loved, had gotten her first pet—a little dog—and was working in a top Boston law firm. She was well positioned economically and emotionally going into the pandemic.

> I was extremely lucky, to not lose my job and also to not have the kind of job where I'm required to be at a place. I've been able to just fully work from home, for almost a year now, without it changing anything about my job. I got a pay cut for a little while, which, again, it was nothing, you know what I mean? It was not—it wasn't anything that changed my quality of life in the way that I know some people have had to deal with in the middle of COVID-19. I have felt extremely lucky that I haven't been affected in that way.

Julia reflected on "how crazy" it was that her grandfather had been a *bracero* (guest worker) in the fields of California and now she had a law degree and a fancy job. Educational mobility had changed her life. Yet her mobility had not erased all of her family's struggles or her worries about her family. Nor had it lessened the care work she did for them. For Julia, the main benefit of educational mobility was knowing that she was going to be okay and that she was finally in a position to help her family be okay too. Her family was still poor, but they were more secure than they would have been without her professional position. To be sure, COVID then added further nuance to her thinking about educational and social mobility.

SURVIVING IT ALL

My research confirms what public health specialists have declared: for the socially marginalized, the impacts of the pandemic have been horrific. While Latinos as a demographic have been hit hard, within that group the undocumented and those in mixed-status families have been hit harder still. The impacts have been physical, in the form of death and illness, as well as mental and social. Indeed, mental health emerged as one of the most challenging aspects of the pandemic for the individuals and families in this study. The financial stress accompanying the virus both caused and exacerbated the mental health stresses that many experienced.

The places where families lived shaped the virus's impact on their lives and their ability to navigate the pandemic. Those who lived in global cities like New York, Houston, Los Angeles, and Chicago were the first hit by the virus and, at least initially, the hardest hit. Parents who were essential workers in these and other large cities had to take public transportation and go to work in tight spaces, often without any protection. And if and when they did get sick, as members of Alberto's family did, they received little assistance from underresourced and overcrowded hospitals and health clinics. Few had health insurance. Living in a more remote area was a protective factor at the beginning of the pandemic. But that protection did not last for long. Once the pandemic spread beyond large cities, those who lived in secondary cities, small towns, and rural areas were also hit hard and typically had no access to adequate local and community supports, unlike those who lived in major urban areas. Thus, place ultimately neither protected nor disadvantaged anyone, though the ways in which people experienced the virus were place-specific.

Wherever they lived, youth in this study emphasized that COVID had heightened the responsibility they felt as caretakers within their families. They displayed a critical understanding of how their educational privileges had better situated them to confront the crisis. The safety net they had created for themselves also helped to protect their families. This is to say, youth felt the responsibility to use their privilege to help their families through the crisis however they could. And yet they also came to realize that, although they were better positioned than their family members, they were still unable to protect their families as much as they wanted. Yes, they were able to create a safety net, but the net still had some gaping holes. Youth in this sample were discouraged, and some were grief-stricken, when they could do nothing but stand by and watch when family members fell through those holes.

For some, confronting the pandemic from a familial standpoint was comforting. Youth said that with the onset of COVID they realized how much they missed their family and yearned to be with those they loved. They similarly described a growing appreciation for their loved ones. Yet others talked about the stress and anxiety that came with the responsibility they felt for their parents and siblings in a context that was so uncertain. The expectation of reciprocity within immigrant families in this study was both a support and a burden in youth's lives, and COVID only intensified this expectation. As of this writing, youth continued to push ahead, striving for their goals, but also in some cases adapting them in order to meet new familial obligations and realities.

Chapter 6 | Redefining Success

I HAVE BEEN awed and inspired by the achievements of the youth I got to know over the course of this project. As of 2022, the vast majority had graduated from Amherst College and those who had not were poised to do so soon. Graduates had gone on to medical school, law school, PhD programs, and graduate school. Others had staked their claims in finance and marketing, tech, education, activism, and the nonprofit sphere. Two had been awarded Fulbright fellowships, and one had participated in Teach for America. They had achieved much of this while navigating a pandemic. The purpose of this chapter is not to detail these significant outcomes but instead to explain the process and consideration they brought to constructing their goals and how they came to define success. Family, community, and immigration are central to this story.

When I asked participants in this study about their goals and plans for the future, most prefaced their response by returning to the narrative of the immigrant bargain.[1] They would remind me that their educational successes were built on their parents' sacrifices. And so, as the vast majority looked to the future, they did not plan or dream as individuals but as members of an immigrant family for whom they felt a responsibility. This finding fits with the recent work of the anthropologist Andrea Flores, who found that aspiring immigrant youth in Nashville, Tennessee, redefined success and belonging to center family, care, and connection.[2] Just like Flores's interlocuters, participants in this study welcomed their responsibility to family, even though it was typically accompanied by complicated emotions and a heightened pressure to do well.

As I show throughout this book, by graduation time most participants had become critical of simplistic feel-good narratives that conflated educational and social mobility. Those who became more conscious of their own and their family's subordination also came to recognize the potential disjuncture between pathways that would lead to their personal intellectual and professional satisfaction and those that were most likely to uplift their families financially. Thus, some paid back their parents' sacrifices by sacrificing their own desires and passions and pursuing post-college paths that would earn them the most money and security. This choice compelled some to abandon their individualized conceptualizations of success and to aspire instead to do what they thought was best for their family. Others explained to family and peers that financial wealth might never be in the cards and that instead they were choosing to do meaningful work that would provide security.

No matter what they decided for their future, most participants were optimistic. Amherst had provided them with opportunities, connections, and skills, and they were confident that they could employ them to better their own life and their family's life.[3] Hope and optimism were basic nutrients that they relied on as they constructed their plans and that they were not willing to eschew, even knowing that the path to social mobility might be long, slow, and difficult.

In addition to centering family in their goal construction, several participants included their community and the greater society in their aspirational narratives about the future. At Amherst they had learned about the systemic roots of the inequalities and marginalization that impact low-income immigrant communities, and they yearned to do work that would lead to social change. Some pursued pathways to academia, nonprofits, activism, or policy work, areas where the link between their work and social change was direct. Others were headed toward jobs in finance, tech, or the corporate world, believing that they could use any wealth accumulated to spur development in their own and other low-income communities. Youth were ambitious and confident that they could make a difference.

In 2020 and 2021, when I returned to a subset of my sample to inquire about how they were faring in the context of COVID-19 and the accompanying economic crisis, our conversations were a bit more sobering. By this time, most had graduated from Amherst. Thus, I was able to see how their lives had progressed after graduation as well as how the pandemic was impacting their progress. It quickly became clear that while an elite college degree and the networks that Amherst provided had translated into basic protections, their educational mobility had not erased all barriers, especially for those who were undocumented. Despite ongoing barriers and some skepticism, every participant I interviewed believed that ultimately they were going to find a path that would benefit not just themselves but also their family members. In the midst of the pandemic, hope and optimism seemed more essential than ever.

PAYING IT BACK AND PAYING IT FORWARD

Maria was part of the 1.5 generation—those who came to the United States as children. Her migration started not in a poor community, as was the case for most 1.5-generation and adult participants in this study, but in a gated urban community in Colombia. Maria told me that for as long as she could remember she had aspired to reclaim the status and material comfort that her family had enjoyed before coming to the United States. When she, her mom, and her brother migrated from Colombia to New England, they left behind a life of upper-middle-class luxury. As she explained it, "We were surrounded by wealthy people. I guess we were probably wealthy too." In Colombia, Maria's mom had not worked outside of the home but devoted her time instead to Maria and her older brother.

Three weeks before Maria was born, her dad was killed for his role in a narco-trafficking scheme. Though Maria never had the opportunity to know him, the money he gained through his informal economic work padded her early childhood with material comforts. But because of the war and her father's involvement in the narco-economy, Colombia was never a secure place for their family. So when Maria's mom was presented with the opportunity to travel to the United States with her children on a tourist visa, she grabbed it. It all happened very quickly. "One day my mom just sat us down and said we're traveling to the United States. I have the opportunity and we have to go now." Maria was nine.

They settled in a small industrial city in southern New England (where Maria's mom still lives). At the time of their migration, unemployment and crime were high in the city, and there were few opportunities for residents to better their circumstances. Maria's family experienced downward social mobility—from a gated community to public housing, from social status to social stigma. Maria's mom, despite having earned a college degree in Colombia, did not speak English and had no internationally recognized credentials. She got a job in a nail salon and had to learn how to navigate life as an undocumented immigrant living paycheck to paycheck. Even as a young child, Maria recognized all that her mom had sacrificed and how hard the transition to the United States had been for her.

> I'm always trying to tell her, like, "You did it. You lost part of your life having to come here and work under the table." But she doesn't see it that way. She doesn't see all the hard work or all the things that she had to sacrifice. I don't think she saw it as, like, "Oh, this is something I've never done and it sucks." I think for her it was just like, "Oh, this sucks, but I have to do it for my kids."

Her mom's sacrifices guided Maria's educational decisions as she moved through childhood and into high school and shaped her goals and what she envisioned for her future. Most importantly, Maria became determined that she would not be poor as an adult and that her mom would not be poor when she was old. When Maria, her mom, and her brother obtained U.S. residency and new doors of opportunity opened, Maria made it her mission to attend a top-ranked college. She was a strong student, and the counselors at her magnet school supported her decision to aim high. Maria was not principally motivated, however, by her own academic passions and interests. She was driven instead by her desire to secure a path to financial success and ultimately to be able to give back to her mom and to her community.

> College wasn't the main goal, it was just, like, sort of the process. And that's how I always understood college. Like, it was just a step for me to become financially stable, to become wealthy. That's always been the goal since high school. . . . Growing up, it was just like, "I want to be wealthy so I can first of all give back to my mom, but then give back to the community, because that's why I'm here."

Like other participants in this study, Maria expressed a fervent loyalty to those who had helped her along her path, aware that her immigrant family and community formed the base of her mobility ladder.

At Amherst, Maria double-majored in economics and law, jurisprudence, and social thought in the belief that these majors would provide her with the best career opportunities. Outside of class she read voraciously, focusing on texts about race, class, and inequality. With each text she devoured, she became more conscious of the inequities structuring her home community and her immigrant family's experiences. Eventually she became an activist and an outspoken campus leader on racial and immigrant justice issues.

And then, in a moment of exhaustion and high anxiety following a major campus protest in which she had played a leadership role, Maria decided that she needed to step back to reflect on where this activist path was taking her. After "doing the math," she concluded that her activism was taking her away from her primary goal, which was to pay back her family and community. As much as she wished it were otherwise, she believed that they needed her wealth more than they needed her ideals. So she switched her focus from activism to a career track that she believed would launch her into the upper class. In her telling of it, she buckled down and started to look at Amherst differently, not as a place of social inequality but as a place whose resources and networks could help her, her family, and ultimately her community get ahead.

> I realized I either tap into these resources and get a good job, or I come back home to nothing. Like, I have to be able to provide. . . . My brother and I chose majors that would lead us to good jobs. . . . I tell my mom, "You don't have to worry about your future because I'll be working and I'm going to make sure you're fine." I know that I'm my mom's provider in the future . . .

so for me it wasn't a choice. It was like, you either do or you don't. And when I did the finance track, when I did interviews, I always felt uncomfortable. I always felt insecure. Like, I looked around and I'm like, "This is definitely not my place." But it was just like, was there a choice? No . . . this is what I have to do.

When Maria graduated from Amherst, she had already secured a consulting job with a top firm in a large northeastern city. There she would be close to her brother, who was also working in consulting. Their plan was to earn as much money as possible so they could get themselves and their mom on a secure financial footing, and then they would start a company together through which they could lead development efforts in their home city. When we last spoke, Maria was working closely with her brother to devise a retirement plan for their mom while strategizing about their own entrepreneurial futures. They were aiming for the kind of financial success that would enable them to provide for their mom, live comfortably themselves, and be social change agents.

Like Maria, all the youth I interviewed were savvy about what was necessary to translate an elite degree into future social mobility and to contribute to meaningful social and community betterment. Many bemoaned the guidance of academic advisers who urged them to follow their passions; they felt that they needed to be more practical, to choose pathways to securing their economic future and living near family. This is not to say that aspiring youth did not nurture their intellectual desires and interests along the way. Most told me that they loved the rigorous academics of Amherst and made a point of taking courses and choosing majors aligned with their intellectual curiosity. Nevertheless, they felt that they could not afford to make academic and career decisions based solely on what interested them. Lacking an economic safety net, they knew that their dreams and their plans had to be realistic and low-risk. Not all of them were as determined as Maria was to become "rich," but they were certainly committed to making practical choices that would protect their own and their family's material well-being.

For example, both of Angelica's parents had demanding low-wage jobs that provided no flexibility, and so the household depended on her labor and organizational leadership. Angelica continued to fulfill many of her familial obligations while she was at Amherst, and she never lost sight of her responsibility to her younger siblings. She passed up opportunities like summer internships and study abroad so that she could be home with her family when school was not in session, and she remained on call for them when it was. Angelica felt frustrated by the burden of these responsibilities, but she was also grateful for her parents' hard work and the opportunities that their sacrifices had afforded her. Her story is a powerful example of the complexity of family loyalty and the stress that can result when expectations of reciprocity are high.[4]

> My goal was always, I need a job that pays well. Once I got into a college, it became getting a very well-paying job. You know, getting something that will make me a lot of money rather than something that I want to do. You know, maybe what I want to do will give me a lot of money. Maybe I'll be one of the fortunate few that happens to, but I don't have the luxury of, like, thinking about, you know, what do I want to do. . . . At first, I thought maybe math will get me somewhere, because you need math everywhere. But then, when I chose my major my adviser said, "Do something that you love. Do something that you're passionate about, because this is the one chance that you get." But I needed to find something that will make me money, because that's what my family needs. . . . And then, you know, now as a senior, people are asking me, "What are you going to do after graduation?" . . . I'd say, "I'm going back to California," because I really have no other option. . . . Even though things are tense with family, you know, I have my younger siblings to think about. And I always feel that responsibility. I know my counselor and adviser and other people don't approve of this. They're like, "You need to be your own person. You need to move away from that." But if I do, who's going to take care of them? You know, who's going to do all these things for them? Someone has to do it. And my parents can't do everything. And so maybe if I'm there I can help alleviate some of that pressure, even if it's at my expense.

Although Angelica's relationship with her parents was often stressed, she was committed to helping them and even more committed to supporting her siblings. Mostly, she wanted her siblings to have an easier time than she did navigating home and high school and constructing plans and goals for the future. When she considered her future plans, it was them she thought about first. So Angelica went home after graduation, molding her goals and plans to fit her family's needs.[5]

When Angelica first arrived home in 2018, she felt at a loss. She missed the structure of her classes and schoolwork, and she was anxious about finding a job. She had not built networks at Amherst, but she realized that she could still tap into her networks in California. So she reached out to every high school teacher she knew to ask if they had any job leads. Her AP math teacher got back to her quickly to tell her that her alma mater was hiring tutors. She applied, was hired immediately, and went to work in the same building that had been her high school home. To her surprise, she loved the job. After a year of tutoring, Angelica applied for a dual graduate degree program in math and education, was accepted, and began combining a high school student teaching job with graduate school classes. She came to appreciate that, while teaching would never make her rich, it would give her security and allow her to stay near her family. As a bonus, the work would be meaningful, allowing her to give back to the community in which she came of age. Plus, if teaching failed to cut it financially, she would have a master's degree in math and could go into accounting, which was certain to pay a higher salary.

Much of the meaning that Angelica gleaned from teaching high school emanated from the connections she felt to her students. Like her, they were Latino and working-class, and many had undocumented parents. Angelica understood their struggles and the challenges they would face throughout their lives, and she felt tremendous joy when they responded to her with trust and to her teaching with enthusiasm and interest. She felt like she was making a difference.

When COVID hit, Angelica watched with frustration and sadness as many of her students were forced to attend school from crowded homes where stress was high and food was insecure. She became more politicized and more critically conscious of the inequalities that framed the educational system, her community, and her own life.

> There are some kids who have told me, "Ms. S, I'm sorry, but, like, I can't pay attention right now because my little sister's crying and my mom's at work, so I have to take care of them." I'm like, "Just go do what you need to do. The notes will be in class. If you need help, I can make myself available. The priority is your well-being and your family's. . . . We'll work through it together." But you know, it's given me a glimpse into what I went through in high school, but in a completely, you know, next-level way, because I didn't have to do it online. You know, I had all these responsibilities too, and at least I got to escape for a bit. They don't have that. You know, they're trapped . . . and I don't know, it just makes me angry.

Angelica's heightened consciousness about her students' hardships and her own opportunities made her responsibility to her own family feel a bit less burdensome. She found it emotionally easier when she had to rethink her goals after using the money she'd been saving for life after graduate school to support her family instead when her parents' hours were cut back during the pandemic. She was grateful that, although remote teaching was difficult for many reasons, it allowed her to be an advocate for struggling students and to be home with her siblings, where she could assist them with school during her breaks. Angelica redefined success to encompass caring for those she loved. Ultimately, she came to appreciate that her education had given her the best shot of anyone in her family at securing a good job and weaving a family safety net, and she came to accept the reality that for now it was up to her to play the provider role. All the while, she continued to advocate for her students and siblings, both paying it back and paying it forward.

Zaida, like Maria and Angelica, went to college expecting that her education would put her on the path to social mobility and that she would be able to pay back her parents' sacrifices. Since attending high school in Miami, Zaida had wanted to work in the criminal justice system. Her interest was sparked when one of her closest teenage friends went to prison. At Amherst, Zaida never lost sight of her goal, doing everything she could to support her friend and others like him who had been impacted by the underresourced and biased criminal justice system.

> I took a class in prison last semester, and I have my friend who is in prison, and . . . I want to work in prisons and kind of helping them, like the whole transition process back into the community. . . . Like, if I want to do boots on the ground work, it's like a master's in social work. . . . So I'm kind of leaning towards that.

There was one problem with this goal. Zaida knew that this professional path was certain to disappoint her parents, who assumed that a college education would lead to a high-paying job. Social work would not be that. When she was first thinking about college, she had believed the same thing. Yet she eventually came to realize that, even if she ultimately decided to go to law school (her parents' preference), it would be a long time before she'd be "rich." So one step in constructing her goals and future plans was explaining to her mom that, while she was confident that, as an educated person, she would have financial security, she was never going to be wealthy.

> And they're like "Yeah, when Zaida starts working she's going to buy me a car." And I actually want to do that and just, like, have enough money to, like, if I can't live with them, to be able to support them, like, the most I can. So then, like, my mom can stop working and just chill. Because she always comes, she's always joking . . . "My daughters are not going to help me once they have money." . . . I think my mom's very supportive of whatever I do. She's very much like, "Okay, yeah, that's good." Because we're still, like, doing well in school, we're not like other kids she sees nowadays. So she really supports all of it. But I think she also kind of confuses the fact that we're getting a higher education. She thinks that's, like, an automatic way

to get rich. I'm like, "No, Mom, I'm probably not going to be making that much money. . . ." When I told her I wanted to continue school, she's like, "Why do you need to continue school? You've already been there for four years." I was like, that's not, that's not really realistic. I mean, for some careers it is. For the econ major, that's totally different. But I think that's the only thing, so, like, immigrants assume once you have a college degree . . . I don't even think they really understand that master's and doctorates exist. They think once you do your four years, you're going to be chillin'. I'm like, no.

When we last spoke, Zaida was positioned to graduate from Amherst with a double major in psychology and Arabic. She had thrived at Amherst, acing her courses, working as a research assistant in the psychology department, and serving as a student leader in one of Amherst's equity and inclusion initiatives. As graduation approached, Zaida was weighing a decision about where to go to graduate school. She had applied to all the top social work graduate programs in the country. Not surprisingly, she was accepted to all of them. But while the Ivy League and other elite programs beckoned, Zaida felt pulled toward home. Her dad's mental health was not good, her mom missed her, and others in her family needed her support. Ultimately, Zaida bucked much of the advice she received to grab the opportunity to study in one of the country's top programs; if she did, she was told, many doors of opportunity would open. Instead, Zaida decided that it was time to go home. She would study at a state university that had a strong program and had offered her a robust financial aid package.

When I was doing the whole grad school process, I think my outlook on, like, academics and stuff changed a little bit. Because, like, when I applied to Amherst, at that point it's like, "Yeah, I just want to leave Florida." You know, experience something else. I'm over it, like, I'll just go wherever, wherever it takes me. And then now for grad school, my top pick is actually a Florida school, because I'm kind of just thinking my immediate goal is to be able to have a job that I can pay their [her family's] rent. . . . But I think I'm kind of set on the fact that I want to settle here for now, just to be able to help financially.

It wasn't the glitziest choice, but Zaida decided that going to school near home was the best choice for her and for her family and community. She had never looked back and was confident that she would find as much meaning and security in prioritizing family and home as she would have found if she had followed an individualized, Ivy-covered pathway.

ASPIRATIONAL LIMITATIONS: UNDOCUMENTED IMMIGRATION STATUS AND COVID

Although the immigrant bargain and giving back to family and community were central to the aspirational narratives I collected, not all youth were able to make good on the bargain, even with an Amherst degree. Participants' intersecting social positions—their race, class, gender, and legal status—shaped the ease or difficulty with which they moved through and beyond college and their opportunities to fulfill their end of the bargain. While my data show that any of these social positions could produce barriers to achievement, having an undocumented legal status emerged as the most obstinate challenge, and one that was intensified by COVID.

The sociologist Roberto Gonzales argues that because having an undocumented immigration status affects opportunities and outcomes with such breadth and depth, it operates as a master status, or the central identity category, in the lives of undocumented individuals and can override the privileges connected to other social positions like race, class, or gender.[6] While this argument does not point to a universal experience of living without documentation, it does suggest that legal status is perched atop an identity hierarchy. The experiences of the undocumented and DACA participants in this study support this conceptualization. Despite dreaming big and achieving impressive academic success, being undocumented or having DACA status dampened some youth's future prospects by limiting their ability to reach their mobility goals. Being undocumented in the time of COVID added yet another barrier.

Carlos left Honduras in 2006 to reunite with his mother and siblings, who had migrated to the United States several years earlier. After he failed to secure a tourist visa, his mom paid for him to travel undocumented with a *coyote* through Guatemala and Mexico to the U.S. border. The harrowing trip took two months. Carlos was detained at the U.S. border, where he was treated "like a dog" by border officials, he said later. When he was eventually released, he joined his mom and siblings in a small New England city. Not speaking a word of English, Carlos enrolled in public school. His entry into education was rough, but he ultimately did well academically. He received DACA status while in community college and transferred to Amherst that same year, graduating in 2017.

Amherst was not easy for Carlos. While he made good friends and took advantage of the "amazing academic opportunities" that Amherst provided, he struggled with depression and a persistent feeling of alienation. As he explained it, the trauma of being separated from his mom and siblings when he was young, living through two major earthquakes, and then having to endure a difficult border crossing had left their mark. Doubting that any other Amherst students could understand his life, he often felt very much alone. To make matters worse, he was living in the legal limbo of DACA status, which had become even more precarious with the election of Trump. As such, Carlos approached his postgraduation life with trepidation. He had ambitious goals—to be a broadcast journalist and live in Paris—and was highly motivated to help support his mom and grandmother, but he also knew that, at least for the time being, the cards were stacked against him.

> I graduated in December of 2017. At the time I was dealing with a lot of mental health disorders. A lot of it had to do with politics and how I felt that . . . everything was just coming to an end. And though I should have been very excited about my post-Amherst life, I knew that jobs that I applied to, that I interviewed for, would be asking about immigration status. . . . Trump had just won, and it was very early in his presidency, so DACA was even more at risk at the time. And like with my past, with anxiety and depression, that made everything just more stressful. . . . The only work that I could find was . . . being a teaching assistant [in an elementary school] . . . but that wasn't full-time. It was an on-call type of position. . . . Everyone imagines that you graduated from Amherst, and now the world's been opened up to you. It's not always the case.

Being overqualified for the jobs that he could find depleted Carlos's motivation. After a couple of years working in temporary positions, he decided that his best bet was to go to graduate school in pursuit of his goal of working in media broadcasting. School was the only place he knew where his status would not get in his way. Or so he thought. Carlos did his research and applied to the best programs he could find within a couple hours' drive from home. That way he could attend school and still help his mom and grandma. He orchestrated his plan perfectly. Then his DACA status emerged as a barrier.

> I got accepted into a really good graduate program. I got a fellowship, like, the President's Fellowship, which is rarely awarded and that would cover like half of my tuition for my master's in journalism. . . . However, because of DACA, I couldn't get a loan for the other part. So I did get accepted, I did get financial aid. But then I can't even get loans because of my status. So I had to say no.

Carlos was heartbroken and drained. He was determined and smart, and he had a prestigious college degree. He "had done everything right." And yet he found himself stuck. While his goals and plans were on hold, the bills kept coming. His family still needed his financial contribution. So he went back to waiting tables, the job he had while in community college. He became more depressed as he constantly had to answer questions from friends, family, and even strangers about why, with an Amherst degree, he was working as a server in a restaurant.

> And there are also, like, the cultural norms, cultural expectations, that can add stress to the whole situation. Like, if you go to college, you're expected from your family to get a good job. [They ask,] "Why aren't you working in your field?" And then, after a while, I had to return to working in a restaurant. And even the local people were like, "Oh my God, you went to Amherst. What are you doing here?" And having to explain was just so hard.

Carlos waited tables for several months, all the while applying to different positions in nonprofits and community groups, which he had been advised would be more open than private industry to hiring someone with DACA status. In the process, he pushed aside his thoughts of going into media and broadcasting and began to pursue a new goal. He would become a social worker, with the intent of putting his own life experiences to work by helping others who were similarly marginalized. Finally, after what he said seemed like forever, he got a job working for an antipoverty nonprofit organization in a large Latino community near his home. Carlos found meaning in the work, and now feeling more optimistic than he had in a long time about the future, he allowed himself to start thinking again about graduate school. He decided to apply to social work programs. This time around he did research in advance about which programs offered need-blind aid to undocumented and DACA students.

Unable to change his status, Carlos crafted his aspirations and definition of success to fit what was possible. He set his sights on becoming a mental health counselor for queer, undocumented youth—those who were facing the same identity struggles that he had faced during his own coming of age.

> I want more tools to be able to advocate at a greater level. Because I understand that . . . the more letters you add to your name, it definitely helps when it comes to the impact that your activism can have. And on an individual level, I want to be able to help those communities that lack access to mental health services—undocumented, migrant, LGBTQ communities that have been fleeing from discrimination. There were a lot of people that . . . came in the caravans that had experienced multiple, multiple hardships. . . . I want to become a therapist, a mental health counselor, to be able to help these communities. And part of me also wants to be able to do activism that causes, like, a greater impact, because there is a lack of opportunity. . . . So there's a

lot of things that led me to social work. And I do feel like the more I learn the more it allows me to not only advocate for myself but to advocate for my community.

Carlos's post-Amherst path was characterized by adaptation and resilience in the face of dashed dreams. When we last spoke in 2021, he had just begun graduate school for social work on a full-ride scholarship. He was still struggling with his mental health. COVID had been particularly tough on him and his family. He had lost his stepdad to the virus and become the sole income earner when his mom lost her job. Still, he assured me that he was doing all right. As difficult as the last few years had been for him, he told me that he was certain they would have been a lot worse if he had not graduated from college and had a degree that carried some prestige. He also felt really good about embarking on a career that would allow him to be a community leader and social change agent. Carlos's plan was to keep chipping away at the barricades in front of him. He reflected, "Is there another choice?"

Cesar also had DACA status. He migrated from Nayarit, Mexico, to Los Angeles with his mom when he was in elementary school. Although he did not endure the level of immigration-related trauma that Carlos did, he described feeling a general and persistent sense of insecurity from being undocumented. He too struggled while at Amherst. He had a close group of friends, all low-income and Latino, who kept him sane. "We all were struggling," he explained to me, "so we could just totally be ourselves."

Despite struggling socially and emotionally, Cesar did well academically in college. On paper he looked well positioned for medical school, which had long been his goal. And yet, following graduation, he came to realize that he faced barriers that he had not taken into account.

> After graduating, I was kind of at a loss about what my next step should be. Originally my plan had been to attend medical school. . . . But I'm undocumented. And I had heard a lot of horror stories . . . about how difficult it is to get into medical school if you are, and how difficult it is to get financial aid. . . . And to be honest, I think I let that fear sort of stop me from applying. Because, you know, people say that being undocumented stops you from going to college and succeeding in college. I was able to do that. But I think med school is even more daunting, so I sort of let that affect me, and I decided to not go.

Cesar tucked away his dream of medical school and started to think about other possible paths. In the meantime, he needed a job. He found one in a law firm. After a short stint there, he moved to another job, with the

City of Los Angeles. This job came with fantastic benefits and job security. It was not his dream job, but he reasoned that it was much better than most, and he appreciated the progressive politics that enabled him to be hired for a city government job despite having DACA status.

As Cesar launched into his new administrative position, he continued to ponder his STEM-based aspirations, trying to strike a mental balance between ambition and realism. He yearned for some guidance but didn't know where to turn. Though a good student, he had never felt comfortable reaching out to his professors, and he had not found a postcollege mentor.

> I majored in neuroscience, and it is something that still is interesting to me. I've sort of been toying with the idea of mixing that with technology and maybe doing AI learning, machine learning, which is, you know, sort of where it is headed. But I don't think there's someone that I could candidly ask for advice for something like that. And so, I guess, that's sort of where some of my hesitation comes from. . . . I'm the oldest and a lot of my friends are also first-generation, and so no one really knows how I would get that started. . . . Also, my path right now has sort of been survival, and I think sometimes I let that hold me back in regard to, you know, furthering education or things like that. . . . I know that I have Amherst, you know, a title of being an Amherst graduate, in my corner. And sometimes I wonder if that's enough to keep me going. . . . But I have to think about the fact that I am undocumented, and so insurance and benefits like the ones I have are incredible. Going to school and not having health insurance and all these things sort of compacting together, where, like, if something happened, like, I had to pay for a surgery and I was in school, I don't have the social support to be able to recover from that.

Cesar understood the barriers that were in his way. He recognized that not building relationships with professors at Amherst had left him without a mentor, and that his strong friendship groups with other low-income Latinos, while meaningful, were not that helpful in navigating a new career path. With this reality check, he decided, at least for the time being, to enjoy the security and opportunity he did have.

> Thankfully, this is a job that I can do from home, so COVID hasn't impacted me very much. I guess the way it has impacted me the most is that it's put my thoughts about going [back] to school sort of in the background, because it seems like, right now, you know, other members of my family aren't working, it's just me and my brother. And so, we're sort of having to keep the family going. And so, any thoughts about further schooling have kind of gone onto the back burner. . . . My brother and I help pay the meager cost for

our family, the rent and some of the bills and stuff like that. . . . My mom is also undocumented. . . . I constantly worry about her. She doesn't have a pension, and so how are we going to provide for her in the long run? And so, yeah, I'm trying to make my way into this world, but at the same time . . . I have my family to consider.

In this context, as his gratitude for his job security increased, his goals around neuroscience and AI moved further to the back of his mind.

Cesar was similar to many of my undocumented participants who told me that COVID prompted them to put their plans and goals on hold. COVID was a stark reminder of the precarity of undocumented life, and thus it motivated them to focus on their basic health and security as well as that of their family members. As I detailed in the last chapter, many of my participants' parents were essential workers in jobs with few protections against the virus and limited economic security. Although educational mobility was not enough to allow participants to overcome all the barriers of living with an undocumented status, it did allow almost all of them to secure remote work that provided a steady income and basic protections. During COVID, Cesar, like most participants, came to appreciate this privilege as never before.

U.S. citizen youth with undocumented parents also felt the weight of their precarious legal status increase during COVID. If they had been concerned only about their own security and well-being, they could have evaded the "multigenerational punishment" of undocumented migration, which placed their parents' legal vulnerability on their shoulders.[7] Most of them had graduated from Amherst and gone into professional jobs or graduate school and were thus in the privileged position of working or studying remotely. Yet every participant I interviewed during the pandemic told me that they felt the responsibility to use their own advantaged position in the labor market, or in graduate or professional school, to help protect their parents and other family members whose lives and work were more precarious. The implication was that they had to pragmatically analyze their goals in the evolving context of intensified stress, anxiety, and heightened family responsibility.

Isabela was in her second year of a doctoral program in pursuit of her goal to become a professor when COVID struck. As mentioned earlier, Isabela's mom, Victoria, being undocumented, did not qualify for federal support when she lost her job and then returned to work on reduced hours. Before COVID, Isabela's academic aspirations made practical sense. Though she knew she would never get rich as an academic, she believed that a PhD would put her in a position to get a good-paying job with the promise of tenure and meaningful work that would help make the world a better place for immigrant families. This security would, in turn, benefit her mom and her sister. She was committed to taking care of both of them. With COVID came the reminder of how uncertain the academic market could be. Many colleges and universities put hiring freezes in place in addition to temporary holds on the admission of new doctoral candidates. This new academic landscape shifted how Isabela thought about her future. Besides adding urgency to her plans, COVID also raised doubts.

> COVID shifted my perspective in the way that, now I'm thinking, like, well, maybe I don't go into academia because it's looking kind of grim. Some people are talking about the job market for us being bad. So I think that's part of the reason why I'm like, well, maybe I wouldn't be opposed if I'm not in academia beyond grad school. But in another way . . . it just heightens the urgency. . . . I need to stick to this timeline. Like, I can't mess up. . . . Like, I can't take a break. I need to get through this. . . . I mean, it's just more urgent because I don't know how long my mom's job is going to be there. I don't know anything. So I just need to, like, get it together and stick to a plan.

The urgency Isabela felt was intensified by her mom's mental health struggles. Isabela wanted to be home with her to lend direct support. But during the first year of the virus, travel restrictions prevented it. Then Isabela got COVID, which made her yearn for home even more. Ultimately, however, she decided that it would be best for everyone if she "stuck to her plan," which was to get through graduate school and get a job as quickly as possible. In the meantime, she would take on as much graduate student teaching as she could and send whatever money she could back to California to ease the burden she knew her mom and sister were carrying as they struggled in the virus's wake.

Noel, like Isabela, had academic ambitions. His goal was to become an immigration scholar and find a teaching position that would allow him to mentor aspiring youth from backgrounds similar to his own. He decided to go to graduate school, even knowing that the academic job market could be volatile and that there was no way to eliminate that risk. At the same time, the possibility of doing work that he loved and having the security of tenure encouraged him to continue his academic pursuits. Before COVID, he was confident of the viability of his plan. But COVID raised the stakes of his decision-making. Like Isabela, he felt new urgency and doubts. Then, just as COVID shut down the campus, Noel's biological dad, with whom he had recently reconnected and become close, was cited for an immigration violation and found himself at risk of being deported. Noel wanted to stick to his plan, and COVID and his dad's unfortunate encounter with Immigration and Customs Enforcement (ICE) added urgency to it.

COVID has added pressure to my goals. . . . It's just like, I have that feeling like there's not going to be any jobs by the time we graduate, so I'm using grad school as a security blanket. . . . Many people tell you like, "Yeah, you should take a break after you graduate, you know you've got to make sure that you want to do this or that you're willing to put yourself through six more years of this." And it's hard because . . . who can afford to take a year off? Or who can afford to be able to say, "I want to take a year off and, like, think about what I want to do?" . . . So, yeah, COVID has only exaggerated the need for me to get this [graduate school] done, done and over with.

Noel's words remind us that reflection is a privilege. Enjoying extended decision-making time is a privilege. Noel did not have the luxury of stepping back, pausing, and thinking about his future. His family was counting on him—there were bills that needed to get paid—and he had goals that he was anxious to reach.

Noel decided to keep moving forward. With his mom and dad's blessing, he applied to all the top graduate programs in his field and was accepted to most of them. In the end, however, he decided not to attend the top-ranked program, or the program with the adviser with whom he most wanted to work. Instead, he chose the program that offered him the largest stipend and was located in the place with the lowest cost of living. This formula would allow him to pursue his doctorate while helping his family financially and saving money for the future.

Indeed, as the narratives I collected make clear, the aspirations of this group of high-achieving, ambitious youth were centered foremost on pragmatic concerns and family responsibility, and for several, on a commitment to social change. While they had all achieved educational mobility, they had not yet fulfilled their end of the immigrant bargain. As youth planned their future, it was with an eye toward the impact of each step they took on the well-being of the family, kin, and community that had helped them along the way.

ALWAYS STRIVING, BUT NEVER ALONE

From the first interview I completed for this book, I have been struck by the thoughtfulness of my participants. Although they were still coming of age themselves, most tried to see the world from the perspectives of their immigrant parents and grandparents, and they took these perspectives into account as they made decisions about their own future. As such, few solely centered their own interests or passions when planning for the future. Instead, they positioned their own desires in relation to the needs and expectations of their parents and elders. And then, when they had determined the right balance, they constructed their goals and aspirations and redefined success on their own terms.

As youth moved through Amherst and beyond, their critical understanding of their social position and their family's and their prospects was both sharpened and heightened, and they came to more clearly see the inequalities that structured their lives. This consciousness in turn nurtured their commitment to family and community. I do not mean to romanticize immigrant families and communities. Instead, I would argue that the teamwork that enables migration, settlement, and survival in a new country remains central to the decision-making of the 1.5 and second generations even after they achieve individual educational mobility.

Some, like Angelica, initially resented the responsibility they felt to their immigrant family. They felt misunderstood by their parents as well as by their peers, professors, and advisers, all of whose expectations, frustratingly, were often in conflict. For example, while the message they got from parents was that family always came first, at school they were told that this was "their time" and they should do what was best for themselves as individuals. Knowing that they could not satisfy everyone sometimes triggered anxiety and stress. Even when they felt anxious and stressed, however, family obligation tended to win out eventually over the seduction of individual pursuit. Only follow-up research will tell if this tendency held.

The way youth formed their aspirations and planned their future depended a lot on the mosaic of their identities. Angelica, for example, told me that she thought she would have felt more freedom to carve a path independent of her family and community if she had been a son instead of a daughter. Nuances in social class mattered too. Those who came from the poorest families tended to feel the most stress as they calculated how their future path would pay off in terms of financial security. Yet the social position that intervened most by far in goal construction and future planning was legal status. Undocumented and DACA students confronted the most persistent barriers to meeting their goals. Independent of how well they performed in school, most told me that their aspirations had been limited by their undocumented status. Being undocumented limited the perks and options usually forthcoming with an Amherst diploma. Ben, a Colombian student, told me that he had wanted to pursue the humanities but took a corporate job because it had headquarters in Bogota; if he were ever deported, he would be in a place where he could still work. Carlos felt that he was not called back for interviews after he revealed his legal status, and Cesar put his medical school dreams on hold because he knew how difficult it would be to qualify for financial aid. I was often overwhelmed by the resilience demonstrated by undocumented students as they recalibrated their goals to fit the evolving legal and political realities of their lives.

COVID shifted opportunity structures and upped the stakes of success for everyone I interviewed. Whether from worrying about their own jobs and careers or about their parents' health and well-being, stress among youth was high. Here again, those who were most socially marginalized and vulnerable before COVID struggled the most. And yet even these youth were resilient, revising their plans, adjusting their expectations, and figuring out new ways forward. Extended adolescence had no place in the stories I collected; instead, those I interviewed were rushed into early adulthood by circumstances.

There is much that policymakers can learn from the life paths and goals of the high-achieving Latino youth whose stories I have shared. I conclude with suggestions for social, policy, and cultural changes that would harness the ambitions, smarts, and insights of this aspiring group of young people, while protecting the families and networks that are the core of their success.

Chapter 7 | Moving Forward

WHEN I FIRST met Gaby in 2016, she was obviously struggling. As I detailed in the opening of chapter 1, she felt out of place at Amherst and was torn between her shifting interests and passions and her family's expectations. She felt that she owed it to them to be successful, but what success looked like was unclear to her then. It needed to include financial security, to be sure, but she was searching for meaning beyond that.

When I spoke with Gaby again in 2021, much of the angst she was experiencing in 2016 had dissipated. So much had happened over the course of five years. Gaby had ultimately decided to follow her heart and leave STEM and premed to pursue her interests in education and the humanities—fields that she was confident would give her the best shot at achieving self-fulfillment while helping to support her family and contributing to social change in her community. She graduated from Amherst in 2018 with top grades and "the best friendships in the world." She went on to win a Fulbright, and she navigated the pandemic while supporting her mom through health struggles and surgery. Then Gaby set her sights on getting a doctorate in cultural and ethnic studies. She was not the same person who arrived at Amherst in 2014, she assured me. Her politics had changed. Her goals and visions for the future had changed. And her relationships had changed.

As we finished our conversation, I asked Gaby what parts of her educational journey stood out most. As I had come to expect and appreciate, Gaby paused for a moment to fully take in the question. She then shared a coherent string of reflections. She started by talking about how hard it had been getting to Amherst from a public high school. She thought that, if she had not learned about QuestBridge, she would never have found her way. But even after finding her way, the academic learning curve was steep—steeper than she had ever imagined it would be. And she was unprepared for the emotional shock of moving into an elite space. Especially during her first year, she remembered, she had to constantly fight against feelings of inadequacy. Her memory of how hard it had been to move away from her family and then to later realize that she was growing apart from them emotionally and intellectually would forever be seared in her mind. If her heart was still not completely at peace, it was because of her still rocky relationships with her dad and her brother.

Gaby went on to describe her love-hate relationship with Amherst. There had been much to love. Her college experience gifted her with incredible relationships. The classes she took and the professors she met transformed her thinking, stoked her passions, inspired new goals, and gave her the tools to pursue them. She would also be forever grateful that she received a debt-free education that helped set her up for a materially secure life. But her time at Amherst was also really hard, and she harbored some resentment.

The diversity among Amherst's students was incredible, Gaby said, but in her view, there was not enough acknowledgment by students, faculty, and staff of the inequality underlying that diversity. She explained that it was difficult to go to school with wealthy peers who had no understanding of poverty, racism, or the roots of inequality and no reason or desire to learn about them. She also resented having her identity reduced to "low-income," "first-generation," or "Latina" when she saw identity as much more nuanced. She believed that these nuances produce radically different experiences among students and are commonly overlooked. Indeed, confirming Jack's findings, she knew that her experience coming from public high school was different from that of Latinos who went to prep school.[1] Relatedly, her experience as a U.S. citizen was radically different from that of undocumented students. She went on to thoughtfully reflect that she was privileged in some ways and subordinated in others, noting that the fluid collage of her identity continued to change shape, especially with respect to social class. She now hovered in a liminal space between financial insecurity and membership in a cultural elite. To be sure, even though Gaby had added an Amherst degree and a Fulbright to her list of achievements and filled up her stores of cultural capital, her family's material struggles and the growing anti-immigrant sentiment in society were still obstinate markers of her subordination.

Gaby's post-Amherst story and reflections, while unique in their particularities, paralleled in many ways the other stories I collected during this research. For the most part, as I detailed in the last chapter, the youth in this project had thrived. They were, in no uncertain terms, extraordinary, having overcome formidable obstacles to achieve academic greatness. And yet, as Gaby's story suggests, their academic achievements had not erased the core challenges of growing up in a marginalized immigrant family.

Most of them had arrived at Amherst aware that they had seized opportunities to which their family and community members did not have access, but they were optimistic that their opportunity was part of a progressive movement toward equity. Fueled by the immigrant bargain, they entered college believing that their academic success could lift up their families too, and they were committed to doing the work to ensure that this happened. To be sure, there were those who, after graduating from Amherst, had already embarked on a professional path that would enable family uplift. But this was not likely to be the path for all of them, at least not for a while. For most, I imagine, financial security will be tenuous upon first arrival. And so, it is not surprising that when I asked youth who had graduated from Amherst—many of whom had moved on to graduate school or a professional position—if they identified differently now in terms of social class, most of them, like Gaby, said that they felt situated in an in-between space. Although they believed that, as individuals, they would continue an upward climb, they still linked their identities to their financially strug-gling families and communities, and they were less certain than they had been upon entering Amherst of their ability to lift up their families with them. Indeed, almost all clearly acknowledged—and this troubled many of them—the disconnect between their newly minted elite educational status and the persistently marginalized status of their family and home com-munity. Through their studies and, as importantly, their coresidency with wealthy, White, non-immigrant students, they had come to a more sophis-ticated and fine-tuned understanding of opportunity and mobility.

And so it is not surprising that many talked about redefining success in a way that centered family and community and, for some, also included social and community change efforts. A big takeaway from this research is that these youth, despite their immersion in an elite space, had not forgotten where they came from. If anything, they had come to appreciate their communities more.

The youth who participated in this study also had not forgotten the familial sacrifices that had propelled them onto their mobility paths. The vast majority told me that they would feel successful only when they had achieved enough financial security to take care of their parents well enough to allow them to stop working and to rest. Continuing to center family, how-ever, had not lowered the price of mobility. For many students, educational mobility had been accompanied by a growing rift between them and their closest family members as their studies and life away from home changed their perspective on the world and in many cases shifted their identity. These familial rifts had been accentuated by the pressure some youth said that they felt to be doing more with their degree and achieving material success faster. They understood that their success depended on the employ-ment opportunities that they could access, their networks, and the general state of the economy as much as it did on their smarts and hard work. They understood that college graduation did not represent the finish line, but rather a starting gate at the beginning of the next phase of their climb. Many said that they were frustrated that their family members did not share this understanding or perspective. Instead, their parents and some siblings saw college as the final box to check on the path to financial prosperity and failed to understand why their newly graduated child or sibling could not buy a house, pay off all debts, and acquire more comforts. My participants recognized that a major source of this gap in understanding—which was yet another product of the structural inequality undergirding their experiences—was the divergence between them and their family members in experiences and education. Many said that they had come to accept that bridging that gap would be difficult, if not impossible.

INSTITUTIONAL POLICY CHANGES

Experiences of educational mobility are framed by relationships and interactions between multiple layers of federal, state, local, and institutional policies, what Tanya Golash-Boza and Zulema Valdez term "nested contexts of reception."[2] Although each of these levels can be analyzed separately, it is critical to recognize that, because they are nested, a policy change at one level rarely overrides the policy implications that manifest at other levels, especially the local and institutional levels. Amherst can offer full tuition coverage and generous financial support for undocumented students, for example, and the institutional leadership can sign on—as they seemingly always do—to lobbying efforts to support DACA and undocumented youth. And yet ultimately Amherst does not get to decide who can reside in the United States "legally," or what employment opportunities are accessible to undocumented students after graduation; nor can they protect students' family members from detention or deportation. Although Amherst has the resources to offer low-income students a debt-free education, they cannot provide the money necessary to remove the relentless financial strain experienced by many working-class immigrant families. This would require large-scale structural change that Amherst can vocally support through its mission and advocacy—as I encourage them to keep doing—but that cannot be directly implemented by one institution.

Whereas this research suggests that radical structural changes are necessary on the federal and state levels to expand opportunities and security for aspiring youth and families, I have focused here on something closer to home for me—the institutional level of policy. Instead of making outright policy recommendations, I highlight themes that could help guide policy-making discussions and decision-making in regard to upwardly mobile Latino youth. Most of these themes, while situated at the institutional level, point to the need to recognize impacts on the lives of aspiring Latino youths and their families of federal, state, and local policies.

Clearing and Expanding Opportunity Pathways

College debt is soaring, and the competition to get a high-paying job is tougher than ever.[3] At such a time, it is hard to ignore the unique opportunities opened up by need-blind admissions and a prestigious diploma from an elite school that promises a high degree of social mobility.[4] Those graduating from elite colleges and universities today are likely to become tomorrow's leaders within government, industry, and academia.[5] As such, the commitment of these schools to diversifying their student bodies suggests that the upper echelon of society will also become more diverse. Would such diversification thus signal the democratization of opportunity? Yes and no.

My findings suggest that Latino youth leaving Amherst have a sophisticated understanding of inequality and discrimination and experience navigating both in daily life, and it will certainly contribute to democratization when they bring this understanding, along with deep stores of knowledge, skills, and passion, to their careers. Their narratives also suggest that they will commit time and energy to expanding opportunities to youth whose background is similar to their own. This too is an exciting prospect.

Yet, while I celebrate the diversification of the elite, I recognize that the mobility pyramid is built on the exclusion of those who may be just as smart and hardworking, but who cannot secure the right kinds of social and human capital to move into the elite realm. This certainly seemed to be the case for some of the siblings in this study whose talents and intellect were not recognized for a variety of reasons and who thus stayed behind while their brother or sister surged ahead. If this difference was notable within my small sample, we can assume that it is common in the larger society. Until educational mobility is socially supported as a family and community endeavor, there is the risk of new inequalities developing and the current inequitable system being reproduced under the celebratory veil of diversity.

It would be wrong for the takeaway from this research to be that highly selective schools should be the primary measure of educational mobility or success. Diversifying private, elite higher education cannot be the sole answer to generations of exclusion and discrimination. To be sure, public colleges and universities serve as mobility platforms for many more young people than do highly selective schools.[6] Yet public universities and community colleges typically do not have the high endowments of private, elite institutions, and thus they are unable to offer the same kinds of need-blind aid or to put the same support structures in place. There are, of course, exceptions. As of this writing, Oregon, Nevada, Arkansas, New Jersey, Maryland, Tennessee, Rhode Island, Delaware, Kentucky, and Indiana have programs covering two years of tuition at participating schools. But if you are an aspiring child growing up outside of these places, you are out of luck. This is to say that the landscape of higher education is inherently unequal and opportunities are place-specific. I encourage private institutions to use their influence to support robust funding for public higher education, from community colleges to major research universities. Such funding has taken a major hit over the past decades.

Elite institutions could do even more, however, than express solidarity. It would be a radical but prudent and sensible move for progressive, wealthy private institutions, which can serve only a minority of aspiring young people, to engage in public-private partnerships, perhaps with institutions from their own state, region, or city. Such partnerships would help democratize the opportunities for mobility. It would also lessen inequalities within families, like those in this sample that had one sibling going to an elite private school and the other enrolled in a community or state college.

Institutions of higher education should also pay close attention to the intricate formula that supports educational mobility. The youth in this study all thrived academically in high school, had family support, *and* had the social capital that enabled them to find highly selective schools with need-blind policies. Only when family networks, local school networks, and elite recruitment networks converged was entry into a highly selective college possible for them. To increase access to higher educational opportunities, admissions teams must recognize these three tiers as operating concurrently. Pipeline programs remain excellent ways to identify high-performing marginalized students, but they tend to be centered in large urban areas and thus should not be the central focus of recruitment. The life stories I collected suggest that highly selective schools must cast a much wider net if they want to attract the best and brightest. A lot of progress has been made recently on some great efforts at Amherst to broaden recruitment to include rural, suburban, and geographically isolated places that have traditionally been off the radar screen. Yet more work is needed, not just at Amherst but at other schools that share Amherst's mission of increasing access, and a major shift of resources to such efforts will also be required.

For now, getting into an elite institution from a geographically remote place remains difficult—a crapshoot in some situations. For example, I was surprised and dismayed to learn about the centrality of testing for youth in these areas. Before conducting this research, I would have cheered the end of standardized admission exams because of how they benefit the most affluent—those who are able to invest time and money in learning how to test well.[7] Now I am ambivalent. Several participants in this study who were from remote areas told me that they were able to access elite recruitment networks only because they performed well on these tests. Remember how Noel thought about whether to "check the box" on the PSAT? Despite his hard work and academic success, this critical move was what opened the world of elite education and need-blind admissions to him. This is to say, until highly selective schools are able to broaden their recruitment reach into remote and rural areas, college entrance exams might remain the only way in which some students can access them. I would advise admissions teams to include this finding in their debates about the pros and cons of test-optional admissions.

Recognizing the Centrality of Family in the Lives of Youth

When I began this research, I intuited that family would be an important theme, but I did not imagine that family would play the starring role in the life histories I collected. Yet early on in the research it became clear that youth constructed their identities and aspirations and understood their accomplishments and experiences through the lens of their immigrant families. This was not just the case for some participants in the study. It was the case for everyone I interviewed. Most recognized their parents' immigrant sacrifices as essential to the opportunities they now had. Yet, while the American Dream and immigrant bargain narratives that filled their childhoods had been inspirational, most came to recognize through their education and through their experiences living away from home that these narratives were blind to the structural barriers that made family mobility so much more difficult than individual mobility. Moreover, many came to see more clearly that their individual educational opportunities had shifted the social structure of their family, creating new inequalities.

These realizations, generated by a heightened critical consciousness, motivated and complicated students' paths to and through Amherst. They had to learn how to live, strive, and thrive in two radically different worlds, that of home and that of school. Making this adjustment even more difficult for students was that many of their parents and siblings never had the opportunity to visit or experience even a small piece of Amherst. This lack of exposure widened the understanding gap between participants and their families. Youth talked about these realities as a significant part of the high price of educational and social mobility.

I feel grateful to work at an institution that is devising and implementing policies with the aim of lowering the emotional price of educational mobility. When I started this project, Amherst already had robust resources in place to support students of color, low-income students, and immigrant students. They also employed a lawyer who was available to assist undocumented students with immigration-related matters. Yet many of the students I interviewed early on still felt lost, marginalized, and unhappy. So they organized. They were part of a larger movement of students who expressed their frustrations and difficulties to the college leadership. The leadership listened and worked with students, faculty, and staff to make significant changes. For example, now the immigration lawyer invites family members to participate in their meetings with students. The college covers all costs. There is also now an immigration office on campus with a staff member whose charge is partly to develop programming and supports for undocumented students. This office also helps teach U.S. citizen students about resources and supports that can help their undocumented family members. The first-year dean, Professor Rick López, himself an Amherst alumnus and once a first-generation Latino college student, has transformed Amherst's orientation program to be more inclusive of immigrant students and parents. There are now welcome sessions for parents, conducted in Spanish, and events at which Latino students, faculty, and staff are on hand to welcome Latino parents. These are just a select few of the investments that all institutions could make to enhance inclusion of immigrant families.

COVID exacerbated and exposed inequalities between students from families of privilege and students from marginalized families. When campuses across the country shut down in the spring of 2020, some students returned to fully furnished private bedrooms that could serve as home offices, in houses that were wired with high-speed internet, and with parents who worked remotely and were able to protect themselves and their families from the virus by comfortably barricading themselves at home. Other students returned to crowded houses or apartments, with no quiet or private places to attend class remotely or study, and with parents who were essential workers and thus constantly at risk of exposure to the virus. Amherst and other wealthy institutions with the means to do so allowed students who needed to stay on campus to do so, and emergency funds and technology were made available to assist students and families, but the broader inequalities framing students' lives persisted outside of the realm of school support. It is simply not possible for progressive elite schools with large endowments to erase these larger inequalities. I do think, however, that it's imperative for institutional leaders in higher education to recognize the nested nature of inequalities and the undue toll that the pandemic and accompanying economic crisis has had on their most vulnerable students. They should know that, while they are protecting the students at risk in their campus communities, those students are worrying about and often caring for their family members who lack such protection. Students and graduates who have moved home or far from campus carry similar responsibilities.

Recognition of the familial contexts and complexities of the lives of upwardly mobile youth should be accompanied by programs to educate faculty and staff about these contexts and complexities. It would be important, for example, for them to learn that second-generation immigrant students who are U.S. citizens and have undocumented parents are likely to share their parents' fears and uncertainties about that undocumented status. It would also be helpful for faculty and staff to understand how much work students do outside of school to support their parents and siblings; they should know that this work is essential to family well-being, though it often takes away from time students would otherwise spend on their studies. This is also work that takes up emotional space and energy. Faculty and staff who understand the centrality of family relationships might be able to advise their students more appropriately and support students more effectively in their goal formation. This kind of consciousness raising among faculty and staff could also foster greater empathy for students and enhance their appreciation of student accomplishments, resilience, and resourcefulness, thus strengthening, in turn, their individual relationships while building community.

Addressing Inequalities and Understanding Gaps within Residential Communities

One of the most common challenges that youth described when talking about their transition into college was confronting wealth and Whiteness. That they often characterized this challenge as a confrontation, rather than a meeting or an introduction, is telling. For most youth in this study, wealth and Whiteness had come to stand in for entitlement, as well as ignorance of race and class inequalities. Although several of the youth I interviewed talked about confronting overt racism, more common were participants' stories about students who did not recognize their own privileges and who seemed to have no idea about the inequalities and injustices contextualizing the campus community and the world beyond it. More troubling still, they seemed to have no interest in doing the work necessary to educate themselves and help dismantle the inequalities.

This entanglement of lack of recognition, no critical consciousness, and no interest in self-education lay at the heart of the microaggressions that made many participants in this study feel socially excluded. Among these many microaggressions were assuming that everyone had been exposed to the same types of cultural and educational capital and that everyone's parents went to college; being very comfortable literally taking up a lot of space on campus and unaware that not everyone felt the same; disrespecting custodial and dining hall staff and not realizing that the parents of some students worked in similar jobs; and perhaps most importantly, having no critical understanding of the mythological aspects of meritocratic thinking. Indeed, entitlement comes easily to those who believe that they and their families worked harder and are smarter than everyone else and thus deserve their privilege and wealth. Feeling entitled, they do not understand that they have peers whose families worked just as hard but have not had the same access to opportunity and material well-being.

Without a collective understanding of the inequality at the base of diversity, and without a desire to dismantle it, it is hard to imagine students ever being able to build trust and friendships across difference. Institutions of higher education, however, are well positioned to make relevant changes. Amherst has an open curriculum: outside of a student's major and first-year writing seminar, there are no required classes. But while classes are not required, there are ways to incentivize students to take classes that focus on inequality and the core elements of democratic communities. Perhaps schools like Amherst that do not have general education requirements could offer a certificate program or tie certain honors distinctions to having taken courses that focus on inequality. Ideally, these courses would address the systemic causes of the -isms that make campus life difficult for students from marginalized backgrounds. Of course, not all faculty are positioned to teach classes in these areas, but many are, and many others are eager to learn how to address these difficult topics effectively.

One of my first research assistants, Elaine Vilorio, suggested to me that colleges not just offer optional "bridge" programs for marginalized students in the summer, but programs for the most privileged students as well. Such programs would give these students the space, resources, and guidance to think deeply and critically about the diversity and inequality of elite residential communities. My hunch is that many students would be eager to participate in such programs, which would attract students who are concerned about equity and social justice and who recognize the inequalities on campus but do not know how to engage the related issues from their own positions of privilege. This type of program would give interested students a structured way to gain this consciousness. It would also, importantly, encourage the most privileged among us to do more of the work to combat social injustices on our campuses and in the larger society. If more students developed their critical consciousness about social inequality, it would be much easier to build community across difference.

Elite schools have the resources to train and hire the faculty and staff necessary to carry out consciousness-raising programs. Indeed, I encourage institutions to make substantial investments in endeavors like the ones I have imagined. It is a great injustice that while youth from marginalized backgrounds have to develop their own critical consciousness just to understand their life situation and that of their families, other students are never asked to think about the inequalities on which their advantages are based. Institutional curricular innovations could lead to radical change in the experiences of marginalized students at elite schools. The payouts in terms of equity, inclusion, and the creation of genuinely strong and caring diverse communities promise to be great. The lessons thus learned at an elite school might eventually pervade other social realms as students of all backgrounds graduate and move into their professional lives with a better understanding of their own position in the social world and that of others. We can hope that at least some would enter their adult lives with a commitment to doing the social change work necessary for achieving true equity.

But if discussions of this kind of curricular change are even to begin, institutions must elevate humility as a core community value. I have learned from my participants how important it is to recognize how little we know or understand about others' lives and experiences. The prerequisite for listening, reflecting, and doing the hard work necessary to learn about inequality is a desire to understand and a willingness to unlearn misconceptions about how hierarchies form. Instead of touting the importance of rankings, accolades, and traditional success, institutions could talk more about the importance of humanity and community, while working hard to nurture both. I have been inspired to watch Amherst move in this direction. And let's be clear—those who have been the most entitled should do the bulk of this work. Imagine what an institution-wide critical consciousness about inequality could do for community building and social justice.

RECOGNIZING THE COMPLEXITY OF LATINO BACKGROUNDS AND IDENTITIES

The youths whose stories structure this book were all Latino, first-generation college students who identified as low-income and who shared experiences rooted in this identity. Most could relate to the stresses of financial insecurity and the challenges of navigating a college culture and community radically different from where they grew up. Most dedicated at least some of their time at Amherst to helping family and community members back home, and they considered the needs of their close family members when planning for their future. Many had experienced the stress and fear connected to being undocumented or having a close family member who was. And at least at some point, the majority had felt alienated and misunderstood at an elite school. Yet there were important nuances in these youth's identities, backgrounds, and experiences that had shaped their pathways to and through college. It is important for leaders of higher education, as well as the faculty and staff who work directly with students, to recognize these nuances and take them into account when creating policies and programs to support this demographic.

A major factor differentiating youth's educational pathways is the kind of high school institution they attended. Jack has made clear the numerous ways in which this factor impacts an individual's experience of an elite school.[8] Perhaps most significantly, low-income students who attended an elite preparatory high school arrive at Amherst already having confronted wealth and Whiteness. They also knew the rules of the elite game—like attending office hours, networking, and accumulating cultural capital as a means of enhancing their opportunities for future social mobility. Those who went to underresourced public schools reported feeling much more alienated and shocked upon arrival at Amherst, and they struggled more.[9]

Another major difference between students at elite schools is in legal status. Undocumented or DACA students need different services and supports than do U.S. citizen students. The pressures and uncertainties that accompany this status can make it difficult to plan for the future and to focus on school. Although having access to legal counseling is critical for these students, that alone is not enough. Undocumented and DACA students would also benefit from robust resource centers with easily identifiable staff and faculty members who support them, as well as a point person who has the resources to organize dinners, meetings, and social gatherings. Amherst College has done a lot of this work, to the great benefit of its undocumented and DACA students. Indeed, those I interviewed early in this study—who attended Amherst before an immigration office was created—reported having had a much harder time, and having been much more isolated socially, than did those who attended Amherst when this office and staff were in place.

U.S. citizen students with undocumented family members may also benefit from these supports and may want to join in some of the community-building activities, though their experiences should be recognized as essentially different. Indeed, DACA students and undocumented students have different needs and different levels of security. Campus leaders, faculty, and staff who can recognize these differences will be better able to support students in the ways they need and deserve.

Race and class differences also matter. "Low-income" can feel like a catchall category. While there were youth in this sample who lived in a house their family owned, there were many others who only knew rentals and constant negotiating with landlords. Some youth in this sample had been food- and housing-insecure, and others identified as solidly working-class. Race and ethnic differences also have important experiential impacts. Youth who identified as White or light-skinned Latinos told me that they assumed they had fewer barriers to overcome than did those who identified as Black or Afro-Latino. Providing forums where students can freely and critically explore their nuanced identities is beneficial. Youth talked about how the classes, affinity groups, and friendship groups that provided these opportunities were transformative, empowering, and affirming.

Finally, it is important for faculty and staff to recognize that the places where youth grew up will shape their experiences of college as well as their plans for the future. Those from large cities are much more likely, for example, to feel out of sorts when they first arrive at Amherst. As Fiona said, "And I hated the birds! . . . And then the cicadas. I was like, what are they?" That Amherst did not jibe with her geographic habitus accentuated the loneliness she felt. Of course, it was not just that Fiona was from a big city. There are many students on elite campuses who are from big cities. It was that she had not traveled much outside of New York City, and so the rurality of Amherst felt shockingly different.

Students from more remote areas have different, but just as significant, challenges. I heard most often from these youth that they did not know anyone who could relate to the place they called home. Many were from places to which travel was difficult, so going home for breaks or holidays was sometimes prohibitively expensive. But perhaps most importantly, students from remote places knew that after graduation it would be hard for them to go home and find work or other educational opportunities that were meaningful and lucrative. As Noel so aptly noted, "To make this big migration to Amherst puts a lot of pressure on those of us from rural communities. To experience social mobility, you have to be prepared to leave your roots behind." The more college and university faculty and staff can recognize the ways in which place shapes students' perspectives, the better they will be able to support students.

EXTENDING SUPPORTS BEYOND GRADUATION

Youth in this study learned through their time at Amherst that their academic work was only part of what was necessary to win a financially secure and meaningful future. Most entered Amherst never having heard about internships or career mentors, and they were shocked when they met peers who had already had internship experiences in high school—yet another marker of inequality.

One of the most impactful programs I learned about over the course of my research was the Meiklejohn Program at Amherst. This program for first-generation and low-income college students recognizes the importance to their success of building up stores of social capital and gaining internship experiences, while also being encouraged to build community. During my research, those in charge of the program came from backgrounds similar to those of the student participants. A shared background between leaders and participants helps build the "in-group identity" that Smith considers so important to the mobility of aspiring youth.[10] The Meiklejohn Program, and the incredible work of its leaders, has not only notably improved inclusion at Amherst but also empowered students on their mobility paths beyond graduation.

Staff willing to keep working with students from marginalized families after they leave campus can help make up for the social capital deficits they have experienced. Indeed, just as cross-class actors helped youth move from high school to college, so too they are invaluable as students move from college into their next professional or academic phase. This research points to the importance of focusing resources and recognition on the staff who are doing this important work. It is not an exaggeration to say that they are invaluable to the experiences of aspiring low-income Latino youth.

As I hope this book has made clear, COVID added another barrier for aspiring youth to overcome. Those who graduated in 2020 and 2021 were hit especially hard, as they had to move into a professional world that was in the midst of crisis and transition. At the beginning of the pandemic there were few jobs at the levels that graduates were pursuing, and some graduate and doctoral programs had stopped accepting applications. Perhaps most difficult, students who had appreciated the material and mental health supports they received at Amherst lost those supports upon graduating. Meanwhile, their caretaking responsibilities for family and kin had intensified during the pandemic. All of these factors inevitably conspired to disrupt youth's mobility pathways.

Although institutions of higher education could not realistically fix all of the impacts of the COVID crisis, this research points to the benefits that would come from making need-based emergency funds available for all alumni. Most participants in this study did not need these funds offered by Amherst, but some did. Those who were still students told me that they did not know how they would have made it without the college's extra support. Whatever colleges and universities can do to support alumni through a crisis makes a huge difference in the lives of those who are struggling—and have struggled—the most.

FINAL THOUGHTS

As I finished this manuscript, it was reunion weekend 2022, and I was delighted to see some of the early participants in this study as they returned to campus. Their stories, reflections, passion, and energy reminded me why

I decided to embark on this project years ago. They were on a path that few would ever be able to travel. Having been born into and grown up in immigrant families that lacked financial and often legal security, they saw education as the key to their mobility and well-being and that of their families. I was reminded during reunion weekend that their vision and motivation had not changed. Their consciousnesses, however, had become more critical. As I engaged with them in fun and meaningful catch-up conversations, they made me feel hopeful, grateful, and inspired.

As I have documented, the participants in this study were extraordinary young people. And yet, there is much more work to be done to give them support and appreciation that matches the generations of family work and struggle that have supported and guided them so far. The bulk of responsibility rests with those of us who have not borne this generational burden to educate ourselves on the complexity, difficulty, and rarity of American mobility stories and then to do the work to broaden and strengthen access to mobility pathways for all youth seeking a more secure future for themselves and for their families.

Appendix A | Demographics of Study Participants

Pseudonym	Gender Identity	Legal Status or Place of Birth	Ethnic Identity	Home in the United States	Mother's Highest Level of Education Completed	Father's Highest Level of Education Completed
Luna	Woman	Citizen	Mexican	Chicago, Illinois	Some high school	High school
Lisa	Woman	Citizen	Mexican	Maryland	High school	NA
Gloria	Woman	Citizen	Mexican	Chicago, Illinois	High school	High school
Sony	Nonbinary	Citizen	Puerto Rican	Holyoke, Massachusetts	Middle school	High school
Emily	Woman	(Born in Ecuador)	Ecuadorean	North Bergen, New Jersey	High school	High school
Laura	Woman	(Born in Colombia) (green card in 2012)	Colombian	Deerfield Beach, Florida	Some college (Colombia)	Some college (Colombia)
Ben	Man	(Born in Colombia)	Colombian	Palm Beach, Florida	College (Colombia)	College (Colombia)
Ana	Woman	(Born in Puerto Rico)	Cuban and Puerto Rican	Fort Worth, Texas	Some college (Puerto Rico)	NA
Brenda	Woman	Citizen	Mexican	Wyoming	NA	NA
Amanda	Woman	Citizen	Salvadoran and Colombian	New York City, New York	Some high school	Primary school
Carlos	Man	(Born in Honduras)	Honduran	Northampton, Massachusetts	Some high school	NA
Tito	Man	(Born in Peru)	Peruvian	Bradenton, Florida	High school	High school
Maria	Woman	(Born in Colombia)	Colombian	Rhode Island	College (Colombia)	NA
Ernesto	Man	(Born in Colombia)	Colombian	South Carolina	High school	Some college (Colombia)

Name	Gender	Citizenship	Ethnicity	Location		
Eli	Woman	Citizen	Ecuadorean	New York City, New York	High school; had returned to college	Some high school
Samantha	Woman	Citizen	Mexican	New York City, New York	High school	High school
Silvia	Woman	Citizen	Dominican	Hackensack, New Jersey	High school	College + (Dominican Republic)
Jaime	Man	(Born in Dominican Republic)	Dominican	Galloway, New Jersey	NA	NA
Fiona	Woman	Citizen	Mexican	Bronx, New York	Primary school	Middle school
Ricardo	Man	Citizen	Mexican	Waukegan, Illinois	Middle school	Middle school
Francia	Woman	Citizen	Dominican	Bronx, New York	Primary school	NA
Isabela	Woman	Citizen	Mexican	Santa Ana, California	Middle school	Some high school
Julia	Woman	(Born in Mexico)	Mexican	San Diego, California	High school	High school
Cecilia	Woman	(Born in El Salvador)	Salvadoran	Virginia	High school	NA
Rebeca	Woman	Citizen	Mexican and Belgian	Taos, New Mexico	College (Europe)	High school
Cesar	Man	(Born in Mexico)	Mexican	Los Angeles, California	High school	NA
Kevin	Man	(Born in Mexico)	Mexican	Oklahoma City, Oklahoma	Middle school	NA
Miguel	Man	Citizen	Dominican	New York City, New York	High school	NA

(continued)

Pseudonym	Gender Identity	Legal Status or Place of Birth	Ethnic Identity	Home in the United States	Mother's Highest Level of Education Completed	Father's Highest Level of Education Completed
Iván	Man	Citizen	Puerto Rican and Honduran	Carlisle, Pennsylvania	High school	NA
Alberto	Man	(Born in Guatemala)	Guatemalan	Houston, Texas	Middle school	High school plus military (Guatemala)
Omar	Man	(Born in Mexico)	Mexican	Evanston, Illinois	Primary school	Middle school
Rosa	Woman	Citizen	Mexican	Englewood, California	Middle school	NA
Layla	Woman	(Born in Dominican Republic)	Dominican	Queens, New York	Primary school	Primary school
Sandra	Woman	Citizen	Ecuadorean	Newark, New Jersey	Nursing school (Ecuador)	Middle school
Dianis	Woman	Citizen	Dominican	Boston, Massachusetts	High school	Some high school
Heidi	Woman	Citizen	Mexican	New Brunswick, New Jersey	High school	Some high school
Angelica	Woman	Citizen	Mexican and Guatemalan	Santa Ana, California	Primary school	Primary school
Beatriz	Woman	(Born in Brazil)	Brazilian	Melrose, Massachusetts	College (Brazil)	College (Brazil)
Naomi	Woman	(Born in Dominican Republic)	Dominican	Lowell, Massachusetts	Some college (Dominican Republic)	NA

Name	Gender	Citizenship	Nationality	Location	Education 1	Education 2
Nora	Woman	(Born in Dominican Republic)	Dominican	New York City, New York	Some college (Dominican Republic)	Some college (Dominican Republic)
Teresa	Woman	Citizen	Mexican	Chicago, Illinois	High school	High school
Llaria	Woman	Citizen	Dominican	Mission Hill, Massachusetts	College (Dominican Republic)	High school
Lucy	Woman	Citizen	Salvadoran and Black American	Taylorsville, North Carolina	High school	NA
Franchesca	Woman	Citizen	Dominican	Annapolis, Maryland, and West Palm Beach, Florida	Some high school	High school
Noel	Man	Citizen	Mexican	San Angelo, Texas	Some high school	NA
Paola	Woman	Citizen	Mexican	Santa Barbara, California	High school	High school
Antonio	Man	(Born in Mexico)	Mexican	New Jersey	Some high school	Some high school
David	Man	Citizen	Dominican and Honduran	Village of Pelham, New York	Primary school	Middle school
Camila	Woman	Citizen	Mexican	San Diego, California	College (Mexico)	NA
Jon	Man	Citizen	Dominican	Washington, D.C.	Primary school	Primary school
Gaby	Woman	Citizen	Nicaraguan	Highland, California	General education degree (GED)	General education degree (GED)
Ramon	Man	Citizen	Dominican	Kissimmee, Florida	High school	NA

(continued)

Pseudonym	Gender Identity	Legal Status or Place of Birth	Ethnic Identity	Home in the United States	Mother's Highest Level of Education Completed	Father's Highest Level of Education Completed
Kimberly	Woman	(Born in Panama)	Panamanian	Panama	Some college (Panama)	NA
Edith	Woman	(Born in Venezuela)	Venezuelan	Doral, Florida	College (Venezuela)	College (Venezuela)
Bridget	Woman	(Born in Colombia)	Colombian	Palm Harbor, Florida	Some college (Colombia)	College (Colombia)
Violeta	Nonbinary	Citizen	Nicaraguan	Miami, Florida	Some college (Nicaragua)	Some college (Nicaragua)
Fidel	Man	Citizen	Dominican and Cuban	New York City, New York	Some college (Dominican Republic)	High school
Zaida	Woman	Citizen	Honduran and Cuban	Miami, Florida	Primary school	High school
Leisy	Woman	(Born in Dominican Republic)	Dominican	Rahway, New Jersey	Some college (Dominican Republic)	NA
Leo	Man	Citizen	Mexican	Edinburg, Texas	High school; had returned to college	High school

Appendix B | A Methodological Roadmap

At its core, this book is a life history study of the educational mobility experiences of Latino students who were the first in their families to graduate from college. The book's argument is built from in-depth interviews I did with sixty students, as well as interviews I did with members of a subset of their families. This book also has a deep ethnographic grounding. The research was generated from Amherst College—where I am a professor and where my youth participants were then students—and the majority of interviews took place there. While I intentionally did not center my ethnographic observations or community engagement methods in the text, they guided my research, analysis, and writing from start to finish.

In my first semester teaching at Amherst in the fall of 2014, I taught "Latino Migration: Labor, Lifestyle, and Illegality," an introductory seminar that drew twenty-five students, mostly Latino. It was in this class that I began to learn about Latino students' experiences of educational mobility. Sometimes in class discussion, and also during office hours, students opened up to me about their pathways to Amherst and the challenges of navigating the college while trying to maintain close ties to their families back home. Much of what I learned caught me off guard. I was a new faculty member, and very much in a honeymoon phase. I was in awe of the thoughtfulness, intelligence, and engagement of my students, the rich diversity of the campus community, and the bounty of resources the college had to offer. Struggling students did not fit within this narrative.

During this semester, I started to journal about the stories that students were sharing with me about their experiences as upwardly mobile children of immigrants. I also started to keep track of the difficulties that I was observing in some of their academic lives. I distinctly remember being surprised when one of my best students stopped attending class. When I reached out to check in on her, she explained that things were not going well at home and she was contemplating taking a leave. She ultimately took that leave, assuring me that she would be back. She did come back the next academic year, and she later graduated. But her iterative path signaled how hard the journey had been, and I started to realize that she was not the only one for whom this was the case. I spent a lot of time thinking about this journey. At the time I did not have plans to embark on a research project or to write a book. I just wanted to better understand the lives of the students in my classrooms so that I could more effectively teach and support them.

The next semester I taught another immigration seminar, "Gender, Migration, and Power: Latinos in the Americas," and had another fantastic group of students, again mostly Latino. It was during a conversation with one of those students, Jeremy Paula, that the idea for this project was born. "Why doesn't anyone write about us?" he asked. He was smiling and his voice had a joking tone, but there was an underlying seriousness to his question. He went on to say, in so many words: "It seems like no one is writing about low-income Latinx kids who have 'made it,' who have defied the grim statistics and predictions. . . . Why isn't anyone telling our stories?" He went on to explain that when he did see representations of his educational mobility story in print, they were often superficial celebrations. He made sure I understood that the story was much more complicated. And then he repeated his question: "Why isn't anyone writing about it?" I pondered Jeremy's question for the next several days. He was right. As far as I knew, no one was writing about this.

I invited Jeremy to meet with me the next week so that we could talk more. His question had inspired me. I wanted to write about Jeremy and the other students like him I was getting to know. But I wasn't sure if the idea had legs. More to the point, I was not sure that I, a White and non-Latino professor, was the one to tell these stories. And I was not sure what it would look like to do a study in the school where I was teaching. But I also did not know how else to do it. I was who I was, and I was where I was. Learning about students' pathways to an elite college and the complexities of those pathways would require great trust. Even though I felt that I was building that trust within the Amherst community, such a project would also introduce the challenges of managing that trust. It would be a tricky dance. Jeremy agreed to explore the possibility with me.

Drawing from the start-up research funds that Amherst provided me, I asked Jeremy if he wanted to be my research assistant. Before deciding if this research project was possible or the right thing to do, I needed to know more about what work had already been done. So Jeremy and I began delving into the literature on second-generation youth and educational mobility. We started with Vivian Louie's book, *Keeping the Immigrant Bargain*. After finishing it, Jeremy told me that it was the first time he had seen himself and his family represented in academic literature. He had related strongly to the stories of college-bound youth who were motivated to do well to pay back their parents' sacrifices. We kept reading about second-generation youth, looking at work by Robert Smith, Philip Kasinitz, Mary Waters, Roberto Gonzales, and Leisy Abrego. We also started exploring the scholarship on low-income youth in elite spaces, beginning with the then-new work by Anthony Abraham Jack. Although we discovered that research was underway, there was simply nothing that merged the intersecting realities of being a low-income student at an elite college and a child of Latinx immigrants. Jeremy and I met regularly to talk about what we were learning and to identify gaps in the literature.

The next fall I asked another student, Elaine Vilorio, to join Jeremy and me in our exploration. Elaine was taking a class with me, and we were working closely together on a committee to launch a Latinx and Latin American studies major at the college. She had impressed me with her smarts, insights, and passion to develop policy-relevant knowledge based on Latinx lives. Elaine was enthusiastic about joining our reading group and brought great energy and commitment to our venture. In the meantime, I kept teaching immigration classes and thus hearing more students share bits and pieces of their story and their family's story. I had come to feel confident that there was an important book here; I just didn't know yet exactly how to go about it.

Elaine, Jeremy, and I decided to organize two focus groups of low-income, Latino Amherst students who identified as first-generation college students. Our goal was to learn what they had to say about their own pathways to Amherst and their experiences of educational mobility and to get a sense of how comfortable they would be sharing this information. Just as important was my need to know how Latino students would feel about me leading research on this topic. By this time my classes were quite well known among Latino students on campus, but I knew that in many ways I would always be an outsider among them.

After going through the institutional review board process and creating a script, Jeremy and Elaine recruited students for these focus groups and then facilitated the conversations. I was there, but mostly in the background, piping up once in a while. Both focus groups lasted over two hours and would have gone on much longer if we had not had to stop them because of the late hour. Students wanted to talk. I was struck by their honesty and depth of thought in response to the questions we were posing. Clearly, they had thought a lot about their educational pathways, but no one had ever asked them about those experiences. At the end of both focus groups, Elaine and Jeremy asked the students how they would feel about me overseeing the project. They gave me a genuine endorsement, saying that the principal researcher's identity did not matter; all that mattered was the researcher's intent and skill. I decided in that moment that I would work with Latino students throughout the research process as a means of ensuring that the research was grounded in the community and that there would be checks on my power within the process.

While launching this research, I was still teaching courses, many of which were focused on immigration. I decided that I would not use anything I heard in classes or during office hours in the book. The only exceptions—and there are a couple—occurred when a student asked to be interviewed for the book and then gave me permission to use a recap of a conversation we had had before the interview took place, or when a general observation from teaching helped contextualize a theme. Other than these exceptions, I used only my ethnographic observations from teaching and being immersed in the college community to better understand what I was learning in the life history interviews. I did, however, take detailed field notes when I visited students' homes to interview their family members, and I include these ethnographic data in the book.

As soon as this research project formally took root, I reached out to my dean and provost, Catherine Epstein, to tell her about it. I wanted to identify Amherst College in the research, and I wanted her consent. I knew it was not a usual practice to name the institution, but it felt appropriate, and even necessary, not only because of the close work I was doing with Amherst students but also because it was my relationship with the college and the trust I had built in the community as a faculty member that had made the project possible. I was committed to being transparent with leaders of the college in the same way I was committed to being transparent with the students I was interviewing. Catherine expressed enthusiasm about the project, especially the possibility that it would generate critical research that Amherst faculty and staff and other leaders in higher education could use to better serve students. I have kept both Catherine and the dean of admissions, Matthew McGann, in the loop throughout the project. Matt shared admissions policy information with me and helped me understand the mission guiding the college's policies. There is nothing about this project that is meant to be a surprise attack on the administration. There is also nothing I omitted or sugarcoated so as to protect the college.

Since this project's inception, it has been a coproduction of knowledge between me and a rotating research team of Amherst students. After Elaine and Jeremy graduated, I invited two more students to work with me. Then another student approached me to ask if they could join the team. By the end of year two of the project, I had a dedicated group of four students working with me. And so it went for the next three years.

Most of the students who joined the project as research assistants, though not all, were Latino, from a low-income background, and the first in their family to go to college. Several were undocumented or had DACA status, or they were the children of undocumented parents. All shared a deep commitment to understanding how to enhance equity and opportunity in higher education. My student assistants took on various components of the research depending on their interests. Some did interview recruitment. Some helped me with the literature review. Others researched pipeline programs for low-income students and did a historical dive into Amherst's student demographics. Others helped me code interview transcripts. They were also my technical support team, helping me navigate Dedoose, which we used to code and organize all the interview and demographic data. A few of my research assistants also participated in life history interviews with me after asking to be interviewed; these students did not analyze their own transcripts. Relatedly, we code-named the transcripts so as to protect students' identities.

I was transparent with each student I interviewed about who was on my research team at that time, and I got their consent to share insights from the interviews anonymously with the team. There were a couple of times when an interviewee requested that no student research assistant have access to their transcript and I abided by that request. I tried to interview students when they were juniors and seniors, and because there was a necessary time lag for interview transcription, most students had graduated before their interview transcripts were coded.

Most importantly, my student research assistants thought and theorized alongside me. We met as a team every Friday morning to discuss findings and share insights. I learned a lot in these meetings. It was here, for example, that we started talking about the importance of place. I remember clearly the meeting when one of my students who had grown up in a small, remote city started comparing stories about his high school experience with another student who had grown up in New York City. The radical differences in their pathways mirrored what we were starting to see in the interview data. Place seemed to matter a lot. From that conversation we decided to facilitate two focus groups. One would be with students from global cities, and the other would be with students from rural, suburban, and second-tier cities.

It was also during these weekly meetings that the idea was born to interview parents and siblings. Family had emerged early on as a central theme in the life history interviews. Indeed, much of our discussion about the data was focused on family. And in our meetings, students shared their own stories of family. "It's everything," I remember one student saying. As such, we concluded that a story of Latino educational mobility would not be complete without the actual voices and perspectives of youth's family members. Inspired by Joanna Dreby's work, in which she did "constellation interviews" with family members in order to get generational perspectives, we decided to ask ten students to invite their parents and siblings to join the project. I would visit their families in their homes, during which time I would get a chance to see and know them and their communities directly. Each student we approached with the idea responded eagerly. And so I was able, with support from the Amherst Faculty Research Advancement Program, to travel around the country to interview students' family members. This turned out to be one of the most powerful aspects of the research.

In the spring of 2020, I had completed all of my life history interviews and had only one more family constellation interview on my agenda. We were wrapping up the data analysis, and I had identified the themes that would anchor each chapter. I was scheduled for a sabbatical leave the next year to write "the book." Then COVID hit. As cliché as it has come to sound, it really did change everything. At first, I tried to ignore the call from the Russell Sage Foundation for research proposals to add a COVID angle to research on social inequalities that was already underway. I kept reminding myself that I was done and ready to write. But I actually knew that my project needed COVID to be part of it, and I knew my project fit RSF's funding parameters well. I applied, got the funding, and decided to defer my leave for a year so that I could return to a subset of my sample for two waves of interviews looking at the impact of COVID on their educational pathways and well-being. Like the family constellation interviews, I believe that adding this component transformed the project.

For the COVID component of the project, I recruited two of my early research assistants, Elaine Vilorio and Alyssa Snyder, both of whom had graduated and had ambitions to pursue academic tracks in sociology, to join me as post-bacs. They agreed, and together we embarked on the recruitment of forty of the original sixty interviewees. After dividing the sample among us, we each conducted the interviews over Zoom. The three of us also met regularly over Zoom to discuss our findings.

In the end, I am proud to have completed a book that yields insights into the educational experiences of aspiring Latino youth that I hope will guide policymakers and leaders within higher education toward adopting more socially just supports for them and their families. I am just as proud to have been part of a collaborative process centered in a community about which I care deeply and guided by young people whose intelligence, resilience, and commitment are changing the world.

Notes

INTRODUCTION

1. Hondagneu-Sotelo 2007.
2. Goldrick-Rab 2016.
3. Carnevale and Fasules 2017.
4. Abrego 2011; Gonzales 2016.
5. Benson and Lee 2020; Byrd 2021; Jack 2019; López 2020.
6. Warikoo 2016.
7. Ashikenas, Park, and Pearce 2017; López 2020.
8. Dhingra 2020; Greder and Arellanes 2018; López 2020; Louie 2012; Schmalzbauer 2008, 2014; Vazquez 2011; Yoshikawa 2011.
9. Chetty et al. 2017; Torpey 2018.
10. Kao, Vaquera, and Goyette 2013; Zhou and Bankston 2016.
11. Armstrong and Hamilton 2013.
12. Rendón 2019.
13. Chetty et al. 2022.
14. See also Louie 2012; Suárez-Orozco and Suárez-Orozco 1995.
15. Sy and Romero 2008; see also Greder and Arellanes 2018.
16. See Abrego 2014; Dreby 2010; Menjívar, Abrego, and Schmalzbauer 2016.
17. Kibria 1993, 22.
18. Coe 2014, 5.
19. Marrun 2018.
20. Smith 2006.
21. See also Abrego 2019; Flores 2021; Louie 2012; Suárez-Orozco and Suárez-Orozco 1995.
22. Smith 2008.
23. Louie 2012; Smith 2006; Suárez-Orozco and Suárez-Orozco 1995.
24. Dominguez 2011; Dominguez and Watkins 2003; Menjívar 2000.
25. See also Baker and Robnett 2012; Turcio-Cotto and Milan 2013.
26. Abrego 2019.
27. Dreby et al. 2020.

28. Feliciano and Lanuza 2017.
29. Bickham Mendez and Schmalzbauer 2018; Flores 2021; Gonzales and Burciaga 2018; Martinez and Salazar 2018.
30. Smith 2008.
31. Mattern and Wyatt 2009.
32. Schmalzbauer and Andres 2019.
33. See also Hurst 2010; Jack 2019.
34. Jack 2019, 22.
35. Ahmed 2012; Aries and Berman 2013; Benson and Lee 2020; Jack 2019; Lee 2016; Pan and Reyes 2021; Warikoo 2016.
36. Aries and Berman 2013; see also Lee 2016.
37. See also Lee and Kramer 2013.
38. Hurst 2010.
39. Jack 2019.
40. Jack and Black 2022.
41. Venzant Chambers et al. 2014.
42. Byrd 2017, 2021.
43. Pan and Reyes 2021.
44. Ahmed 2012; Benson and Lee 2020; Byrd 2021.
45. Warikoo 2016.
46. Pan and Reyes 2021.
47. Feliciano 2005.
48. See Dreby 2010.
49. Ibid.
50. Opal 2002.
51. López 2020.
52. Ibid.
53. Hoxby and Avery 2012.
54. Jack 2019.
55. Jaswal 2019.
56. Chetty et al. 2017.
57. Jaswal 2019.

CHAPTER 1   PATHWAYS TO AMHERST

1. Sassen 2001.
2. Hoxby and Avery 2012.
3. Rendón 2019; see also Dominguez and Watkins 2003.
4. See also Lee and Zhou 2015.
5. Louie 2012; see also Smith 2006, 2008.
6. Gonzales 2016; Louie 2012; Smith 2008; Zambrana and Hurtado 2015.
7. Smith 2008.

8.   Jack 2019.
9.   Hoxby and Avery 2012; see also Goldrick-Rab 2016.
10.   Louie 2012; Smith 2006, 2008.
11.   Hoxby and Avery 2012.
12.   Sassen 2001.

CHAPTER 2   A NEW WORLD

1.   Jack 2019.
2.   Romero 2011.
3.   Capps, Fix, and Zong 2016.
4.   Ahmed 2012; Jack 2019; Warikoo 2016.
5.   Chetty et al. 2017.
6.   Khan 2011.
7.   Jack 2019.
8.   Jack 2019; Khan 2011.
9.   Bourdieu 1977.
10.   Curl, Lareau, and Wu 2018; Hurst 2010; Ivemark and Ambrose 2021; Lee and Kramer 2013.
11.   Curl, Lareau, and Wu 2018.
12.   Khan 2011.
13.   Rivera 2015.
14.   Benson and Lee 2020; Jack 2019.
15.   Schmalzbauer 2014.

CHAPTER 3   THE PRICE OF MOBILITY

1.   Rodriguez 1982, 5.
2.   Reyes 2018.
3.   Menjívar, Abrego, and Schmalzbauer 2016.
4.   Louie 2012; Smith 2006.
5.   Rodriguez 1982, 77.
6.   Ibid., 78.

CHAPTER 4   SIBLINGS

1.   Conley 2003.
2.   Conley 2004.
3.   Louie 2012.
4.   Torpey 2018.
5.   Chetty et al. 2017.
6.   Abrego 2019.

7.   Estrada 2019.
8.   Kovacs 2022.
9.   Anzaldua 1987.
10. Lopez 2003.

CHAPTER 5   COVID-19 RUPTURES

1.   Menjívar 2006.
2.   Hill and Artiga 2022.
3.   For the Urban Institute's Health Reform Monitoring Survey, see https://
     www.urban.org/policy-centers/health-policy-center/projects/health-reform
     -monitoring-survey.
4.   Parolin 2021.
5.   Barofsky et al. 2020.
6.   Enriquez 2015.
7.   Dreby 2015.
8.   Keeter 2020; Purtle 2020.
9.   Pew Research Center 2020.
10. Purtle 2020.

CHAPTER 6   REDEFINING SUCCESS

1.   Louie 2012; Smith 2006.
2.   Flores 2021.
3.   Franceschelli and Keating 2018.
4.   Dominguez 2011; Menjívar 2000.
5.   Flores 2021.
6.   Gonzales 2016.
7.   Enriquez 2015.

CHAPTER 7   MOVING FORWARD

1.   Jack 2019.
2.   Golash-Boza and Valdez 2018.
3.   Goldrick-Rab 2016; Rivera 2015.
4.   Chetty et al. 2017.
5.   Jack 2019.
6.   Chetty et al. 2017.
7.   Lemann 1999.
8.   Jack 2019.
9.   Jack and Black 2022.
10. Smith 2008.

References

Abrego, Leisy J. 2011. "Legal Consciousness of Undocumented Latinos: Fear and Stigma as Barriers to Claims-Making for First- and 1.5-Generation Immigrants." *Law and Society Review* 45(2, June): 337–70.

———. 2014. *Sacrificing Families: Navigating Laws, Labor, and Love across Borders.* Stanford, Calif.: Stanford University Press.

———. 2019. "Relational Legal Consciousness of U.S. Citizenship: Privilege, Responsibility, Guilt, and Love in Latino Mixed-Status Families." *Law and Society Review* 53(3, September): 641–70.

Ahmed, Sara. 2012. *On Being Included: Racism and Diversity in Institutional Life.* Durham, N.C.: Duke University Press.

Anzaldua, Gloria. 1987. *Borderlands/La Frontera: The New Mestiza.* San Francisco: Aunt Lute Books.

Aries, Elizabeth, with Richard Berman. 2013. *Speaking of Race and Class: The Student Experience at an Elite College.* Philadelphia: Temple University Press.

Armstrong, Elizabeth A., and Laura T. Hamilton. 2013. *Paying for the Party: How College Maintains Inequality.* Cambridge, Mass.: Harvard University Press.

Ashikenas, Jeremy, Haeyoun Park, and Adam Pearce. 2017. "Even with Affirmative Action, Blacks and Hispanics Are More Underrepresented at Top Colleges than 35 Years Ago." *New York Times,* August 24.

Baker, Christina N., and Belinda Robnett. 2012. "Race, Social Support, and College Student Retention: A Case Study." *Journal of College Development* 53(2, March/April): 325–35.

Barofsky, Jeremy, Ariadna Vargas, Dinardo Rodriguez, and Anthony Barrows. 2020. "Spreading Fear: The Announcement of the Public Charge Rule Reduced Enrollment in Child Safety-Net Programs." *Health Affairs* 39(10, October): 1752–61.

Benson, Janel E., and Elizabeth M. Lee. 2020. *Geographies of Campus Inequality: Mapping the Diverse Experiences of First-Generation Students.* New York: Oxford University Press.

Bickham Mendez, Jennifer, and Leah Schmalzbauer. 2018. "Editors' Introduction: Latino Youth and Struggles for Inclusion in the 21st Century." *Ethnicities* 18(2, April): 165–77.

Bourdieu, Pierre. 1977. *Outline of a Theory of Practice.* Cambridge: Cambridge University Press.

Byrd, W. Carson. 2017. *Poison in the Ivy: Race Relations and the Reproduction of Inequality on Elite College Campuses.* New Brunswick, N.J.: Rutgers University Press.

———. 2021. *Behind the Diversity Numbers: Achieving Racial Equity on Campus.* Cambridge, Mass.: Harvard Education Press.

Capps, Randy, Michael Fix, and Jie Zong. 2016. "Fact Sheet: A Profile of U.S. Children with Unauthorized Immigrant Parents." Washington, D.C.: Migration Policy Institute (January).

Carnevale, Anthony P., and Megan L. Fasules. 2017. "Latino Education and Economic Progress: Running Faster but Still Behind." Washington, D.C.: Georgetown Center on Education and the Workforce. https://cewgeorgetown.wpenginepowered .com/wp-content/uploads/Latinos-FR.pdf.

Chetty, Raj, John Friedman, Emmanuel Saez, Nicholas Turner, and Danny Yagan. 2017. "Mobility Report Cards: The Role of Colleges in Intergenerational Mobility." Working Paper 23618. Cambridge, Mass.: National Bureau of Economic Research (July).

Chetty, Raj, Matthew O. Jackson, Theresa Kuchler, Johannes Stroebel, Abigail Hiller, Sarah Oppenheimer, and the Opportunity Insights Team. 2022. "Social Capital and Economic Mobility." Cambridge, Mass.: Opportunity Insights. https://opportunityinsights.org/wp-content/uploads/2022/07/socialcapital _nontech.pdf.

Coe, Cati. 2014. *The Scattered Family: Parenting, African Migrants, and Global Inequality.* Chicago: University of Chicago Press.

Conley, Dalton. 2003. "The Panel Study of Income Dynamics." Working paper. New York: New York University, Center for Advanced Social Science Research.

———. 2004. *The Pecking Order: A Bold New Look at How Family and Society Determine Who We Become.* New York: Vintage Books.

Curl, Heather, Annette Lareau, and Tina Wu. 2018. "Cultural Conflict: Implications of the Changing Dispositions of the Upwardly Mobile." *Sociological Forum* 33(4, December): 877–99.

Dhingra, Pawan. 2020. *Hyper Education: Why Good Schools, Good Grades, and Good Behavior Are Not Enough.* New York: New York University Press.

Dominguez, Silvia. 2011. *Getting Ahead: Social Mobility, Public Housing, and Immigrant Networks.* New York: New York University Press.

Dominguez, Sylvia, and Celeste Watkins. 2003. "Creating Networks for Survival and Mobility: Examining Social Capital among African-American and Latin-American Low-Income Mothers." *Social Problems* 50(1, February): 111–35.

Dreby, Joanna. 2010. *Divided by Borders: Mexican Migrants and Their Children.* Berkeley: University of California Press.

———. 2015. *Everyday Illegal: When Policies Undermine Immigrant Families.* Berkeley: University of California Press.

Dreby, Joanna, Sarah Gallo, Florencia Silveira, and Melissa Adams-Corral. 2020. "Nací Allá: Meanings of U.S. Citizenship for Young Children of Return Migrants to Mexico." *Harvard Educational Review* 90(4, Winter): 573–97.

Enriquez, Laura E. 2015. "Multigenerational Punishment: Shared Experiences of Undocumented Immigration Status within Mixed-Status Families." *Journal of Marriage and Family* 77(4, August): 939–53.

Estrada, Emir. 2019. *Kids at Work: Latinx Families Selling Foods on the Streets of Los Angeles.* New York: New York University Press.

Feliciano, Cynthia. 2005. *Unequal Origins: Immigrant Selection and the Education of the Second Generation.* El Paso, Tex.: LFB Publishing.

Feliciano, Cynthia, and Yader R. Lanuza. 2017. "An Immigrant Paradox: Contextual Attainment and Intergenerational Educational Mobility." *American Sociological Review* 82(1): 211–41.

Flores, Andrea. 2021. *The Succeeders: How Immigrant Youth Are Transforming What It Means to Belong in America.* Berkeley: University of California Press.

Franceschelli, Michela, and Avril Keating. 2018. "Imagining the Future in the Neoliberal Era: Young People's Optimism and Their Faith in Hard Work." *Young* 26(4, suppl., September): 1S–17S.

Golash-Boza, Tanya, and Zulema Valdez. 2018. "Nested Contexts of Reception: Undocumented Students at the University of California, Central." *Sociological Perspectives* 61(4, August): 535–52.

Goldrick-Rab, Sara. 2016. *Paying the Price: College Costs, Financial Aid, and the Betrayal of the American Dream.* Chicago: University of Chicago Press.

Gonzales, Roberto G. 2016. *Lives in Limbo: Undocumented and Coming of Age in America.* Berkeley: University of California Press.

Gonzales, Roberto G., and Edelina M. Burciaga. 2018. "Segmented Pathways of Illegality: Reconciling the Coexistence of Master and Auxiliary Statuses in the Experiences of 1.5-Generation Undocumented Young Adults." *Ethnicities* 18(2, April): 178–91.

Greder, Kimberly, and Jordan Arellanes. 2018. "Investing in Future Generations: Realities and Goals of Latino Immigrant Families." *Diálogo* 21(1, April 1): 89–100.

Hill, Latoya, and Samantha Artiga. 2022. "COVID-19 Cases and Deaths by Race/Ethnicity: Current Data and Changes over Time." Kaiser Family Foundation, August 22. https://www.kff.org/coronavirus-covid-19/issue-brief/covid-19-cases-and-deaths-by-race-ethnicity-current-data-and-changes-over-time/.

Hondagneu-Sotelo, Pierrette. 2007. *Doméstica: Immigrant Workers Cleaning and Caring in the Shadows of Affluence.* Berkeley: University of California Press.

Hoxby, Caroline, and Christopher Avery. 2012. "The Missing 'One-offs': The Hidden Supply of High-Achieving, Low-Income Students." Working Paper 18586. Cambridge, Mass.: National Bureau of Economic Research (December).

Hurst, Allison L. 2010. *The Burden of Academic Success: Loyalists, Renegades, and Double Agents*. Washington, D.C.: Lexington Books.

Ivemark, Biörn, and Anna Ambrose. 2021. "Habitus Adaptation and First-Generation University Students' Adjustment to Higher Education: A Life Course Perspective." *Sociology of Education* 94(3, July): 191–207.

Jack, Anthony Abraham. 2019. *The Privileged Poor: How Elite Colleges Are Failing Disadvantaged Students*. Cambridge, Mass.: Harvard University Press.

Jack, Anthony Abraham, and Zennon Black. 2022. "Belonging and Boundaries at an Elite University." *Social Problems* (September 10). DOI: https://doi.org/10.1093/socpro/spac051.

Jaswal, Sheila. 2019. "Being Human in STEM: Moving from Student Protest to Institutional Progress." *Diversity and Democracy* 22(1, Winter): 21–24.

Kao, Grace, Elizabeth Vaquera, and Kimberly Goyette. 2013. *Immigration and Education*. Oxford: Polity Press.

Keeter, Scott. 2020. "People Financially Affected by COVID-19 Outbreak Are Experiencing More Psychological Distress than Others." PEW Research Center, March 30. https://www.pewresearch.org/fact-tank/2020/03/30/people-financially-affected-by-covid-19-outbreak-are-experiencing-more-psychological-distress-than-others/.

Khan, Shamus. 2011. *Privilege: The Making of an Adolescent Elite at St. Paul's School*. Princeton, N.J.: Princeton University Press.

Kibria, Nazli. 1993. *Family Tightrope: The Changing Lives of Vietnamese Americans*. Princeton, N.J.: Princeton University Press.

Kovacs, Kasia. 2022. "The Pandemic's Impact on College Enrollment." *Best Colleges* (blog), May 6. https://www.bestcolleges.com/blog/covid19-impact-on-college-enrollment/#:~:text=According%20to%20the%20National%20Student,fell%20 4.4%25%20in%20the%20fall.

Lee, Elizabeth M. 2016. *Class and Campus Life: Managing and Experiencing Inequality at an Elite College*. Ithaca, N.Y.: Cornell University Press.

Lee, Elizabeth M., and Rory Kramer. 2013. "Out with the Old, in with the New? Habitus and Social Mobility at Selective Colleges." *Sociology of Education* 86(1, January): 18–35.

Lee, Jennifer, and Min Zhou. 2015. *The Asian American Achievement Paradox*. New York: Russell Sage Foundation.

Lemann, Nicholas. 1999. *The Big Test: The Secret History of the American Meritocracy*. New York: Farrar, Straus and Giroux.

Lopez, Nancy. 2003. *Hopeful Girls, Troubled Boys: Race and Gender Disparity in Urban Education*. New York: Routledge.

López, Rick. 2020. "Creating a Place for Latinidad at an Elite Liberal Arts College: Amherst College, the 1970s through Today." In *Amherst in the World*, edited by Martha Saxton. Amherst, Mass.: Amherst College Press.

Louie, Vivian S. 2012. *Keeping the Immigrant Bargain: The Costs and Rewards of Success in America*. New York: Russell Sage Foundation.

Marrun, Norma. 2018. "'My Mom Seems to Have a Dicho for Everything!'": Family Engagement in the College Success of Latina/o Students. *Journal of Latinos in Education* 19: 1–17.

Martinez, Lisa M., and Maria Del Carmen Salazar. 2018. "The Bright Lights: The Development of Oppositional Consciousness among DACAmented Latino Youth." *Ethnicities* 18(2, April): 242–59.

Mattern, Krista, and Jeff Wyatt. 2009. "Student Choice of College: How Far Do Students Go for an Education?" *Journal of College Admission* 203(Spring): 18–29.

Menjívar, Cecilia. 2000. *Fragmented Ties: Salvadoran Immigrant Networks in America*. Berkeley: University of California Press.

———. 2006. "Liminal Legality: Salvadoran and Guatemalan Lives in the United States." *American Journal of Sociology* 111(4, January): 999–1037.

Menjívar, Cecilia, Leisy J. Abrego, and Leah C. Schmalzbauer. 2016. *Immigrant Families*. Oxford: Polity Press.

Opal, J. M. 2002. "The Making of the Victorian Campus: Teacher and Student at Amherst College, 1850–1880." *History of Education Quarterly* 42(3, Autumn): 342–67.

Pan, Yung-Yi Diana, and Daisy Verduzco Reyes. 2021. "The Norm among the Exceptional? Experiences of Latino Students at Elite Institutions." *Sociological Inquiry* 91(1, February): 207–30.

Parolin, Zachary. 2021. "What the Covid-19 Pandemic Reveals about Racial Differences in Child Welfare and Child Well-Being: An Introduction to the Special Issue." *Race and Social Problems* 13(1): 1–5.

Pew Research Center. 2020. "Health Concerns from COVID-19 Much Higher among Hispanics and Blacks than Whites." Pew Research Center, April 14. https://www.pewresearch.org/politics/2020/04/14/health-concerns-from-covid-19-much-higher-among-hispanics-and-blacks-than-whites/.

Purtle, Jonathan. 2020. "COVID-19 and Mental Health Equity in the United States." *Social Psychiatry and Psychiatric Epidemiology* 55(8, August): 969–71.

Rendón, María G. 2019. *Stagnant Dreamers: How the Inner City Shapes the Integration of Second-Generation Latinos*. New York: Russell Sage Foundation.

Reyes, Daisy Verduzco. 2018. *Learning to Be Latino: How Colleges Shape Identity Politics*. New Brunswick, N.J.: Rutgers University Press.

Rivera, Lauren. 2015. *Pedigree: How Elite Students Get Elite Jobs*. Princeton, N.J.: Princeton University Press.

Rodriguez, Richard. 1982. *Hunger of Memory: The Education of Richard Rodriguez.* New York: Bantam Books.

Romero, Mary. 2011. *The Maid's Daughter: Living Inside and Outside the American Dream.* New York: New York University Press.

Sassen, Saskia. 2001. *The Global City: New York, London, Tokyo.* Princeton, N.J.: Princeton University Press.

Schmalzbauer, Leah. 2008. "Family Divided: The Class Formation of Honduran Transnational Families." *Global Networks* 8(3): 329–46.

———. 2014. *The Last Best Place? Gender, Family, and Migration in the New West.* Stanford, Calif.: Stanford University Press.

Schmalzbauer, Leah, and Aleli Andres. 2019. "Stratified Lives: Family, Illegality, and the Rise of a New Educational Elite." *Harvard Educational Review* 89(4, Winter): 635–60.

Schmalzbauer, Leah, and Manuel Rodriguez. 2023. "Pathways to Mobility: Family and Education in the Lives of Latinx Youth." *Qualitative Sociology* 46: 21–46. DOI: https://doi.org/10.1007/s11133-022-09523-5.

Smith, Robert. 2006. *Mexican New York: Transnational Lives of New Immigrants.* Berkeley: University of California Press.

———. 2008. "Horatio Alger Lives in Brooklyn: Extrafamily Support, Intrafamily Dynamics, and Socially Neutral Operating Identities in Exceptional Mobility among Children of Mexican Immigrants." *Annals of the American Academy of Political and Social Science* 620(1, November): 270–90.

Suárez-Orozco, Carola, and Marcelo Suárez-Orozco. 1995. *Transformations: Migration, Family Life, and Achievement Motivation among Latino Adolescents.* Stanford, Calif.: Stanford University Press.

Sy, Susan R., and Jessica Romero. 2008. "Family Responsibilities among Latina College Students from Immigrant Families." *Journal of Hispanic Higher Education* 7(3, July): 212–27.

Torpey, Elka. 2018. "Measuring the Value of Education." Washington: U.S. Bureau of Labor Statistics (April).

Turcio-Cotto, Viana Y., and Stephanie Milan. 2013. "Racial/Ethnic Differences in the Educational Expectations of Adolescents: Does Pursuing Higher Education Mean Something Different to Latino Students Compared to White and Black Students?" *Journal of Youth and Adolescence* 42(9, September): 1399–1412.

Vazquez, Jessica M. 2011. *Mexican Americans across Generations: Immigrant Families, Racial Realities.* New York: New York University Press.

Venzant Chambers, Terah T., Kristin S. Huggins, Leslie A. Locke, and Rhonda M. Fowler. 2014. "Between a 'ROC' and a School Place: The Role of Racial Opportunity Cost in the Educational Experiences of Academically Successful Students of Color." *Educational Studies* 50(5): 464–97.

Warikoo, Natasha K. 2016. *The Diversity Bargain: And Other Dilemmas of Race, Admissions, and Meritocracy at Elite Universities.* Chicago: University of Chicago Press.

Yoshikawa, Hirokazu. 2011. *Immigrants Raising Citizens: Undocumented Parents and Their Young Children.* New York: Russell Sage Foundation.

Zambrana, Ruth, and Sylvia Hurtado. 2015. *The Magic Key: The Educational Journeys of Mexican Americans from K-12 to College and Beyond.* Austin: University of Texas Press.

Zhou, Min, and Carl L. Bankston III. 2016. *The Rise of the New Second Generation.* Oxford: Polity Press.

Index

Tables and figures are listed in **boldface**.

study, choosing, 80, 167–69; social
connections and networking through,
6, 64–65; traveling away from family
to attend, 10, 33–35, 74, 77. *See also*
adapting to college; educational
mobility pathways; elite colleges
college visits, 24, 26, 43
community networks. *See* social
supports and mentors
conformity, 59–65
Conley, Dalton, 104, 130
Coronavirus Aid, Relief, and Economic
Security Act (CARES, 2020), 137
COVID-19 pandemic, 22, 134–62;
Amherst College and, 134, 142,
144–45, 158–59, 189–90, 195; college
enrollment rates and, 114; economic
impacts of, 138–44; educational
mobility and, 137, 158–61; family
caretaking responsibilities and,
151–58, 169, 177–78; goals of
students, effect on, 177–79;
inequality, exacerbating, 135–36,
189–90; institutional policy changes
and, 189–90; mental health impacts
of, 144–50; study methodology,
effect on, 15–16, 208;
undocumented immigrants and,
135–37, 141–44, 150
critical consciousness of inequality:
bridging two worlds and, 73–74;
COVID-19 pandemic and, 169;
developing, 190–92; familial price of
education mobility and, 188; guilt
and, 10; lack of, 13; sibling
educational mobility and, 131; social
mobility and, 4; U.S. citizenship vs.
undocumented status and, 9
cross-class actors: educational and
social mobility, facilitating, 27, 35–36,
39, 42, 195; friendships and social
networks, 6, 64–65; geographic

location benefits and access to, 45;
lack of access to, 44. *See also*
preparatory and pipeline programs
cultural capital, 12, 40, 53–54, 62–63,
190
cultural scripts and norms, 59–65,
149–50, 193
Curl, Heather, 61

DACA (Deferred Action for Childhood
Arrivals) students: at Amherst,
support for, 188–89, 193; financial
aid for, 39, 42, 44, 173–74; immigrant
bargain and, 28–32; institutional
support for, 185, 193; limitations on
goals of, 172–76, 180, 193; Trump
administration order rescinding
status of, 134, 150
DAPA (Deferred Action for Parents of
Americans), 108
demographics of study participants,
198–202
discrimination, 39. *See also* race and
racism
Doméstica (Hondagneu-Sotelo), 1
domestic ethnographies, 15–16
double consciousness, 49–50
doubly disadvantaged students: elite
college experience and, 12, 49, 55–57;
inequality, experience with, 73;
privileged poor vs., 12, 53–55, 59–60
Dreby, Joanna, 9, 208

economic mobility. *See* social mobility
educational mobility pathways, 21,
24–47; convergence of networks for,
45–47, 187; COVID-19 pandemic
and, 137, 158–61; education as
pathway to success and, 2, 8–10,
28–29; elite college network,
accessing, 39–45; family support
and, 7–8, 27, 28–35, 45–46, 187;

Made in United States
North Haven, CT
19 March 2025

66980485R00145